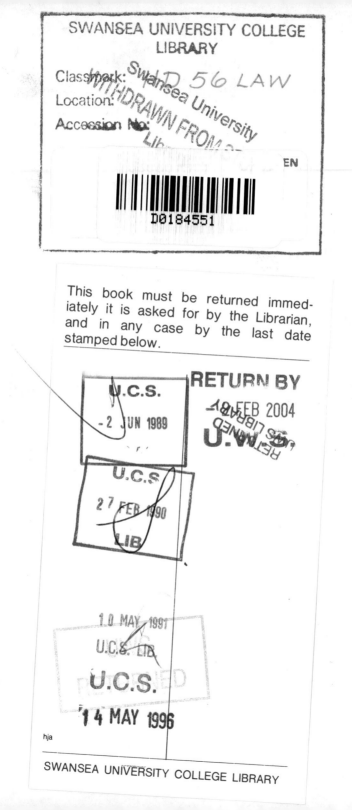

CORPORATE STRUCTURE AND PERFORMANCE

CORPORATE STRUCTURE & PERFORMANCE

The Role of Owners, Managers and Markets

By Michael L. Lawriwsky

CROOM HELM
London and Canberra

ST. MARTIN'S PRESS
New York

© 1984 M. Lawriwsky
Croom Helm Ltd, Provident House, Burrell Row,
Beckenham, Kent BR3 1AT
Croom Helm Australia Pty Ltd,
28 Kembla Street, Fyshwick, ACT 2609, Australia

British Library Cataloguing in Publication Data

Lawriwsky, Michael L.
    Corporate structure and performance.
    1. Industrial organization (Economic theory) —
    Mathematical models
    I. Title
    338.7   HD2326
    ISBN 0-7099-1645-0

Library of Congress Cataloguing in Publication Data

Lawriwsky, Michael L.
    Corporate structure and performance.

    Based on thesis (doctoral) — University of Adelaide,
1980.
    Bibliography: p.
    Includes index.
    1. Industrial productivity.   2. Performance.
3. Industrial organization.   4. Industries, Size of.
I. Title.
HD56.L39   1984   338.7   83-24748
ISBN 0-312-17001-7

Typeset by Leaper & Gard Ltd, Bristol
Printed and bound in Great Britain

CONTENTS

LIST OF FIGURES

LIST OF TABLES

To Maria and Lubomyr

PREFACE

The behavioural and performance consequences of the separation of ownership and control have been widely recognised as having the potential to revolutionise the theory of the firm, as well as the current approach adopted in studies of industrial organisation. That such a separation exists throughout Western capitalist economies is indisputable; its progress has been traced in a number of published works. Whether it is of real consequence to theoreticians or policy makers has, by contrast, been a flashpoint of contention. Here empirical researchers over the last 25 years have been content to replicate again and again studies which have sought to test for performance differences between 'owner-' and 'management-controlled' corporations. Using different samples and methods of measurement, a set of conflicting findings has emerged. As a result, the profession has made little progress towards reaching a consensus on this issue. In the meantime the last few decades have witnessed developments which threaten to alter the basic parameters of the separation thesis. Here I am referring specifically to such factors as the exit of small private shareholders and the concomitant growth of financial institutions which has resulted in a trend back to concentrated ownership.

This book makes two contributions to the literature; one theoretical, the other methodological. At the theoretical level it is argued that it is not control type *per se* which is critical in determining the performance of the firm. Instead it is proposed that the prime determinants of observed performance are the interrelationships between internal organisational structure, the product market and the capital market. However, these interactions will be modified by control type, firm size and maturity. Thus, interest is directed at decisions taken at the firm level by top management in response to their incentive structure and internal and external constraints on their behaviour. The major methodological innovation of this study is that it explores the interactions between stockholders, managers and markets. That is, it first examines the ways in which these factors influence behaviour and performance *within* control types before comparisons *between* control types are attempted. It is argued that only in this way may differences (or lack of differences) in performance be fully understood.

The book is based on my doctoral dissertation, which was submitted to the University of Adelaide in 1980. While structured around an empirical study employing Australian data, the theoretical basis of the book is a discussion of the modern corporation, and some emphasis is given to the remarkable similarities in developments taking place in other Anglo-American economies as well as continental European economies.

I owe an eternal debt to David K. Round, my thesis supervisor, for his continual encouragement and incisive comments on successive drafts of the original thesis. It was in my formative years as an undergraduate at the University of Adelaide that David Round, who was then pioneering the empirical application of the structure-conduct-performance triad in Australia, stimulated a keen interest in that field. I am also indebted to Drs John Hatch and Ian McLean for the advice they gave as co-supervisors and to Professors G.C. Harcourt, D.R. Kamerschen, D.C. Mueller, E.A. Russell, Z.A. Silberston and E.L. Wheelwright and Mr R.R. Hirst for the encouragement and comment they provided. I would also like to express my gratitude to Professor F.G. Davidson, who pointed out a number of shortcomings in the expression, presentation or logical progression of the penultimate draft of this book. My most fundamental intellectual debt, though, is to Brother Michael Flaherty, who taught me the love of learning.

The ownership and control data upon which this work is based are among the most comprehensive ever to be compiled in Australia. The task of gathering and collating this data set was one of considerable proportions, involving several inter-state visits. Here thanks are due to the staffs of the corporations, chartered accounting firms and corporate affairs offices in each state for the assistance they provided while searches of publicly available records were made. In particular, I would like to acknowledge the work of Judith Herman, my research assistant, who read and arranged thousands of microfilmed records and made most of the tedious calculations. I am grateful to the Department of Economics at the University of Adelaide for providing funds for this assistance.

Invaluable computing assistance was provided by Michael Petty of the University of Adelaide and Terry Tremayne of La Trobe University. Thanks are also due to Julia Anderson, Sandra Barnes, Helen Cook and Heather Watkins of the School of Economics at La

Trobe University for typing the manuscript.

Finally, I would like to express special thanks to my wife, Maria, who not only accepted my periods of absence from the hearth, but also actively assisted at various stages.

Note on Terminology

In Britain the owners of corporate equity capital are referred to as shareholders. In the United States they are called stockholders. Elsewhere, these terms appear to be used interchangeably and no particular convention is adopted in this book.

1 INTRODUCTION

The Issues

> firms are not, regardless of what economic theory may suppose,
> undifferentiated, profit maximizing agencies which react to given
> market situations in ways which are independent of their organ-
> ization ... management ... is influenced not only by market
> pressures, but also by considerations internal to the firm
>
> (E.S. Mason, 1939)

The above quotation, from a paper delivered by Mason at a con-
ference of the American Economic Association (AEA) in 1938,
indicates that the pioneer of the market structure-conduct-
performance paradigm recognised the importance of the missing
corporate structure-performance link. However, the seminal works
of Mason (1939, 1949) and Bain (1951, 1956) were unable to
incorporate this linkage since the structure-conduct-performance
triad was primarily geared to analysis at the market level. It also failed
adequately to integrate the vital stock market influences which
interact with 'internal considerations' to bring about the allocation of
resources which they sought to explain.

In a more recent symposium of the AEA, two of the three papers
considering the state of research in industrial organisation
(Grabowski and Mueller, 1970; Grether, 1970) independently
arrived at the conclusion that future research should, within the
context of large, diversified corporations operating oligopolistic
markets, become more aware of 'internal organizations, policies and
strategies' (p. 85) as essential to gaining an improved understanding
of corporate performance. In addition, Grabowski and Mueller
sounded a note of caution with regard to the role of econometrics in
the study of industrial organisation. That is, unless a suitable way of
analysing firms according to their internal structure can be found,
empiricists may be forced to abandon econometric techniques in
favour of the older case-by-case approach, where the unit of analysis
would be the large diversified firm. This is because the cross-sectional
studies which have characterised empirical research in the field make
the implicit assumption that all firms in a sample react to external

1

shocks on the basis of similar behavioural parameters.

The phenomenon referred to as the 'separation of ownership from control' has occupied a central position in economists' perceptions of factors internal to the firm since the publication of Berle and Means's (1932) *The Modern Corporation and Private Property* a half-century ago.[1] The central thesis of their book was that, owing to the rise of the joint stock corporation, over a number of years the gradual diffusion and dispersion of stockholders would eventually result in a situation where professional managers come to dominate the affairs of the corporation. As an indication of the importance of these developments, Berle and Means estimated that in 1929 up to 44 per cent of the 200 largest corporations in the United States were subject to management control. The secular trend to greater dispersion of shareholdings has, since that time, been documented in many capitalist economies.

But such a trend would not be of very much interest to economists, apart from any associated redistributions of wealth, if there were no behavioural or performance consequences. In the period after the Second World War several alternative theories of the firm emerged in response to the observation that the traditional dual entrepreneurial functions of ownership and management had become separated. In most of these models professional managers were seen to derive utility from the size of the corporation, due to the salary, power and prestige afforded by size. Hence, managers were assumed to be striving to maximise the rate of growth of the firm subject to some minimum profitability or valuation constraint which would satisfy shareholders and provide the desired degree of security from takeover (e.g. Baumol, 1959; Marris, 1964). Other theorists speculated that when market constraints are absent, managers may allow costs to rise (Leibenstein, 1966), or seek discretionary expenditures on staff and emoluments (Williamson, 1964).

The alternative theories of the firm were criticised by orthodox economists (e.g. Baldwin, 1964; Solow, 1968) who argued that there remain significant market restraints on managerial behaviour. Managers must seek profits and win customers and capital in order to survive in the long run. On the other hand, economists of more 'radical' persuasion (e.g. C. Wright-Mills, 1972) have argued that the profit motive of old is still prevalent, since even 'unpropertied managers' are part of the capitalist class and despite their background will have interests identical with it.

The large number of empirical studies examining performance

differences due to the separation of ownership from control have not resolved the conflict. On the contrary, the lack of consensus in the findings of empirical research has sparked more controversy. Nyman and Silberston (1978) have charged that the cross-sectional methodology employed by empirical researchers is defective and have opted for a longitudinal case-by-case approach. An even more fundamental criticism has more recently been made by Francis (1980), who claims that most firms are unlikely ever to be controlled by managers. Instead, they will be controlled by ownership interests of some kind; by a family, by industrial capital or by financial institutions.

The performance consequences resulting from different corporate ownership structures is the subject of this book. A model of corporate enterprise is developed which extends the traditional market structure-conduct-performance model of industrial organisation to take account of the internal organisation of firms, firm maturity and capital market restraints on managerial decision-makers. While the foundations of the model are derived from the 'new' or 'managerial' theories of the firm, attention is focused not on the establishment of *a priori* hypotheses regarding the relative performance consequences of a separation of ownership from control, but on the more fundamental question of the effectiveness and operations of the various incentives, market and non-market restraints acting on managers.

The new theoretical and empirical approaches adopted in this study allow us to consider some fundamental questions which have arisen owing to developments in corporate securities markets in the past 20 years. Foremost among these are the implications of the decline of the individual investor and concurrent rise of financial institutions for the behaviour and performance of the corporation. Close co-operation between financial institutions and corporate management have long characterised the French, German and Japanese economies. Some observers have held that this has contributed to the generally fine performance of those economies. In the Anglo-American economies some isolated studies have investigated the effects of financial institutions on capital market efficiency and some useful case-study material has been documented. However, no cross-sectional study has considered the effects of financial institutions on corporate profitability, growth or payout policy. Similarly, the performance implications of intercorporate shareholdings have received limited attention in the literature.

The empirical work is based on comprehensive data on the

ownership structures of 226 listed Australian corporations. However, the theory is meant to be general in that it is structured on the assumption of an advanced capitalist economy, with its attendant cultural setting and institutional framework. Since cultural and institutional differences as well as timing differences in the process of capitalist development do occur between such countries, it is perhaps appropriate at this point to establish the international perspectives of this study.

The fundamental message of this book is that it is not the separation of ownership from control *per se* which is important, but rather the tradeoff between managerial incentives and market restraints. Cultural influences and tradition are important in determing the managerial reward system which develops in any country. In this connection we find that France and Germany (Dyas and Thanheiser, 1976, pp. 310-14) are similar to Australia, with a relatively small proportion of total executive remuneration being composed of non-salary incentive rewards. Experience in the United Kingdom, however, suggests that variable reward systems are more popular there, but still fall short of the extensive schemes practised in the United States.

The available evidence suggests that in Western Europe, as in Australia, families have tended to retain control of public corporations for a longer period than in the United States. Similarly, the concentration of institutional stockholdings has been higher in Europe and Australia. While Nyman and Silbertson (1978) found the registers of a number of UK corporations were dominated by financial institutions, the concentration of such holdings is even higher in Australia. In this sense, Australia is well advanced in relation to the trends to institutional dominance which are developing in the US and UK. Yet the extent of institutional control in Australia is still far less extensive than that already apparent in Germany. Again, in terms of organisational structures, and in the extent of diversification, the US is ahead with more conglomerates and the concomitant growth of multi-divisional structures. Holding company structures are relatively more common in Europe and Australia.

International similarities and differences also appear at the board of directors level. The US, UK and Australia have one board composed of external appointees who may or may not represent specific interests and some executive directors. Since 1966 France has operated an optional two-tier system based on the German model. In a formal two-tier system an executive board performs its duties under the direct control of a supervisory board (Grossfeld and Ebke, 1978). The legal system may exert other influences on control arrangements. In Germany, for example, the corporation law grants power of veto to stockholders with a holding of 25 per cent or more, which helps facilitate bank control. On the other hand, continental European laws tend not to place as much emphasis on the anti-trust aspects of interlocking directorships as the US laws do (when, in fact, there is less reason to have them in the US) and there is less emphasis on insider trading provisions.

All in all, the capital markets of the US, UK and Australia are freer, with more trading and a greater flow of information. This extends also to the market for corporate control. Takeover raids are much less common on the European Continent. However, mergers do take place after deliberations between parties as to the commercial advantages. Probably the main reason for the absence of market raids is the fact that the concentration of stockholdings is greater on the Continent; however, it might also reflect the thinness of capital markets, or even cultural traits. Thus, the market for corporate control is a phenomenon largely restricted to the Anglo-American economies (Daems, 1978; Davies, 1982).

The upshot of this discussion is that the process of capitalist development has been and will continue being uneven between capitalist countries. It is influenced by the size of the economy and by its cultural, legal and institutional framework. Bearing in mind the differences and similarities outlined above, it would appear that the present study, in employing Australian data, will provide particularly useful insights into aspects of the corporate structures developing in Australia, Canada, the US and the UK, in short, the Anglo-American economies. However, one cannot rule out the applicability of various aspects of the analysis to continental Europe.

The structure of the book is as follows. The 'managerial growth hypothesis' and a number of the empirical studies which it spawned are examined in Chapter 2. On the basis of a literature review and sensitivity analysis of the data, it is concluded that new theoretical and methodological approaches are required. The new theoretical structure is outlined in Chapter 3. In chapters 4 through 7 the new methodology is employed in a series of empirical tests of the main hypotheses. The final chapter presents the conclusions and implications for the study of industrial organisation, for the theory of the firm and for the main players — shareholders, managers and policy makers.

A New Approach

The approach adopted in this book is based on the traditional market structure-conduct-performance triad. Given the basic conditions of demand and supply, the primary causal link in the traditional model is assumed to flow from market structure, to conduct to performance. Various feedback loops are also envisaged; conduct may affect structure through artificial product differentiation and advertising cost barriers to entry; predatory pricing behaviour might alter the number of sellers; research and development could alter the basic technological conditions. However, much of the empirical work in this field has taken the view that conduct is the inevitable result of structure. Increasingly, though, this contention is being challenged, despite the major problem of constructing adequate proxy measures of conduct.[2] But conduct, or decisions taken at the firm level, can have a significant impact on performance once the area of discretion defined by the structural attributes of the market has been determined.

The extended model of industrial organisation which forms the core of this study focuses on the corporation, rather than the market, as the logical unit of analysis. A schematic representation of the model is presented in Figure 1.1. In essence, the model views potential corporate performance as having an upper boundary determined by the degree of discretion (in the product market) which is available to managers. Ultimately this discretion is dependent upon the market power available to the firm, that is, on such factors as market share, concentration and barriers to entry. But the extent to which managers can take advantage of this discretion is defined by the effectiveness of internal and external (stock market) restraints on their behaviour. How managers will use these residual discretionary powers, however, will depend on their incentive structure.

The major difference between the traditional model of industrial organisation and the model developed here is that, in the former, conduct (and therefore performance) is determined solely by market structure, with tacit recognition of the influence that decisions by regulatory agencies could have on the results. In our extended model, observed conduct and performance are the outcome of conflict between internal organisation, market structure (the product market restraint) and the restraints imposed by the capital and corporate control markets. Firm maturity, or the level of investment opportunities, is expected to modify the incentives and restraints originat-

Figure 1.1: An Extended Model of Industrial Organisation

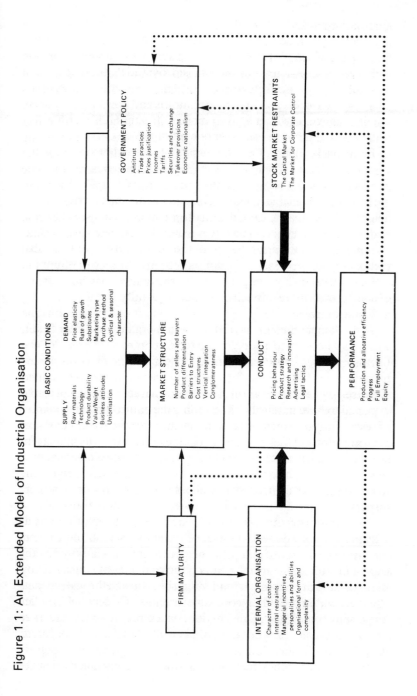

ing from within and outside the firm. Apart from the feeback loops in the traditional model, we now have the non-market corrective mechanism which operates through the internal structure of the firm and the additional market mechanism by which the capital and corporate control markets respond to firm performance. In order to illustrate the workings of these mechanisms and how they may act to modify behaviour within a given market structure it is worth giving some consideration to each component of the model.

In the background of any discussion of internal organisation lies the human factor — the nature of managerial incentives, abilities and personalities and also the incentives of shareholders. For example, the incentives available to managers may include such items as shares held in the company, capital gains from stock options, salary and bonuses. Non-pecuniary incentives will include power and prestige, staff preference, the approbation of the community and other satisfactions of the ego (as, for example, through the achievement of technical excellence). The personalities and abilities of managers are, of course, even more difficult concepts to quantify, but they may play a significant role.[3]

A fundamental element of the internal organisation of a firm is what may be termed as its 'character of control'. The model distinguishes three basic categories, or 'characters of control': (a) private ownership control; (b) company control; (c) management (or dispersed ownership) control. The actual character of control can be expected to have implications regarding the nature and effectiveness of restraining influences. For example, in closely held companies the concentration of votes may mean that the influence of the market for corporate control will have less bearing on the process of adjustment following a poor performance than will internal pressures originating from within the controlled shareholder group (or company). In dispersed ownership companies, however, the external restraint of the market for corporate control may be more pertinent, although its effectiveness may depend on such considerations as absolute size of the firm. The degree of independence from restraints imposed by the capital market might also depend on the character of control. Thus, the allocation of investment funds might be achieved through internal channels within a holding company structure. Closely held private ownership companies might, under some circumstances, prefer to finance internally in order to retain control. Similarly, managers in dispersed ownership companies might be unwilling to engage in external finance if they feel that this will be accompanied by intervention or close scrutiny of their behaviour.

The nature of internal restraints may also be expected to differ according to the character of control. We mean by private ownership companies those in which large private holdings are highly concentrated and organised into strategic blocks of shares. If we speak of private ownership control, then, we are really speaking of control by a minority of well-organised shareholders — not control by all private owners. The same argument applies to those firms which are effectively controlled by other companies. While in the dispersed ownership situation it would be possible for informed and capable investors (such as financial institutions) to unite in challenging management, no such option would normally exist in firms with a highly uneven distribution of share ownership. In these firms the distribution of shareholdings between 'insiders', who are also members of top management, and 'outsiders', who are not aligned with them, may be more relevant. If the definition of owner control is centred on the board of directors and the extent of stockholdings they can be shown to represent directly (i.e. directors as a cohesive group), we must surmise that *these* stockholders can exercise their potential power and can detect whether managers are pursuing their own interests. A similar argument would apply in the case of company control, since a large holding by another firm is usually accompanied by representation on the board. In a dispersed ownership company this role may be played by institutional investors.

However, two qualifications should be noted. First, if managers in these firms are being constrained to 'maximise shareholder welfare', this may only mean that the welfare of that group of shareholders which has the power to control managers is being maximised. For example, the ownership group may be composed of managers and their utility set need not correspond precisely with that of shareholders who are not executives in the firm. The objectives of a dominant company shareholder need not correspond with those of private shareholders. The controlled company might be one of several and its policies be tailored to an overall strategy which is designed to promote the welfare of the group as a whole.[4] Also, the objectives of institutional investors may not coincide with those of small shareholders.

The second point is that the 'power to control' as we define it also implies an ability to retain control were agents outside the incumbent group to make a bid to obtain control for themselves. That is, the term 'control' must imply that the controllers have an area of discretion within which the probability of 'potential controllers' succeeding in their attempts is low. Obviously this probability will be directly related to the discretion which is actually *exercised* by the controllers. And the degree of discretion which can be exercised without attracting a credible bid for control will depend on the extent of that control.

Such controlling power is held by the managers of a firm in which shares are so widely dispersed that it would be very difficult for existing shareholders to mount an effective opposition to it. But the control held by these managers would also — to varying degrees — be subject to limits imposed by outside bidders (i.e. takeover raiders) in the stock market. However, this control is also wielded by a cohesive group of private owners and by a dominant company shareholder. In these cases power derives not from the dispersion of shares, but from their concentration. Thus, what may be termed as 'absolute control' would come when a strongly unified body has possession of close to 50 per cent of a company's voting stock. Here the *limit* to discretion would be set by the product market (i.e. by the outright failure of the company), while the extent to which discretion is exercised would largely depend on the interplay of forces within the controlling body of shareholders. In dispersed ownership companies, however, the extent of discretion will very much depend on firm size, since large size is associated with a degree of freedom from scrutiny by the market for corporate control.

A final element of internal organisation is the organisational structure and complexity of the internal operations of the firm. Organisational complexity may have implications both for the way policy is formulated and the manner of execution. For example policy may be determined by one or a small group of key individuals, or by a process of conciliation and bargaining between executive committees representing a variety of interests within the firm's management structure. The number of hierarchical tiers in the organisation will, on the other hand, determine the extent to which control loss acts to distort the directives which have been issued (Williamson, 1967). We also include in this category the administrative structure of the firm. That is, whether it is organised along functional lines such as finance, production and marketing (the 'unitary' or U-form), or along product lines (the 'multi-division' or M-form) with the responsibility of overall co-ordination residing in the hands of an elite central office staff (see Chandler, 1969; Channon, 1973; and Williamson, 1970, 1973, 1975). The Chandler thesis holds that the form of organisational structure follows strategy (i.e. conduct) in that the multi-division form arises out of the diversification policy pursued by management. However, it is recognised that the multi-division form may also *facilitate* the adoption of a strategy of diversification. Also, it is apparent that the character of control may influence the strategy and structure of the firm. For example, Channon (1973) found that family-controlled firms in the UK tended to remain single product and maintain a U-form structure.

In this framework managers are seen to operate within a rather complex network of incentives and non-market (internal) restraints. But these factors are important in determining organisational objectives (and consequently performance) only in so far as they are allowed to operate by a variety of market (external) restraints. The restraints imposed by the stock market have not received very much attention in industrial organisation studies. Yet we would expect that if managerial incentives to maximise profits were weak and the internal and product market restraints were ineffective, these stock market restraints might prove crucial in determining the actual degree of discretion enjoyed by managers in pursuing alternative objectives.

We should expect firms which compete for funds in the capital market to earn higher future rates of return because of the more objective, stringent investment criteria set in an open market. An efficient capital market will provide funds to those firms which have the most worthy investment projects. Baumol (1965) argued that this capital market discipline was being avoided by a large section of US corporations,[5] and, in view of the results achieved by Little (1962) in the UK, that this was a cause for concern. Little's research suggested an astonishingly inefficient use of shareholders' funds in the investment process — probably because market controls were being avoided.

But Baumol (1965, p. 82) concluded that the stock market's powers to police company efficiency 'may have survived intact', since the value of executive stock options depends entirely on the market's valuation. Another reason was that 'if disaffection among stockholders grows very strong, management's tenure may itself by threatened'. Clearly these were references to the interrelationship between the stock market and a firm's internal organisation, i.e. the incentives available to managers and the internal restraints imposed by shareholders.

Furthermore, the stock market may indirectly influence company behaviour and performance through the market for corporate control. If the current performance and future prospects exhibited by the firm under existing management is lower than could be expected in the light of opportunities which present themselves, the stock market will depress its share price. If this happens, and the costs involved are not excessive, there will exist an incentive for other firms to acquire control of the productive assets of the firm and institute reforms in management. For the acquiring firm the prospect of capital gains may be attractive, whilst the incumbent managers will fear the possibility of loss of tenure, demotion or, at best, the prospect of subservience to the higher management of the acquiring concern. Hence, the effectiveness of the market for corporate control in disciplining the behaviour of individual companies may be paramount in determining their performance.

Another element of the model relates to firm maturity. Mueller (1972) suggested that the implications of the separation thesis (internal organisation) may be modified depending upon the maturity and extent of investment opportunities faced by firms at different stages of their development. This can be seen to alter conduct in two ways; first, by changing the relationship between managerial incentives and company performance; and second, by modifying the restraint imposed by the capital market. Thus, Mueller proposed that shareholders' and managerial objectives will be compatible when a firm is 'non-mature' and its investment opportunities exceed internally generated funds, since both will be keen for the company to grow rapidly. At this stage firms will be making frequent recourse to the capital market for funds and it will be in the managers' best interests not to invest beyond the level where marginal returns are equal to the marginal cost of capital. By contrast, managers in a 'mature' corporation, whose investment opportunities fall short of available internally generated funds and which only infrequently approaches the capital market (lacks restraints), will be motivated, in their pursuit of size and its attendant advantages, to reinvest funds which promise a marginal rate of return which is lower than the shareholders' discount rate. In the context of our model, then, maturity is seen to alter the internal organisation (the relationship between managerial incentives and performance) of the firm and the effectiveness of the capital market restraint in the determination of conduct and performance. At the same time basic conditions and market structure will also be affected by maturity (see Shepherd, 1976). The feedback from conduct to firm maturity indicated in Figure 1.1 shows that research and innovation can transform a mature firm, with low investment oportunities relative to internally generated funds, into a non-mature one.

The final element of the model is the government policy restraint, which is also implicitly contained in the traditional model. For example, policy relating to mergers and monopolies, trade practices, investment and export incentives and the protection of domestic industries from import competition can modify the basic conditions, market structure and conduct of firms. Thus, governments can affect the performance of the company sector and, in line with their policy objectives, adjust the restraints according to observed performance. In the expanded model depicted in Figure 1.1 we observe that government policy may also impinge on internal organisation and stock market restraints. Taxation can affect the incentive structures of managers and shareholders. Relative rates of taxation on dividends and capital gains will affect shareholders' preferences regarding the reinvestment of profits and hence the degree of dependence on the capital market. The imposition of death duties and estate taxes will help to shape the ownership structure within companies which have a dominant private owner-controller. Government legislation regulating the mechanics of takeover bids can influence the market for corporate control. Similarly, requirements for minimum disclosure of financial and other information will sharpen the efficiency of the capital market in its allocative role. Problems of measurement and data limitations militate against the formal incorporation of variables reflecting government policy. Also, it is probable that the large number of separate influences acting on individual firms will be normally distributed and can be consigned to the error term in an econometric investigation.

To summarise, our model provides for three characters of control. Managers in each of these groups of firms are subject to a set of incentives and restraints on their behaviour. However, these incentives and restraints will not be uniform for companies *within* each group. For example, managers' shareholdings will vary and so will the effectiveness of shareholders' power to restrain them. Also, firms of different sizes will be subject to varying degrees of external restraint from stock market influences. Only in those firms which can be shown to be largely independent of internal and external restraints can managers be said to 'control' and this can occur in any of the three groups.

The central point to emerge from the model is that it is not control type *per se* which is critical in determining the performance of the firm. Instead, it argues that the prime determinants of observed performance are the interrelationships between internal organisational structure, the product market and the capital market. However, these interactions will be modified by such factors as control type, firm size and maturity. By removing control type from centre stage and replacing it with the need to analyse carefully the nature of incentives and restraints acting on top management, the major methodological innovations of the present study are logical progressions. First, this means that the individual interactions between stockholders, managers and markets must be explored. Second, it means that the ways in which these factors influence behaviour and performance *within* control types need to be understood before comparisons *between* control types are attempted. Only in this way can differences (or lack of differences) in corporate performance be fully understood.

Data and Definitions

Two major sources of data have been employed in this study. First, the accounts of a sample of companies listed on the Sydney Stock Exchange over the period 1965-6 to 1974-5. These accounts have been arranged into a standardised format by *STATEX*, an investment service prepared and published by the Research and Statistics Department of the Sydney Stock Exchange. This data set relates to some 370 corporations accounting for over 90 per cent of the capitalised value of all corporations listed on that exchange. As a first measure, companies engaged in mining, finance, development and contracting were eliminated in order to confine the sample to manufacturing and service industries. Of the 317 remaining companies, 300 were registered in the south-eastern mainland capital cities of Sydney, Melbourne, Canberra and Adelaide. A sample of 250 companies was drawn from this group, but was reduced by the omission of companies which had changed their accounting date or were not willing to co-operate in the study. The final sample consisted of 226 companies, which accounted for half the paid-up capital of non-mining, non-finance, non-development and contracting companies listed on all Australian stock exchanges in 1975. Of these, 194 were listed continuously.

The accounting data have been standardised in *STATEX* in the sense that certain items appearing in the annual reports of companies have been re-classified according to a set procedure in order to facilitate inter-company comparisons. Detailed definitions of the variables employed are provided in Appendix Table A.1.3. The main financial variables are size, growth, profitability, market valuation, risk and retentions.

The measure of size adopted in this study is *net assets* (NA_o, defined as long-term assets *plus* current assets, *less* current liabilities, *less* other deferred liability. Hence it is a measure of the book value of the long-term capital invested in the company. To circumvent the possibility of any feedback between dependent (profitability) variables and independent (size) variables in later analysis, size is measured at the beginning of a period. The growth measure is the compound annual *rate of growth of net assets* (GNA) over a period of time. It relates the closing value of net assets to the opening value and in so doing is subject to bias arising from the different valuation and depreciation techniques employed by accountants in different companies.

Another variable employed in the analysis is the *external growth rate* (EXG), which measures the contribution to growth of net assets which is made through reliance on external sources of funds. The denominator is net assets at the start of a period, while the numerator is an estimate of the value of external long-term capital raised. More specifically, the latter is defined as funds derived from the issue of ordinary shares, preference shares and long-term debt and increases in minority interests in subsidiaries. The extent of external sources of funds employed in the growth process is held to be an important factor in determining the profitability of uses to which these funds are put. That is, since firms must compete for external funds in an open capital market, only those which promise what the market establishes as a 'reasonable' return given the risks involved will be allocated these funds.

Two measures of average profitability have been calculated. The *pre-tax rate of return on net assets* (RNA) is defined as the ratio of first operating income, *plus* investment income, *plus* non-normal surplus/loss, *less* depreciation, to aggregate net assets. This measure will be used by the financial community to assess the success of managements' policies and strongly influences the terms on which external finance can be attracted. It is our contention that this measure will also be most relevant to a consideration of resource allocation from society's standpoint. Others have proposed that the rate of return on shareholders' equity is the best measure of allocative efficiency (Scherer, 1970, p. 80; Hall and Weiss, 1967, p. 321). However, shareholders' equity is but one of the various sources of capital which finances business and from the viewpoint of allocating the total resources of an economy the *source* of finance is irrelevant (Stigler, 1963, p. 123; Williamson, 1971, p. 411).

The *post-tax rate of return on equity assets* (REA), or the ratio of ordinary dividends and total retained to equity assets, will be of considerable interest to shareholders. The numerator consists of elements which encompass the possibility of current dividends and future capital gains, while the denominator is a measure (albeit an imperfect one) of the net worth of the ordinary shareholders' current interest in the company. The main problem with this measure is that equity assets are extremely sensitive to errors in valuation. This is because ordinary shareholders, in their capacity as the ultimate bearers of risk, are credited with any over-valuation and debited with any under-valuation of the company's assets.

Several writers have expressed the view that an *ex post market rate of return* figure is the most important performance variable in the eyes of shareholders.[6] Such a measure would calculate the rate of return which would discount the dividends and selling price of a share after a number of years back to the original purchase price. However, there are a number of disadvantages associated with this measure. Foremost among these is the fact that it is dependent on 'market expectations' and therefore it is difficult to separate managerial intentions from the resulting figures. If the market accurately foresees the results of managerial actions then all (risk-adjusted) returns should be tending to equality. It is difficult to predict the nature and extent of bias in the data. On the other hand, the shortcomings of accounting data are well known, they are the primary sources upon which management, shareholders and the market act, and it is possible to predict the direction of bias which arises.

Operating risk (SDRNA) is a measure which is meant to reflect the 'business risk' (as distinct from financial risk) associated with the corporate activities of the firm. It is defined as the standard deviation of the pre-tax rate of return on net assets calculated from the residuals around the trend line of earnings over the period. Similar measures have been employed by Fisher and Hall (1969) and by Samuels and Smyth (1968). It is argued that risks encountered in the operations of the firm arise owing to uncertainty about fluctuations in profit rates. Hence, we are interested in the 'pure fluctuations' around expected earnings which can only be calculated once the trend in earnings has been eliminated.

Another two variables which will receive particular attention are the valuation ratio and the retention ratio. The *valuation ratio* (VAL), a term employed by Marris (1964) in his theory of takeovers, is defined as the ratio of the stock market value of the firm's equity capital to the book value of its net assets. If current value accounting conventions were enforced, the denominator could be interpreted as an indicator of the separate economic resources employed by a firm. On the other hand, the numerator is an expression of the stock market's assessment of the company's worth under the assumption that the present management regime will continue into the indefinite future. The *retention ratio* (RET) is defined as the ratio of retentions from normal operations (i.e. excluding windfall gains and losses) to the sum of retentions and ordinary dividends. In this way extra-ordinary earnings and losses have been excluded to give a more valid indication of the 'normal' retention/payout policy pursued by a company.

Another major data requirement was for comprehensive and comparable information on the ownership structures of companies included in the sample. In particular, data identifying the share-holdings of directors and leading executives. Since there existed no central point at which the requisite statistics could be extracted, research had to be conducted around the country in the offices of the companies or their agents. The full data base which was accumulated has been published elsewhere (Lawriwsky, 1978). The question of ownership would be a relatively simple one were it not for the existence of private holding companies, trusts, foundations and nominees. Under the legal system presently enforced in Australia, it is impossible to determine with absolute accuracy the share ownership of all the groups involved. Even if the ownership of all shares could be traced, the question of control would be a perplexing one. Berle and Means (1932, p. 69) defined control as being 'the actual power to select the board of directors (or its majority)'. Since control embodies power, its foundations tend to become deliberately hidden.

Zeitlin (1974) proposed several criteria as indicators of the existence of a *potential* for control. At the very least, he argued, one requires information on the development of the company through the critical phases of its growth, together with a knowledge of the position within the company that institutions, companies or person-alities which played important roles in that development presently occupy. Second, one needs to know what resources any present or potential rivals for control are able to bring to the struggle. Finally, one needs a considerable understanding of the interrelationships between individuals linked through family or professional ties, who may be utilising a complex holding structure to keep control concentrated. In sum, these requirements may be reduced to the task of discovering the 'most effective kinship unit' operating in each case.

While it may be possible by these means to establish the existence of a potential for control by a group of stockholders, others have held that this potential may never be realised. Reeder (1975) considered that this may occur if one or more of the following circumstances is experienced: first, when the owner group or 'kinship unit' does not have the energy to fight; second, when it feels technically incompetent to challenge management; and third, when it is unaware that its interests are being compromised. Since none of these situations are likely to arise when some of the directors represent, or are part of, the owner group, one must consider that reasonable proxy measures for control can be devised by establishing, in each case, the nature and strength of the most effective kinship unit and examining the extent to which directors feature in it.

Thus, the problem becomes one of either establishing a set of arbitrary cut-off points for the percentage of voting stock deemed to be sufficient to exercise owner control (with due emphasis being placed on the peculiarities of environmental and institutional conditions) or applying different cut-off points in each case. Since there will inevitably exist a unique situation in each company, one is tempted to favour the second method. However, this will also involve considerable arbitrariness on the part of the researcher and we have opted for the consistency exhibited in the former method. However, the sensitivity of results to the application of *alternative* cut-off points is considered in Chapter 2.

In comparing the studies by Larner (1970) and Burch (1972) on the ownership and control of US corporations, Reeder (1975, p. 27) concluded that 'for any study to be truly instructive, the criteria used to categorize firms must be explicitly specified, so that the reader can see just what each author himself really means by the term "control"'. This may be done by considering the specific definitions presented below, together with the analysis of the dominant stockholder constraint presented in Chapter 5. The classification criteria are as follows:

1. Private Ownership Control

(a) Majority Ownership. Where directors as a cohesive group[7] or some other identifiable group of private individuals own more than 50 per cent of ordinary shares.

(b) Minority Ownership. Where directors as a cohesive group own between 10 per cent and 50 per cent of ordinary shares. The employment of a 10 per cent cut-off point in Australia can be justified on the grounds that Australian stock exchanges define 10 per cent ownership as a 'substantial interest'. However, further justification, based on theory and empirical observation, is provided in Chapter 5.

2. Other Company Control

(a) Domestic Company. This category is composed of corporations in which another company which itself is Australian owned holds at least 15 per cent of issued ordinary shares and where this is also the dominant holding. A 15 per cent cut-off point is used to eliminate the inclusion of corporations in which a significant holding by another company merely indicates an investment proposition rather than an overt nucleus for the exercise of control.

(b) Overseas Company. A similar definition to that which applies in 2 (a) above is employed here, except that now the controlling company is either a foreign corporation, or one which is controlled by foreign interests. Once again the foreign-owned holding must be the dominant one.

(c) Joint Domestic/Overseas Company. These are companies where there are two or more dominant shareholdings owned by a domestic company and a foreign concern such that joint domestic/overseas control is implied.

3. Management Control

This classification is assigned to companies in which the distribution of shareholdings is so dispersed that none of the above conditions can be satisfied. In many cases the incidence of substantial holdings by banks and other financial institutions may indicate a potential for control, but it is commonly assumed that institutional investors will generally remain passive in the absence of considerable upheavals in performance. This assumption is retained until further tests have been undertaken to establish its validity.

Given the nature and diversity of modern corporate enterprise, the classification of companies into industry groups is bound to be somewhat arbitrary, particularly at the margin. The system employed in this study is the Australian Standard Industrial Classification (ASIC). It should be noted that the level of aggregation is at roughly the two-digit industry level, and it could be expected that much of the explanatory power of industry related factors will be lost at this level. From that point of view a classification of companies at the four-digit level would be preferable since this corresponds more closely with the economists' concept of an industry. However, in Australia assignment of firms to their four-digit ASIC classes is confidential because of the generally small numbers of firms in Australian industries. Moreover, it is possible that even at the four-digit level we may not be defining an industry which is an 'area of close competition' between firms. For the purposes of this study, companies were allocated to two-digit ASIC industries utilising several sources: the *Sydney Stock Exchange Investment Service Sheets, Jobson's Year Book*, and the *Journal of the Associated Stock Exchanges.*

The final dimension is the classification of companies into 'mature' and 'non-mature' categories. Grabowski and Mueller (1975) employed a two-fold classification scheme based on time (companies initiated after 1945) and product structure (companies in which more than 50 per cent of products produced did not exist prior to 1945) to identify non-mature companies.

In Australia, 1939, the beginning of the Second World War, was considered to be a more significant demarcation. The war provided a considerable stimulus to Australia's manufacturing industries and the interruption of imports necessitated home production. During the war, and in the decades following, many new products and industries utilising new technologies were begun, while existing industries were expanded and modernised considerably. 'New' companies created to take over the productive assets of a concern which originated before 1939 were classified as mature, while companies established by 'mature' overseas corporations after that date were deemed to be non-mature in the Australian environment.[8]

To take account of chronologically old firms whose managements appear to have reversed life-cycle forces, the company histories of all 'mature' (by the first criterion) companies, as they appear in the *Sydney Stock Exchange Investment Service Sheets*, were examined and these were supplemented in some cases by information received through enquiries to the companies concerned. Where it could be

Table 1.1: Matrix of Company Classifications, by Industry, Control Type and Maturity

Industry	Majority ownership		Minority ownership		Management		Control type — Domestic company		Overseas company		Joint domestic/ overseas company		Sub-totals		Total
	M	N	M	N	M	N	M	N	M	N	M	N	M	N	
1. Food, beverages and tobacco	3	1	6	2	13		4	1		3			26	7	33
2. Textiles			2		1	2							3	2	5
3. Clothing and footwear						1	1		1	1			2	2	4
4. Paper, paper products, printing	2		3		4		4		2	2	1		16	2	18
5. Chemical, petroleum and coal products	1		4		5		1		6	1			17	1	18
6. Non-metallic mineral products			3		6	2	5		1	2	1		16	4	20
7. Basic metal products			1		1		1				1		4		4
8. Fabricated metal products			7	3	4	2	2		1	3			14	8	22
9. Transport equipment				1	6	1	1		1	1	1		9	3	12
10. Other machinery and equipment	3		9		11	2	1		3	5			27	7	34
11. Plastic and related products			1	1	1				1				3	1	4
12. Wholesale trade			6	1	5		1						12	1	13
13. Retail trade		1	9	1	7		2						18	2	20
14. Transport and storage					3	1	1		2	1			6	2	8
15. Entertainment, hotels, services			2	1	1			3		2			3	6	9
16. Others, construction and wood products				2										2	2
All companies	9	2	53	12	68	11	24	4	18	21	4		176	50	226

Note: M and N denote mature and non-mature firms respectively.

established that a major reorganisation in policy or product structure had been experienced during or after the Second World War, these companies were reclassified as non-mature. As a result of these procedures, 50 of the 226 companies in the sample were classified as non-mature and 176 as mature. The cross-classification of the sample by industry, control type and firm maturity is shown in Table 1.1.

Notes

1. Long before this, however, Adam Smith (1776, p. 700) held reservations as to the efficacy of such separation in promoting optimal performance with regard to the welfare of owners.

2. See Intriligator, Ornstein, Shrieves and Weston (1973, p. 33).

3. Business histories abound with examples of how the personal drive and ambition of leading executives steered the course that the company followed. An excellent Australian example is contained in Snooks's (1973) analysis of W.R. Hume's leadership of Hume Pipes. Francis (1980) has suggested that membership of 'marginal groups' in society, and the need to escape discrimination, may play a significant role in the drive of some entrepreneurs.

4. Brash (1966, pp. 67-70) made this point clear when considering foreign-controlled companies which were reluctant to invite local equity participation in Australia. Executives in these firms were concerned that the pricing and investment policies which suited the overall strategy of the parent might be objected to by minority shareholders.

5. Baumol was referring to Donaldson's (1961) research into the financing arrangements of 20 large US manufacturing corporations. Donaldson found that in only three of these was less than 80 per cent of long-term capital financed internally. However, this scenario conflicts with evidence presented by Lintner and Butters (1955).

6. For example, see Wildsmith (1973, p. 85), McEachern (1975, p. 90), Stano (1976, p. 672) and Holl (1977, p. 208).

7. 'Directors as a cohesive group' includes the directors, their immediate family and known close business associates.

8. Thus, in examining the relationship between foreign investment and firm growth, Penrose, (1956b, pp. 225-6) wrote that a subsidiary of a foreign company, once established, 'has a life of its own, and its growth will continue in response to the development of its own internal resources and the opportunities presented in its new environment'.

2 THE SEPARATION OF OWNERSHIP FROM CONTROL — THEORY AND EVIDENCE

Introduction

Most of the major new managerial theories of the firm based on the observation of a separation of ownership from control were articulated during the 1960s period. The central message was that, while the neo-classical profit maximisation assumption may have been adequate when single-product owner-managed enterprises were the norm, it could not confidently be adhered to in the modern corporate economy. Baumol (1959, 1967), Galbraith (1967), Marris (1964) and Williamson (1967) all offered alternative maximanda which, it was thought, would allow for greater realism in analysing and predicting corporate behaviour and performance.

The emerging managerial literature evoked a sharp response from a number of economists.[1] None of these critics denied that in many cases control has passed from owners to managers. It was their contention, however, that although managers' motivations with regard to profits may seem, superficially, to have been weakened, there do remain important counteracting forces which ensure that the actual behaviour of corporations does not stray very far from that implied in the traditional theory.

During the decade of the 1970s the new managerial theories were subjected to empirical scrutiny. However, the empiricists adopted a rather narrow methodological approach in setting up private ownership-controlled companies as a benchmark reflecting 'shareholder welfare maximisation'. The performance of dispersed ownership (management-controlled) companies was then compared with this in cross-sectional studies which accounted for differing environmental conditions with industry dummies, firm size and/or variables reflecting barriers to entry. The succession of studies covering various periods, employing different samples and alternative definitions of control type in a number of countries have not been able to demonstrate a clear pattern of behaviour. Further research along the same lines does not appear justified.

Rather than embark on an exhaustive review of 'Alternative Theories of the Firm', the next section sketches three models which are of particular interest to this study. Marris's (1964) model is representative of the managerial theories and perhaps, more than any other, has formed the basis of past empirical research which concentrated on control type. Reder's (1947) model illustrates an opposing viewpoint which has been largely overlooked by both theoretical and empirical researchers. Mueller's (1969, 1972) life-cycle model is also introduced as it forms a part of the analysis in later chapters. The next section presents a broad critique of studies testing for differences in performance based on control type. The final section argues for a new theoretical and empirical approach.

Alternative Theories of the Firm

Marris's Growth Maximisation Hypothesis

Probably the most influential growth model of the firm was presented by Marris (1964).[2] It was in many respects similar to Baumol's sales maximisation model,[3] and drew on the earlier works of Gordon (1945), Simon (1957, 1959) and Penrose (1959). Marris also made frequent references to the literature of sociologists and psychologists in what could be termed a multi-disciplinary approach. The central thesis was introduced in an early chapter which discussed the 'changing institutional framework'. Thus, with the rise of functional specialisation in the joint stock company, managers with little, if any, beneficial interest in the company could no longer be expected single-mindedly to pursue profits. The motivational device was portrayed as a managerial utility function, the primary argument of which is the rate of growth of assets of the firm. While managers are largely unconstrained by stockholders or pressures from the product market, they do place some positive value on their security from takeover.

The Marris growth model provided the basic hypotheses of researchers testing the alternative theories of the firm. That is, it provided the expectation that companies controlled by professional managers would earn lower profits, have a lower market valuation and be more risk averse, while growing faster and retaining a larger fraction of earnings than would be necessary for shareholder welfare maximisation. This model and its empirical implications may be summarised with the aid of Figure 2.1. It should be noted that the interpretation shown here is not totally consistent with that originally presented by Marris.[4] However, it is the one which has influenced

Figure 2.1: Marris's Growth Maximisation Model

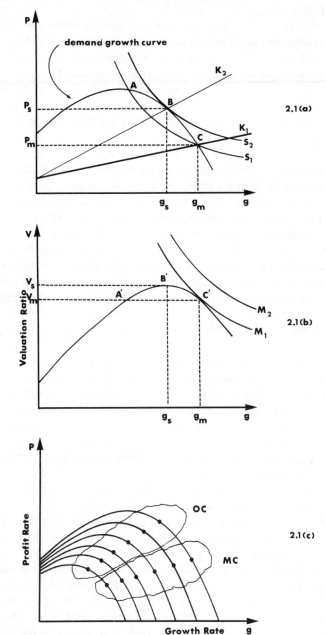

much of the empirical work examining the performances of owner and management-controlled firms.

In Figure 2.1 (a) Marris's 'demand growth curve' shows the relationship presumed to exist between the rate of profit and the rate of growth of assets (or rate of diversification assuming no failures). The rationale for defining its shape is that at low rates of growth the firm will experience the 'temporary monopoly' effect and management may be stimulated by growth so that profitability and growth vary directly, but after a point increasing marketing expenses will come to dominate the former effects, and the curve turns over. The lines K_1 etc., are the 'growth of supply functions', which show the relationship between the rate of profit and the funds which may be forthcoming to finance expansion. The positive slope indicates that with a given retention ratio higher growth can be achieved by earning higher profits or, with given profitability, a higher growth rate may be achieved through higher retentions. Thus, the growth of supply function K_2 requires a lower retention ratio than the function K_1. The introduction of external finance does not alter the basic relationship.

Owing to differential rates of taxation on dividends and capital gains shareholders will show some preference for growth. Shareholders' preferences between growth and profits can be represented by a family of shareholder indifference curves S_1, S_2, etc., in Figure 2.1 (a). The point of tangency, B, with the 'demand growth curve' defines the growth rate which maximises valuation (as mentioned in Chapter 1, the 'valuation ratio' is the ratio of the market value of a company to its book value). This, then, defines the shareholder-welfare-maximisation performance, which would require a growth rate of g_s and profit rate p_s. That combination of profitability and growth, in turn, defines the maximum valuation of the company at point B' in Figure 2.1 (b). A lower indifference curve, S_1, cutting the 'demand growth curve' at points A and C in Figure 2.1 (a) would define another two points on the 'valuation curve' in Figure 2.1 (b) with the same valuation ratio (at A' and C' respectively).

The optimum performance from the viewpoint of professional managers may be established by two methods. First, one could view it as the maximisation of the growth rate subject to a growth of supply constraint such as K_1, beyond which the danger of takeover would be imminent. Alternatively, the managerial utility function could be seen to contain two arguments, the valuation ratio, which would provide a measure of security from takeover, and the growth rate, which is associated with power, prestige and salary. This tradeoff is represented in Figure 2.1 (b) by a family of managerial indifference curves, M_1, M_2, etc., which for consistency show the same result. That is, the highest managerial indifference curve, M_1, is tangent to the valuation curve at C'. Hence, the growth maximisation strategy of managers (m) differs from the shareholder-welfare-maximisation strategy (s) in that growth is higher ($g_m > g_s$), profitability is lower ($p_m < g_s$) and the valuation ratio is lower ($V_m < V_s$). We may also infer, from the positions of K_1 and K_2, that the retention ratio will be higher ($r_m > r_s$).

A fundamental problem of trying to test the growth maximisation hypothesis in a cross-sectional framework is that firms will be operating under varying 'environmental conditions', so that a wide range of growth-profitability tradeoffs will be picked up. The tradeoff between profitability and growth will tend to be swamped by a positive relationship and the spread of observations in the profitability-growth plane will tend to fan out. The latter situation arises because firms operating with extremely high profitability and low growth will be takeover candidates (for not exploiting available opportunities) and so will companies with low profitability but extremely high growth rates (for over-exploiting them).

Holl (1975) has proposed that a cross-sectional scatter of observations for owner and manager-controlled firms might look like that shown in Figure 2.1 (c). In other words, owner-controlled firms would maintain performances close to the shareholder-welfare-maximising ideal, while management-controlled firms would strive for growth maximisation. The loose link here, however, is the assumption that owner-controlled firms (i.e. firms with a concentrated ownership pattern) will necessarily be shareholder-welfare-maximising. Indeed, while the Marris model went into much detail on managerial performance relative to shareholder-welfare-maximisation, the behaviour of owner-controlled companies, and of owner-managed companies in particular, was hardly mentioned.

Reder's Entrepreneurial Control Hypothesis

One writer who did devote some attention to the behaviour of owner-entrepreneurs was Reder (1947). His early analysis appears to have been lost in the rush to find a managerial theory of the firm, when in fact it provides plausible explanations both for the way that owner-controllers operate and why the dispersion of stockholdings takes place. Reder's model, with some adaptation, is presented in Figure 2.2. In essence, it postulates the existence of a tradeoff between greater profits and the maintenance of control by the dominant owner(s). The behavioural hypothesis is that the owner-controller aims to maximise profits subject to retaining control over the firm.

In quadrant I of Figure 2.2, the curve P is a 'valuation curve' which is unlike the one described in Marris's model. Here the curve shows the relationship between the planned rate of growth of the firm over a

Figure 2.2: Reder's Entrepreneurial Control Model

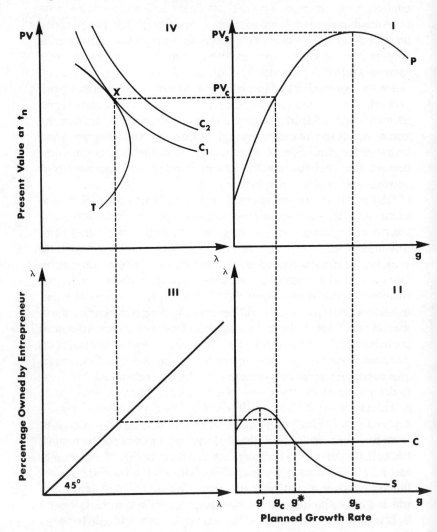

period, $t_o \ldots t_n$, and the present value of the net worth of the firm at t_n (as seen at t_o). Reder does not explain its shape, although one could offer an explanation similar to Marris's 'demand growth curve'. The vertical axis in quadrant II shows λ, the percentage of the firm, which will be owned by the owner-controller at time t_n. The relationship marked S shows how λ will vary depending on the growth rate which is pursued. The S curve will rise at first since at low rates of growth retained earnings may be the only source of finance, or the owner-controller may increase his stake in the firm through purchases or oversubscription to new equity issues. Up to the growth rate g', then, there is no conflict between profitability and control. However, a conflict does develop at high growth rates when greater recourse to external finance is required.

Reder assumed that the owner-controller would maximise the present value of the firm, P, subject to maintaining control. The ultimate constraint, C, was defined as that proportion of the firm's shares which the entrepreneur would need to retain control. The height of C would depend on a number of factors, such as the dispersion of other shareholdings and riskiness of the business. There may be some difficulty here in that the *proportion* of the present value of the firm which may be claimed by the owner-controller ($\lambda.P$) will eventually fall. It may be more valid to interpret P as that portion of the present value of the firm which will belong to the owner-controller at t_n.

If the equity of other shareholders behaves in the same way (although at non-controlling proportions) then g_s may be termed the shareholder-welfare-maximising growth rate. However this is also an oversimplification, as g_s for the owner-controller could differ from that for other shareholders for a number of reasons. Among these we could list different attitudes to risk, different taxation situations and a preference for managerial perquisites.

Reder pointed out that the S and P curves alone are not sufficient to determine what growth rate will be planned by the entrepreneur and merely assumed that it would lie somewhere between g' and g^*, say, at a point like g_c. In order to locate g_c, the optimal growth rate from the viewpoint of the owner-controller, we need to introduce a tradeoff function, T, which describes the relationship between PV and λ. Thus, we are assuming that the owner-controller's utility function has two arguments, the present value of that part of the firm which is owned by him and the percentage of the firm which is owned by him. The first element ties the interests of owner-controllers and other shareholders together, while the latter element indicates a preference for retention of control *through shareholdings.* If this control were lost through dilution, it is apparent that in most cases managerial control could still be maintained as long as no other concentration of shareholdings developed.

The preferences of the owner-controller as between wealth and security of control will be reflected by a family of indifference curves. In quadrant IV the highest indifference curve C_1 is tangent to the tradeoff function at point X and this translates through quadrants I and III to define the optimal growth rate of the owner-controller, g_c in quadrant II. This result shows that the owner-controller's fear of loss of control will cause him to choose a growth rate which is too low to maximise shareholder welfare PV_s, which requires growth rate g_s. Some investment opportunities which are profitable for shareholders (if they result in dilution of equity) will be missed.

This model thus provides a rationale for the observation that dilution of controlling shareholdings does take place over time, even though they may be resisted by owner-controllers.[7] There are other reasons, such as indivisibilities (economies of scale) and changes in technology which will shift the P curve in a way that speeds up the process of dilution. This might explain why dispersion of equity appears to take place more rapidly in some industries. Of course, if the peak of the S function were to occur to the right of g_s there would not be a conflict between shareholder welfare and control maintenance. One reason for not expecting this to be the case generally is that dilution of control has been established as a temporal trend.[8] However, under these circumstances one could propose that a managerial preference for growth among owner-controllers could explain dilution. This illustrates that a vast grey area separates the positions of Reder and Marris, since both are simplifications of reality.

Mueller's Life-Cycle Hypothesis

D.C. Mueller (1972) has suggested that the validity of the ownership and control version of the growth hypothesis varies with the extent of investment opportunities faced by the firm. This may be conveniently shown with the aid of a diagram which originates from Duesenberry (1958). In Figure 2.3 the vertical axis measures marginal rates of return on long-run investments[9] (MRR), the marginal cost of capital (MCC) and investor and manager discount rates (i and m respectively). The horizontal axis measures the volume of investment

Figure 2.3: Mueller's Life-Cycle Model

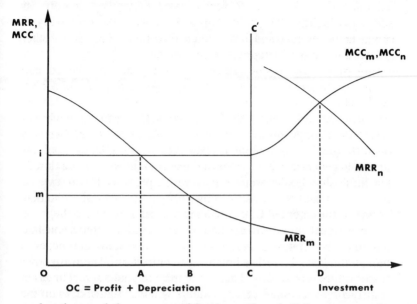

undertaken and the sources of funds employed. OC represents the amount of internal funds (profit plus depreciation) available for investment. The cost of these internally generated funds to a firm which maximises shareholder welfare is the shareholder discount rate, i. This represents the opportunity cost of their funds (given the expected return on investment in another firm or portfolio of firms with comparable risk). The cost of raising new equity capital will equal i plus the cost of transactions, and raising the amount of contractual debt (i.e. the debt/equity ratio) will result in increasing risk premiums. Hence, a rising external MCC schedule is proposed. MRR_n and MRR_m are the marginal returns to investment schedules of non-mature and mature firms respectively.

While 'immaturity' is normally associated with a young innovative firm, it may be possible for a firm, through continual diversification into new products and processes, to remain indefinitely immature (i.e. in the sense that a majority of its products are always in the early stages of their life-cycles). Also, a firm which is chronologically old and stagnating may suddenly become immature by shifting into a new technology.[10] Grabowski and Mueller (1975) felt that while exceptional firms have remained innovative, over time this ability will normally decline. Furthermore, as the firm grows in size and its existing product structure matures, it must increase its rate of diversification for that structure to remain predominantly immature. In addition, Mueller (1972, p. 203) argued that while the availability of capital to the research and development director in a large firm will be greater than to the entrepreneur, the probability that the latter will eventually obtain the necessary funds may actually be greater because of the larger number and variety of sources open to him (also see Mueller and Tilton, 1969, p. 572).

During the early stage of the firm's life-cycle, due to the high levels of investment opportunity prevailing, its MRR schedule (MRR_n) will be such that all profitable investments cannot be satisfied by internally generated funds alone and external finance will be raised. The firm's shareholder-welfare-maximising policy will be to reinvest all its profit and depreciation flow, OC, and undertake external finance to the extent of CD. Assuming that managers have the same time preference for growth as shareholders have for income, it will be in the managers' interest to invest only up to the shareholder-welfare-maximising level. If further investment were undertaken this would reduce future profitability. That is, the real incremental cost in terms of attracting additional external funds would be greater than the incremental revenues generated by that investment, so that future growth would be sacrificed for present growth. In this instance 'both the non-mature growth-maximising and the non-mature stockholder-welfare-maximising firms will undertake the same investment policies' (Mueller, 1969, p. 646). At the immature stage of the firm's life-cycle, then, the interests of managers and shareholders will coincide. Both will be intent on raising sufficient capital to exhaust the available opportunities to maximise both the rate of growth and potential market value of the firm.

With the passage of time, as the firm expands and matures, several changes will occur. The original owner-entrepreneur's equity interest will often be continuously diluted in order to raise additional funds for investment, so that control of the enterprise is likely to pass to management. Managers' freedom from control by shareholders will be enhanced by the fact that a large firm presents a more difficult target for takeover (Singh, 1971; Kuehn, 1972; Holl, 1977). On the other hand, increased size may cause managerial diseconomies to develop (Williamson, 1967). The level of profit and depreciation flows CC' will shift to the right, but the MRR_m schedule will not shift to the same extent. If so, MRR_m will eventually cut the MCC_m schedule to the left of CC'.[11]

In the mature stage of the life-cycle a shareholder-welfare-maximising firm would undertake additional investment only up to the point where the marginal rate of return on investment, MRR_m, equals the shareholders' rate of discount, i. In other words, a shareholder-welfare-maximising management will now be expected to retain OA of earnings, pay out AC as dividends and undertake no external financing.[12] This will allow shareholders, if they wish, to reinvest these funds in other sections of the economy promising better returns. However, in the mature phase of the life-cycle, control is often in the hands of managers, who will be intent on securing their own interest through the pursuit of growth. At this point the conflict with shareholders' interests develops. The cost of using internal funds for a growth oriented management of a mature firm will not be 'the rate of return the stockholders can earn in the market but some much lower, totally subjective value set by the managers'.[13] Hence a mature firm with growth-maximising managers will undertake investment of OB, pay dividends of BC and have a lower rate of return on its marginal investments than a shareholder-welfare-maximising firm.

The shift to growth maximisation over time is likely to be so gradual as to be imperceptible to shareholders. For example, it may take the form of simply not increasing the payout ratio as opportunities for profitable investment decline relative to internal cash flows, or of not increasing it by the necessary amount. The degree of over-investment in growth which results will depend on the difference between i and m and the slope of the MRR_m schedule.

Several seemingly paradoxical features should be noted. First, an immature firm need not be chronologically young, rather it is the firm's economic age which is at issue. Second, Mueller (1970) drew attention to the fact that the separation of ownership from control need not be the overriding factor when considering the growth hypothesis. When managers control an immature firm no conflict of interests is likely to arise as shareholders then gain positive utility from growth maximisation. However, a mature owner-controlled firm may over-invest in growth if the original owners' interests as managers override their interests as shareholders. It is quite possible for owner-managers to have developed similar utility functions to those of professional managers. In addition, the constraints imposed by the dominant shareholder (i.e. the manager himself) and the threat of takeover will be less severe in such firms, so that owner-managers will have relatively more freedom to pursue alternative goals than will their manager counterparts in management-controlled firms. Third, it should be recognised that, in general, it will not be the fastest-growing firms in the economy which are over-investing in growth, since these will most likely be the immature firms. Instead it will be the large sluggish firms which in many cases should not be growing at all. Grabowski and Mueller (1975) and Hiller (1978) have reported findings consistent with the predictions of the life-cycle hypothesis. However, a study by Kamerschen and Kerchner (1978) achieved ambiguous results when testing the hypothesis that in mature management-controlled firms the market would value dividends more highly than retentions.

Tests of the Separation Thesis

Most of the frequently cited empirical research on the separation of ownership from control is summarised in Appendix Table A.2.1. The studies shown there are arranged by country and are in chronological order. The first studies to appear in the United States were conducted by Monsen Chiu and Cooley (1968) and Kamerschen (1968). In deriving conflicting results they set the pace for future research.

While most studies have shown that owner-controlled firms yielded higher profitability, the difference has often been statistically or economically insignificant. The only exceptions to this rule (i.e. where management-controlled firms have been more profitable) have been found in situations where firms have had low market power (Ware, 1975; Sorensen, 1974), or where, as in West Germany, financial institutions have played a significant role in the affairs of industrial corporations (Thonet and Poensgen, 1979). Of the studies examining firm growth, many have found that there was no statistically significant difference based on control type. However, it is important to note that those studies which have found owner-controlled firms to be significantly more profitable (Radice, 1971; McEachern 1975) *also* found owner-controlled firms to grow at a significantly faster rate (Radice, 1971; McEachern, 1978a). In other words, where strong and statistically significant differences in more than one performance variable have emerged, the relationship between these has not been unusual from an economic standpoint. This result indicates that the owner-controlled firms operated with greater 'efficiency' (i.e. on a higher 'demand growth curve') than management-controlled firms.

Similarly, studies examining risk performance have yielded mixed conclusions. But those studies which have examined *both* risk and profitability, and found that significantly higher profits were earned by owner-controlled firms (Boudreaux, 1973; McEachern, 1975), *also* found that these owner-controlled firms were significantly more risky. The same relation holds for retentions and control type. For instance, when McEachern (1975, p. 47) reworked Sorenson's (1974) data excluding low entry-barrier industries he showed that management-controlled firms in the remaining sample earned significantly lower profits and had a significantly *higher* payout ratio than owner-controlled firms. In his own sample McEachern (1975) found that his 'owner-managed' firms, which were significantly *more* profitable than management controlled firms, also had a significantly *lower* payout ratio.

Grabowski and Mueller (1975) have argued that owner-controlled firms will on average tend to be younger and have higher investment opportunities than management-controlled firms. If this were the case, then findings that owner-controlled firms have higher profits associated with higher growth, risk and retentions could not be interpreted as providing support for the separation thesis. Yet only McEachern (1975) attempted to control for this possibility by including a firm age variable in his analysis.

The managerial theories were concerned with large firms operating with some degree of monopoly power. Accordingly, many studies have employed samples composed of large firms, usually the top 200 or 500 US non-financial corporations. Palmer (1973a) limited his sample even further by separating out firms with high entry-barriers in their major industry and Holl (1977) confined his study to those management-controlled firms which in addition could evade the discipline of the market for corporate control. In these studies owner-controlled firms were found to earn significantly higher profits. On the other hand, studies employing a much larger sample (e.g. Kania and McKean, 1976) found no significant differences. But without including a wide range of company sizes and examining for control-type effects within different size categories, it is difficult to conclude that any differences in performances were dependent on control type *per se*. The differences might, for example, have come about through 'survivorability'. That is, within a sample of very large corporations, any remaining owner-controlled companies would need to be exceptional, since in order to grow to that size while retaining ownership control new equity issues would need to be limited and more debt incurred. Such doubts have been raised by

Radice (1971) and Steer and Cable (1978), but no formal tests of the proposition have been undertaken.

Another problem with past studies is that they have assumed that owners, many of whom are also managers, do not derive non-pecuniary benefits from the performance of their firm. Knight (1921) and Schumpeter (1934) recognised that 'empire building' even at the expense of profits may be associated with the egos of owner-managers. Other theorists have also made this observation (e.g. Gordon, 1945; Marris, 1964; Nichols, 1969; Mueller, 1970), but only McEachern (1975) has formally incorporated it in an empirical model.

Several studies separated firms into 'ultimate control' categories. Under such a classification scheme if a firm is controlled through a substantial shareholding by another company which in turn is controlled by a third company, the control type of the last holding company would be assigned to the first two. But it can by no means be taken for granted that the incentives and constraints faced by decision-makers within a particular company-controlled firm are identical to those in the controlling or parent organisation. In fact, Nyman and Silberston (1978, p. 94) have argued that in such firms managerial discretion would be severely limited. It was also reasoned that significant holdings by financial institutions would limit managerial discretion, but no published study has attempted to test this proposition in a cross-sectional framework.

There has also been some disagreement as to what proportion of shareholdings is necessary to constitute control over a corporation and different studies have used varying definitions. Probably the most prevalent definition of ownership control has been that 10 per cent of voting stock be held by a small group of 'related' individuals (e.g. Kamerschen, 1968; Larner, 1970; Palmer, 1973a). Other studies have tested for differences in the performance of two extreme control groups, variously defined (e.g. Monsen, Chiu and Cooley, 1968; Radice, 1971; Boudreaux, 1973). But none of the previous studies has presented a sensitivity analysis of their results employing alternative definitions of management control.

Another controversy surrounds the choice of the appropriate performance indicator. There has been a debate in the industrial organisation literature over whether sales-based or capital-based measures of profitability give the *best* indications of allocative efficiency.[14] The ownership and control studies have been divided as to whether a rate on equity or net assets is superior to an ex-post market rate of return (i.e. the return to an investor from dividends and capital gains). A problem with the market return figure is that it depends partially on market expectations and may be more independent of managerial actions. On the other hand, returns on equity or net assets are subject to the vagaries of creative accounting. Both are subject to the criticism that a risk dimension is not incorporated. It has been argued that the capital asset pricing model (CAPM) will yield a risk-adjusted market rate of return (Bothwell, 1980). However, as Hindley (1970, p. 214) has pointed out, the market may be expected to capitalise the *anticipated* effects of control type. Any differences on the basis of control type which are observed, then, may be due to 'changes in the level of managerial usurpation', or to a change in the control position which has gone unnoticed by the researcher in question.

Caution should be exercised in making international comparisons of studies seeking to uncover performance consequences of the separation of ownership from control. Chandler (1977) stressed that cultural, social and legal differences between the US and European countries have been responsible for chronological disparities in the emergence of managerial capitalism. For example, it was noted that,

> In Europe ... Families identified themselves more closely with the firm that provided the income with which to maintain their status than did families in the United States ... [and where] the owners hired middle managers to co-ordinate flows, the family continued to dominate top management. Often the family preferred not to expand the enterprise if it meant the loss of personal control. (p. 500)

Such a scenario applies equally to Australia which has derived much of its cultural heritage and many of its institutions from European, and particularly British, models. In Australia dominant family shareholdings in firms have invariably been associated with direct representation on the board and an involvement in the managerial decision-making process. This also appears to be the case in the UK (Nyman and Silberston, 1978; Francis, 1980) but not in the US (McEachern, 1975).[15] There also appear to be wide differences in the extent of concentration and control by financial institutions. As a result of bank control, Thonet and Poensgen (1979) found that management-controlled firms are a much less significant feature of the corporate structure in West Germany than they are in the US. The level of concentration of shareholdings by financial institutions in Australia is greater than that of the UK which, in turn, is more concentrated than the US (Briston and Dobbins, 1978, and Chapter 5 below). Another difference between the Western capitalist economies is the attitude adopted toward managerial remuneration. For example, the size and range of executive stock-option and bonus scheme in the US is far greater than in the UK or in Australia (see Chapter 4).

The Need for a New Approach

Two fundamental criticisms were outlined in the previous section. First, that studies have not presented an analysis of the sensitivity of their results to alternative specifications of control type. Second, that concentrating exclusively on the largest corporations in the economy does not allow us a 'cross-sectional snapshot' of the dispersion process. In those limited samples it is difficult to test whether the 'survivorability' argument mentioned above has empirical backing. In the present section a sensitivity analysis is conducted employing the Australian data set.

We shall consider four alternative definitions of management control — denoted MC_1, MC_2, MC_3 and MC_4 — all of which have been employed in previous studies. Specifically, the definitions of these four dummy variables are as follows:[16]

MC_1
$\begin{cases} = 1 \text{ for firms where directors and related interests} \\ \quad \text{held less than 5 per cent of shares} \\ = 0 \text{ if directors and related interests held more than} \\ \quad \text{5 per cent of shares} \end{cases}$

MC_2
$\begin{cases} = 1 \text{ for firms where directors and related interests} \\ \quad \text{held less than 10 per cent of shares} \\ = 0 \text{ if directors and related interests held more than} \\ \quad \text{10 per cent of shares} \end{cases}$

MC_3
$\begin{cases} = 1 \text{ for firms where directors and related interests} \\ \quad \text{held less than 5 per cent of shares} \\ = 0 \text{ if directors and related interests held more than} \\ \quad \text{15 per cent of shares} \end{cases}$

$$
MC_4 \begin{cases} = \text{1 for firms where directors and related interests} \\ \quad \text{held less than 10 per cent of shares and were able} \\ \quad \text{to evade the discipline of the market for} \\ \quad \text{corporate control} \\ = \text{0 if directors and related interests held more than} \\ \quad \text{10 per cent of shares} \end{cases}
$$

In previous studies two of the most frequently used indicators of performance have been the rate of return on net worth (equity assets) and the growth rate of the firm. Most tests have taken the form of regressing these performance measures against a dummy variable reflecting management control. Differences in environmental conditions have been accounted for by the inclusion of industry dummies, firm size and/or industry barriers-to-entry variables.

As estimates of industry barriers to entry at the firm level were not available,[17] the original model was of the form,

$$
P = \beta_0 + \beta_1 \, MC_j + \sum_{k=2}^{k=17} \beta_k \sum_{l=2}^{l=16} ID_l + \beta_{18} \, SIZE + \beta_{19} \, NMAT + \varepsilon
$$

$$(2.1)$$

where,

P	is performance, measured alternatively as REA (post-tax rate of return on equity assets) and GNA (growth rate of net assets) over the period 1966-7 to 1974-5
MC_j	is the management control dummy, where $j = 1 \ldots 4$
$ID_2 \ldots ID_{10}$	are industry dummy variables, where ID_1 (Food, beverages and tobacco) = 0, $ID_1 = 1$ otherwise, etc.
SIZE	is firm size, defined as the reciprocal of net assets in 1966 (NA_0)[18]
NMAT	is the firm maturity dummy, assigned a value of 1 when the firm is non-mature and 0 otherwise.

$\beta_0 \ldots \beta_{19}$ are constants

ε is the stochastic error term

However, when the two-digit industry dummy variables were included in our regressions only one was significant at the .05 level using a two-tailed test. This industry, textiles, had significantly lower profitability and growth. Since the inclusion of the industry dummies did not materially affect the size or significance of the coefficient on MC_j these were dropped from the equation. There is no real theoretical justification for including a textile dummy as this industry was composed of a roughly equal number of management- and owner-controlled firms. Consequently the model reduces to,

$$P = \beta_0 + \beta_1 MC_j + \beta_2 SIZE + \beta_3 NMAT + \varepsilon \qquad (2.2)$$

Following the usual empirical interpretation of the 'alternative theories' we are testing the hypotheses that, (a) management-controlled firms will earn a lower rate of return than owner-controlled firms and (b) management-controlled firms will grow at a faster rate than owner-controlled firms. Therefore, the null and alternative hypotheses are Ho: $\beta_1 = 0$, H1: $\beta_1 < 0$ in the profitability equation and Ho: $\beta_1 = 0$, H1: $\beta_1 > 0$ in the growth equation. No *a priori* hypothesis is made regarding the sign on the SIZE coefficient, since the effects of economies of scale and market power might be countered by X-inefficiency and pursuit of alternative objectives to profit maximisation. When reviewing Radice's 'surprising' results Grabowski and Mueller (1975, p. 405) offered a 'life-cycle' interpretation, arguing that, on average, the management-controlled firms will tend to be more mature and have lower investment opportunities. Therefore, on this count one would expect to find higher profit and growth rates among owner-controlled firms. Still, the application of equation (2.2) to the entire sample gave a surprising result. Management-controlled firms were shown to be *both* more profitable and growing faster than owner-controlled firms. Statistical significance at the .05 level was achieved in every case, except when MC_4 was employed as the definition of management control.

But, as McEachern (1978b, p. 492) has reiterated, the ' "new theories" ... argue that in addition to there being a separation of ownership from control managers must also be relatively free from the product-market constraint ... and this environment is characterized by large firms in less than competitive industries'. Thus a supporter of the managerialist hypothesis would discount this unusual result and insist on a separate test being conducted on the large firms sub-sample.

In fact our sample was stratified into three size categories and the curvilinear SIZE variable in equation 2.2 was replaced by a linear variable NA_0, the value of net assets in 1966. The 'large firms' size category was composed of firms with opening assets exceeding \$20 million in 1966.[19] This corresponds to the top 100 Australian companies at that time. In *proportionate* terms, however, this group is roughly comparable to the top 500 in the US and the top 200 in the UK, which have been the primary subjects of research on ownership and control in those countries. The 'small firms' category was composed of firms with net assets of less than \$5 million in 1966.

A summary of the sensitivity analysis is provided in Table 2.1 which shows the coefficients and 't ratios' obtained on the management-control dummy variables in the three size categories. Considering first the rate of return on equity (REA) column in the large firms sample we find that the negative signs attached to the management-control dummies support the managerialist position. However, the negative coefficients in the growth equations (GNA) run counter to the managerial prediction. Also, the explanatory power was quite low (R^2 ranged from .086, to .182 when MC_3 was employed). The MC_2 definition of management control is similar to that employed in many US studies and the result is not unlike that found by, say, Kamerschen (1968) or Larner (1970). The MC_3 definition approximates most closely the definition employed by Radice (1971), whose sample consisted of large UK firms. This definition has the effect of eliminating what Radice termed 'transitional' control types, those in which the cohesive ownership group holds between 5 per cent and 15 per cent of issued shares. Here the coefficient indicates that management-controlled firms earned a rate of return on equity assets which was 1.5 percentage points less than that earned by owner-controlled firms. But at the same time management-controlled firms grew at a lower rate — 2.4 per cent lower — than did owner-controlled firms. The conclusion is not unlike that reported by Radice.

The fourth definition of management control, MC_4, is similar to the one used by Holl (1977) in the US. There we are testing Holl's hypothesis that management-controlled firms which can avoid the constraint of the market for corporate control and have a significant degree of market power, will earn a lower rate of return than will

Table 2.1: Sensitivity of MC Coefficient to Firm Size and
Alternative Specifications of Management Control

Firm Size	Small		Medium		Large	
Control Type	REA	GNA	REA	GNA	REA	GNA
MC_1	.008	.038	.022	.034	—.004	—.008
	(.415)	(.839)	(2.383)[b]	(2.072)[b]	(.566)	(.587)
MC_2	.028	.045	.027	.032	—.011	—.017
	(2.648)[b]	(1.214)	(2.965)[a]	(1.874)[c]	(1.408)[c]	(1.223)
MC_3	.020	.054	.026	.037	—.015	—.024
	(1.755)[c]	(.970)	(2.625)[a]	(1.780)[c]	(1.850)[b]	(1.466)
MC_4	—.007	.016	.010	.034	—.023	—.027
	(.272)	(.155)	(.747)	(1.717)[c]	(3.223)[a]	(1.661)

Note: a, b and c denote significance at the .01, .05 and .10 levels respectively using a
one-tail test for the large firms sample and a two-tail test for the small and medium-
sized firms samples.

owner-controlled firms in a similar position of market power. The
bias inherent in stating the mangerialist hypothesis in this way can be
seen by comparing coefficients on the control-type dummy variables
MC_2 and MC_4. In the former case, which employs the same definition
of management control based on ownership structure, the profitability of management-controlled firms is 1.1 percentage points
below that of owner-controlled firms. Larner (1970) would argue
that this difference is not very important in economic terms and it is
only barely statistically significant at .10 level using a one-tail test.
Yet in the equation employing MC_4, management-controlled firms
are seen to earn a rate of return 2.3 percentage points less than owner-
controlled firms and this difference is significant at the .01 level.[20]
Holl did not test the proposition that growth rates of firms differed
according to his definition of control type. However, our results
show that these (MC_4) management-controlled firms, as well as
earning lower profits, grew less rapidly. The influence of firm size on
the profitability of these large firms was extremely weak, but size was
generally negatively associated with growth and on one occasion the
size coefficient was significant at the .10 level using a two-tailed test.

Thus, we have found that among the very largest firms in the
economy, depending on the definition employed, management-
controlled firms are shown to be: (a) about as profitable as owner-
controlled firms (MC_1); (b) significantly less profitable at the .10

level (MC_2); (c) significantly less profitable at the .05 level (MC_3); or (d) significantly less profitable at the .01 level (MC_4). The choice, it seems, is up to the researcher.

Before discussing medium- and small-sized firms a digression on the behaviour of the maturity dummy would appear to be in order. For large firms the coefficients relating to NMAT in the profitability equations were all positive and significant at the .10 level. In absolute terms the effect of non-maturity on the average return of equity assets ranged from 1.7 percentage points to 2.4 percentage points. In the growth equations all the coefficients on the maturity dummy had the expected positive sign and were about twice as great as the effect on profitability. However, statistical significance was not achieved. One reason for the lack of statistical significance of the NMAT coefficient in the growth equations and the relatively low t-values in the profitability equations may be the small number of observations. Only three of the 38 large firms were classified as non-mature. Another reason is that we should expect non-mature firms to earn higher marginal rates of return. Thus, Mueller (1969, p. 675) has argued that 'while the correlation between average and marginal rates of return among firms is undoubtedly positive, enough white noise is probably introduced into the data by using the former as a proxy for the desired marginal rates, that the significance of this type of test [of the growth maximisation hypothesis] is placed in some doubt'.

The profitability and growth performances of medium-sized and small owner- and management-controlled firms are now compared. Since the managerialist literature argues that in smaller firms (where competitive pressures are likely to be more intense) managers will have little opportunity to divert potential profits, two-tailed 't tests' are performed on the coefficients of the control-type dummies. Medium-sized firms are defined as those which had net assets of between $5 million and $20 million in 1966. The results show that in terms of both profitability and growth, management-controlled firms outperformed owner-controlled firms. In terms of profitability management-controlled firms earned a rate of return on equity assets which was, depending on the definition used, between 1.0 and 2.7 percentage points higher. Furthermore, this difference was, with the exception of (MC_4), always significant at the .05 level or better. Also, the growth rates of management-controlled firms were always at least 3.2 percentage points higher than those of owner-controlled firms and these differences were significant at the .05 level on one occasion (MC_1) and at the .10 level with alternative definitions.

It is interesting to note that, while the profitability of management-controlled firms which were able to evade the discipline of the market for corporate control (MC_4) was not significantly greater than that achieved by owner-controlled firms, the growth rate achieved by these management-controlled firms was significantly higher at the .10 level. This may indeed indicate that such management-controlled firms were pursuing growth at the expense of higher profitability. However, to conduct such a test on its own would be dubious practice, since the specification of management-control biases the result from the start. In general the signs on the coefficients of NMAT are positive as hypothesised, but statistical significance is not found. Firm size (measured by opening net assets) always had a negative influence on profitability and growth, but the coefficients were never significant.

The next two columns of Table 2.1 show the results of a similar analysis carried out on the small firms sample — those with net assets of less than $5 millon in 1966. In general management-control again has positive effects on profitability and growth, but now the only statistically significant differences are in profit rates. Under definitions MC_2 and MC_3 management-controlled firms earned higher rates of return which were significant at the .05 and .10 levels respectively. The maturity dummy variable is again positive in the majority of cases but never statistically significant. However, the negative influence of firm size on profitability and growth (not shown) was now strong and generally statistically significant at the .01 level.

In sum, our sensitivity analysis has yielded the following results:

(a) Whatever results are obtained in attempts to assess the effects of control type on firm performance, these are quite sensitive to the definition of management control employed. In light of this it is curious that, apart from a limited exercise by Holl (1975), no previous researcher has undertaken such a sensitivity analysis.

(b) In 'large' firms characterised by a high degree of market power, owner-controlled firms earned significantly higher rates of return on equity assets (although the level of significance varied depending on the definition of management control which was used), and higher rates of growth of net assets (although the differences were not statistically significant).

(c) Among 'medium sized' firms the reverse was true, since management-controlled firms earned significantly higher rates of profit, and achieved significantly higher growth rates.

(d) In the 'small' firms sample management-controlled firms again achieved higher profitability and growth, although a statistically significant difference in profits at the .05 level was found only when MC_2 was used as the definition of management control.

(e) On the whole, the highest t-values were achieved when MC_2 was used as the definition distinguishing management- from owner-controlled firms which implies that ownership of 10 per cent of shares was most critical in determining performance, although we have not determined why it was critical.

The findings are consistent with those of an earlier exploratory investigation of large Australian companies conducted by Round (1976a). Similarly, they are consistent with the findings of several US and UK studies. They show how blinkered is the view that results from restricting samples only to large corporations and relying on a single definition of control.

Another important point to emerge from our findings is the apparent interaction between firm size and control type. The size cut-off point employed by most previous studies has probably precluded the discovery of such an effect. However, this effect was found to be significant in the French study conducted by Jacquemin and Ghellinck (1980). Their most substantial finding was that firm size had a significantly greater positive influence on the profitabilty of 'familial' companies. From their results one concludes that among the largest of the top 200 in France, owner-controlled firms are more profitable, while, at the lower range, management-controlled firms were more profitable. No substantial explanation of this 'anomaly' was provided.

Even when considerable differences in performance have been uncovered, most previous studies have shed little light on the fundamental question of *why* the observed differences came about. Thus, upon discovering that the owner-controlled firms in their sample earned higher rates of return Monsen, Chiu and Cooley (1968) qualified their findings in the following terms,

> While our tests show clearly the differences in performance between owner controlled and management controlled firms, they do not, of course, explain why such performance occurs. The hypothesis that seems most convincing to us is that two quite different motivation systems are at work — one for owners and another for managers. (pp. 441-2)

This approach followed a rather indirect course. It made a judgement about the motivation of managers in companies depending on the dispersion of shareholdings in those companies. Supporting studies relating to the linkages between managerial compensation and corporate performance were used to buttress the resulting hypothesis. This was that in firms with a dominant stockholder (owner-controlled firms) managers could be expected to 'maximise shareholder welfare', while in firms without a dominant stockholder (management-controlled firms) managers would be free to pursue their own interests at the expense of the shareholders.

The researchers following this approach have, without exception, made the implicit assumption that motivation and the internal factors restraining its expression have been homogeneous within the 'control groups' identified. Thus, differences in motivations and restraints within these groups have been ignored and in general only variables reflecting the restraint imposed by the product market have been used to control for external influences. This suggests that future research should, instead, proceed from the direct indentification of the incentives and restraints, both internal and external to the firm, which interact in determining its performance. A theoretical model outlining such an approach is presented in the following chapter.

Notes

1. For example, see Baldwin (1964), Machlup (1967), Meade (1968), Peterson (1965) and Solow (1967).

2. See Marris (1964).

3. Baumol (1959, 1967).

4. The version of Marris presented here is a synthesis of Radice (1971), Holl (1975) and Hay and Morris (1979). The latter authors noted the inconsistency between this version and Marris's original work (see Hay and Morris, 1979, fn. 33 on p. 308).

5. McGuire (1964, p. 77) illustrated Reder's model but considered it, along with other 'alternative' theories, as a 'burned out Christmas tree bulb' with its 'brief and transitory moment of glory lost in the glow of the star of profit maximization which remains bright and secure at the top of the tree' (p. 79).

6. Dyas and Thanheiser (1976, p. 37) noted the possibility of such a tradeoff in their study of French and German industry. They also suggested a life-cycle dimension. That is, the willingness to dilute ownership was thought to be greatest in the initial growth phase of the enterprise.

7. Fear of upsetting existing control arrangements was mentioned by the US Securities and Exchange Commission (1971) as one of the main reasons for the low levels of equity funding of investment.

8. Note that the reproductive rate of capitalists might be a factor if family cohesion is not achieved among heirs.

9. That is, such items as fixed capital equipment, research and development, mergers and so on.

10. The classic example cited by Grabowski and Mueller (1975) is that of Xerox, which was a small 50-year-old photopaper manufacturer when its young entrepreneur-managers happened across the Xerography invention.

11. The marginal return schedule for a mature firm (MRR_m) has been drawn in Figure 2.3 in the relative position it would have to CC', although both would be far to the right of their position for a non-mature firm.

12. It should be noted that this does not mean the firm will never resort to raising outside capital once it has begun to pay dividends. It may very well borrow in response to short-run changes in investment opportunities and in order to finance lumpy investment projects, such as a major capital expansion programme or a large acquisition. In addition the necessity to resort to outside capital is increased by stockholder and managerial preferences for a stable dividend policy.

13. Grabowsky and Mueller (1972, p. 11). The amount by which m is lower than i will depend on the degree of managers' empathy to or identification with shareholders, the external opportunities of shareholders and ultimately on the amount by which share price can be depressed without instigating a takeover bid.

14. Bain (1968) suggested a sales-based measure and was supported by Qualls (1972, 1977). On the other hand, Scherer (1970), Stigler (1963) and Williamson (1971) have argued for various capital-based measures.

15. However, in another US study Burch (1972, pp. 101-2) noted that 'with the relatively minor exception of the top 50 transportation companies, something on the order of 80 to 95 per cent of the family controlled firms identified in this study have been dominated by families which have taken an active part in their management over the years'.

16. Note that definitions MC_3 and MC_4 necessitate a reduction in sample size. In MC_3 we eliminate firms in which directors and related interests held between 5 per cent and 15 per cent of shares, while in MC_4 we eliminate management-controlled firms (with less than 10 per cent ownership) which did not evade market discipline. Definition of the latter follows closely that employed by Holl (1977). That is, firms which had below (industry) average valuation ratios in 1966/7 to 1968/9 and did not move closer to their industry average in 1972/3 to 1974/5 were considered to be evading market discipline.

17. Parry and Watson (1977) have estimated a 'cost disadvantage ratio' (Best-X MES) for four-digit manufacturing industries in Australia. Round (1978) argued that this measure — while theoretically superior to minimum efficient scale proxies developed by Comanor and Wilson (1967) or Caves, Khalilzadeh-Shirazi and Porter (1975) — still suffers from significant multi-collinearity with market concentration. In any case, to apply this measure at the firm level would require detailed information on what industry weightings to apply to each firm.

18. The reciprocal of net assets was found to provide the best 'explanation' of profitability and growth, which in the case of profitability is supported by the findings of an earlier Australian study (Phillips, 1978).

19. The choice of a $20 million net assets cut-off point to distinguish 'large firms' is not as arbitrary as it seems. These firms had several performance characteristics which clearly distinguished them from smaller companies.

20. For a further discussion of these issues see Lawriwsky (1980a) and Holl (1980).

3 A THEORY OF CORPORATE PERFORMANCE

Introduction

It is remarkable to note the regularity with which studies of general firm behaviour and performance, in the final analysis, have had to resort to internal factors as explanations of observed performance. In an early study of investment and growth in British industrial firms, Barna (1962) noted a persistence, over a number of years, of profitability and growth performance within firms. Substantial differences in the performance of firms within the same industry, however, suggested that such persistence was not due to factors external to the firm.Therefore, internal factors must have been the cause. He noted that the willingness and ability of different firms to seize upon and exploit opportunities varied greatly according to their basic 'character'.

A later, much more comprehensive study of the growth and profitability performance of British firms carried out by Singh and Whittington (1968) arrived at a similar set of conclusions. Both profitability and growth were found to be persistent characteristics of firms, although profitability was more persistent than growth. This was explained by the fact that growth depends on a firm's *ability* and *willingness* to grow and a firm's ability to grow will be dependent on its profitability. The willingness to grow, however, will depend on 'factors such as the state of competition, the nature of management, the state of demand, and the technological opportunities' and, to the extent that 'the largest firms in an industry would tend to be dominated by managers (as opposed to the shareholders)', by their interest 'in the growth of the firm rather than in its profits' (pp. 149-50).

So far economic researchers have responded to such pleas by attempting to uncover differences in performance between 'owner'- and 'management'-controlled firms. In Chapter 2 we saw that empirical tests of the 'separation thesis' have in many instances met with limited success. It was suggested that a model of corporate behaviour and performance should be developed which approaches the fundamental questions directly. Such a model is presented in this chapter.

The basic outline of the model was described in Chapter 1 in terms of the foundation provided by the traditional structure-conduct-performance paradigm of industrial organisation. A central proposition of the refined model is that researchers cannot infer a direct line of causation from market structure to firm performance. This is because market structure will interact with other influences to determine a firm's conduct and only *after* these influences are considered will its performance become determinate. These influences, both internal and external to the firm, are described in the next two sections. The basic hypotheses to be tested are also presented. In the final section we define in more precise terms what is meant by 'managerial discretion' and outline the approach followed in later empirical chapters.

Internal Organisation

The Incentive Structure

Shareholders. If we assume that there are no significant non-pecuniary benefits attached to the ownership of particular securities,[1] *ceteris paribus*, shareholders will prefer higher profits and stock prices to smaller ones. That is, given the purchase price paid for the shares, and holding risk and other factors (such as marketability) constant, investors will prefer higher profits from which higher dividend payments may be obtained and higher stock prices from which capital gains may be realised. Moreover, unless they are risk preferers or speculators, shareholders will generally favour smaller but more steady *movements* in profits and market prices, to larger, more erratic movements. Thus, long-term shareholders, once they have committed their funds to a particular venture, can only be motivated to maximise the rate of return on their capital, subject to preferences regarding risk and timing of receipts.

Three factors combine to determine the rate of return earned by shareholders, i.e. purchase price, dividends and selling price. But while shareholders are free to choose the price at which they purchase their shares, they can only influence partially the latter two elements. For example, shareholders could endeavour to ensure that the company is being operated by a reasonably competent management which adheres to the principle of reinvestment up to the point where the marginal rate of return on capital is equated with its marginal cost. Thus any surplus funds not returned to shareholders as dividends would become capitalised into the value of the firm at the rate of return which was not less than the rate available to shareholders in alternative projects of comparable risk. However, this 'neoclassical' view is a poor indication of observed experience. In practice the additional complications of capital market imperfections, personal taxation and transactions costs act to modify behaviour.

Although the capital market may provide the 'correct' valuation given the available information, it will not always comprehend accurately the real potential of the resources embodied in the firm. Dividends, rather than retentions, are found to be the operative variable with regard to payout policy.[2] Firms are reluctant to curtail dividend payments or adjust them annually in the light of expectations about the future profitability of investment, since this is likely to create uncertainty in the capital market. While in the neoclassical world the value of the payout ratio is irrelevant to individual shareholders since they can, in effect, 'declare their own dividends' by buying or selling shares,[3] in the real world transactions costs, especially on small parcels of stock, circumscribe such behaviour. In addition, the existence of income taxes makes it expensive for a shareholder to purchase additional stock out of 'unwanted' dividend payments since these will be subject to a higher rate of taxation to that imposed on capital gains and thus may constitute an inferior alternative to the direct retention of these funds by the company.

Since the vast majority of stockholders are normally 'external' to the firm, they have no reliable way of determining whether management is acting to maximise their welfare. They only learn about performance *ex post*, through annual reports, consultants, the financial press and possibly an occasional prospectus. Owing to considerations of security and the conservatism inherent in accounting practice, the picture they receive may give a poor indication of the true situation. In most cases the best that shareholders can do is compare the reported performance of 'their' firm with that of other similar firms, usually in the same industry. The uncertainties that are thereby created will act to minimise the amount of switching they do between the stocks of different companies, as will the fact that the same uncertainties exist everywhere. It is not surprising then, that studies in the US (Nerlove, 1968, pp. 314-15) and the UK (Revell and Moyle, 1966, pp. 31-5) indicate that the common holding period for ordinary stocks averages between five and ten years and often longer periods.[4] There is no doubt that in addition to ignorance, transactions costs and low capital gains taxes act further to reinforce the 'locking-in effect.

As a result of these imperfections stockholders who are outsiders to the firm are often obliged to act in a way which may be indistinguishable from satisficing.[5] Instead of switching from security to security in response to the ebb and flow of market prices (as speculators will do), the majority of stockholders prefer to hold on in the hope that better times will be experienced in the future. When these factors are coupled with the costs involved in organising thousands, and commonly tens of thousands of dispersed, relatively small stockholders, it is obvious that only an extremely poor performance by managers could activate small stockholders to take punitive action through direct confrontation (although such cases are not unknown).[6] However, it is quite likely that prior to such an event the market for corporate control would act first to dislodge management. In that case shareholders would merely have to play a passive role in accepting a takeover offer designed to replace existing management.

Managers. (Both empirical and theoretical deliberation indicate that most elements in a professional manager's utility function can most effectively be realised through an expansion in the size of the firm. Executive salaries have been found to be highly correlated with the size of the firm and length of tenure proves to be quite high among top-ranking executives,[7] indicating the need for a long-term commitment to one firm. In his pioneering work on the nature of professional management, Gordon (1945) argued that its power is derived from position rather than personal wealth and that this power will grow strictly in proportion to increases in the size of the firm. Marris (1964) saw promotional opportunities as being the natural result of an expansion in the number of hierarchical tiers in an organisation and proposed that this can be achieved most efficiently through growth. On the other hand, Alchian (1969) argued that managers compete for promotions and new positions by performing well in their current job and are thereby motivated to perform in the stockholders' interests. Similarly, Fama (1980) has argued that the managerial labour market will tend to eliminate sub-optimal performance. This approach, however, seems to ignore what criteria will be given precedence by top management, who are instrumental in devising incentive schemes. The 'managerial' models developed by Baumol (1967) and Williamson (1964) also related managerial incentives to growth and size variables.

Another common line of argument is that 'unpropertied managers' will lack the motivation to strive to maximise shareholders' welfare because of the absence of strict symmetry in risks and rewards (Monsen and Downs, 1965). If they perform very well in one period they are not likely to have bonuses lavished on them, while shareholders' and the markets' expectations for the future may be raised, applying additional pressure on them. On the other hand, an extremely bad performance may catalyse stockholder rebellion and possibly lead to dismissal.

In 1965 Baumol (1965, p. 81) wrote that 'by far the most important reason for management's concern for the behaviour of the price of company stock is the stock option whose value to the recipient executive depends directly on the performance of the company's securities'. But in an appendix (pp. 83-90) he expressed some doubts as to the ability of stock options to effect a perfect alignment of management and stockholders' interests. That is, since the option does not include payment of dividends until it is exercised, the optimal dividend policy for the option holder need not — in the absence of a special case in which the optimum for both is a zero dividend — be the optimum policy for the stockholder. Williamson (1970, p. 92) added two more reservations which he described as the 'moving equilibrium' and 'free ride' problems.[8] Furthermore, movements in stock prices are often independent of the efforts of management. Other problems with executive compensation plans have more recently been outlined by Smith and Watts (1982).

On the issue of executive stock ownership, Gordon (1945, p. 313) proposed that for it to be 'successful in restoring the profit motive' the gains from ownership must be at least comparable in magnitude to those which are received from salary and bonus. He also doubted that bonus payments in their (then) present form would be effective, since they are normally such a small proportion of total salary, fluctuate much less than do profits and cannot be negative (while profits can). It should also be noted, however, that bonuses which are based on profits by themselves need not be sufficient to ensure the maximisation of shareholder welfare. Once the investment and financing decisions have been made, it may be in the interests of a utility-maximising management also to maximise profits, since they will provide the internal funds necessary to finance further growth, and to pay dividends, which are important for the maintenance of security from takeover.

An alternative viewpoint expounded by Lewellen (1969) holds that, while it is true that in the large corporation there has been a separation of ownership and management *functions*, this has not been sufficient (a) to alienate the pecuniary interests of managers from those of stockholders, or (b) to produce a set of managerial goals which conflict with the attainment of profit maximisation, where profit maximisation is taken to be synonymous with the maximisation of the market value of the corporation's stock. Lewellen's claim was that the total executive compensation package, especially in recent years, has been heavily weighted towards 'ownership' items such as stock options, stock bonuses and profit-sharing plans, which must serve to align closely the objectives of managers and stockholders. His second point was that, while it is true that in most large corporations the *relative* size of stock in the hands of management is small, and so does not constitute a controlling interest, it is nevertheless very important in terms of the *total* personal wealth positions of managers.)

Similarly, Wood (1976, pp. 39-40) has argued that the interests of managers and long-term shareholders will be roughly parallel, since both have a vested interest in the company's profitability. Managers will desire profits because they provide the means to achieving a high rate of growth, while for shareholders profits will signify higher dividends and stock prices. Although there would arise conflicts of interest between managers and stockholders, Wood felt that these would be of minor consequence when compared with the 'community of interest' between them.

The latter point has been stressed by sociologists and 'radical' economists. Such writers as C. Wright Mills (1972) doubt that it would be possible for someone not born into 'the wealthy class' to rise to the top of a large corporation without first having completely internalised the interests and ideologies of that class. Thus, Sweezy (1953, p. 63) concluded that managers are 'utterly unsuited by training and social status to adopt an independent historical position' since their very existence is inextricably tied to the service of capital.[9]

Owner-Managers. By definition, owner-managers are substantial stockholders with a large financial interest in the company. What we have termed 'professional managers' may also possess large holdings, but the distinction is that the shareholdings of owner-managers are the vehicle by which they exercise *control* over the firm. That is, shareholdings of an owner-manager are sufficient to allow him to exercise control in his own right.[10] At the same time owner-managers have access to, on the one hand, inside information which is barred to outside shareholders and, on the other, the pecuniary and non-pecuniary benefits normally associated with the utility functions of professional managers.

Knight (1921) and Schumpeter (1934) recognised that 'empire-building', even at the expense of profits, may be associated with the egos of owner-managers. Other theorists have also made this observation (e.g. Gordon, 1945; Nichols, 1969; and even Marris, 1964), but only McEachern (1975) has formally incorporated it in an empirical model. As McEachern (1975, pp. 66-7) pointed out, owner-managers are likely to be in the highest personal income tax bracket, so that after a corporate tax rate of say 50 per cent on profits had been paid and another say 50 per cent in marginal personal tax, the diversion of a dollar's worth of potential profits to non-pecuniary benefits costs the owner-manager only 25 cents in foregone dividends.

Another view, which appears particularly plausible, holds that some part of the 'equity' of owner-managers derives from their ability to *control*. Thus, Reder (1947, p. 455) speculated that 'in order to keep this control the entrepreneur will fight reorganisations to the bitter end and will reject outside funds which might bring annoying restraints on his freedom of action'. But if a strategy designed to retain control is actively pursued, at some stage a conflict with 'outside' shareholder interests may develop. Hence owner-managers might fail to take full advantage of profitable expansion opportunities since this will often require external finance, and after a point greater external finance will entail a loss of control. More recently, Kamerschen (1970, p. 670) also noted that 'fear of loss of control could ... influence owners to prefer internal over external financing'.

Managerial Incentives and Corporate Performance. In view of the difficulties associated with stock option schemes and the possibility that salary and bonuses may not serve shareholders' interests (see Marris, 1964), the ownership of ordinary shares by management appears to be the most effective means of promoting a 'unity of interest' with the shareholder body. The proportion of shares owned by managers may be small, yet these shareholdings may be large enough in absolute terms to promote 'shareholder-oriented' behaviour. Note, however, that a total unity of interests is possible only if the manager has a 100 per cent ownership stake in the company (e.g. see Jensen and Meckling, 1976).

Other things being equal, we should expect there to be a positive relationship between the absolute value of managers' shareholdings and the rate of return, since their personal welfare will be linked directly with the profitability performance of the firm. However, if managers have large shareholdings and are generally wealthier than the average shareholder, this holds several implications for the retention, risk and growth policies of firms.

First, wealthy managers will be in a higher marginal tax bracket than the average shareholder. If, as Kamerschen (1970, p. 670) has argued, capital gains are allowed preferential treatment over dividends in the tax structure, 'it is possible to provide theoretical support for expecting [these] owners to try to withhold their cash dividends in favour of capital appreciation through productive reinvestment of retained earnings'. Thus, *ceteris paribus*, the retention ratio will be positively associated with the value of managers' holdings.

Second, managers with a large financial interest in their company may be less well diversified than the average shareholder (see McEachern, 1975). Palmer (1973b) has proposed two hypotheses regarding risk. The first was that if large holdings by top management are associated with greater control, lower-level managers will have more to fear from these shareholders and therefore become more risk averse. An alternative hypothesis was that wealthy individuals tend to place their wealth in companies which are less risky for other reasons; for example, companies which are more highly diversified or operating in markets which are naturally subject to lower fluctuations in demand. If either of these arguments is correct managers' shareholdings will be negatively related to operating risk.[11]

Finally, if profitability and retentions are positively related to the value of managers' shareholdings, so too should be the rate of growth of the firms. As has already been indicated, to the extent that a large shareholding by managers is employed as an instrument for maintaining control over the company and for ensuring their positions, growth might not be as rapid as in a company where more external finance is raised. But if those firms in which owner-managers rely on the voting power of their shareholdings are identified, so that this possibility is accounted for, a positive relationship between the value of shareholdings and firm growth will be observed.

One further point which should be mentioned here is that managers will be subject to varying internal constraints. In particular, the performance of managers in company-controlled firms will be more closely scrutinised than that of managers in either concentrated private ownership or dispersed-ownership companies. The performance restraint on managers of company-controlled firms may be in the form of well-defined performance targets set by the controlling company. In that case the discretion of managers will be confined to a lower range of performance values, as for example by a downside limit to the rate of return which can be earned. Therefore, the relationships between the value of managers' shareholdings and firm performance may appear to be weaker in company-controlled firms.

Internal Restraints and the 'Character of Control'

In a tentative classification of firms Nyman and Silberston (1978, p. 94) found it useful to distinguish between alternative control situations on the following basis.

(a) Firms which are effectively owner-controlled by families, individuals, or the board, giving those firms a large degree of discretion.
(b) Firms controlled by outside shareholders such as other firms or financial institutions, severely limiting management discretion.
(c) Firms with no centre of control, where management has significant discretion, within the limits set by the product and capital markets.

The drawback of this classification scheme, however, is that it implies that on the basis of ownership structure we can identify three *discrete* patterns of behaviour. Our approach is similar in that we also classify firms into three 'characters of control': (a) private ownership control; (b) company control; (c) management control. But inherent in our specification is recognition of the fact that the extent of freedom from internal restraints will vary *within* these groups. For example, shareholdings by a cohesive private ownership group or outside company may have different implications for discretion depending on their size. Or, for a given company shareholding, the implications may differ depending on whether the firm in question is domestic or overseas-controlled. Similarly, a given concentration of shareholdings by financial institutions may have a differential impact on managerial discretion depending on the size of the company.

Private Ownership Control. Dominant private shareholdings, which are commonly organised on a family basis, are almost invariably associated with the board of directors (see Burch, 1972, pp. 101-2, and Chapter 5 below). That is, control is exercised by a closely knit group of relatives, friends or business associates which may be termed the 'directors' cohesive group'. The size and composition of this group is bound to vary with time and circumstances. In the early years after the foundation of the company, for instance, there may be one dominant personality or only two or three coalition members. But in the older-established companies there may be many heirs to the original founder's fortune.

Normally the most able (or managerially inclined) members of the ownership group will take up positions on the board of directors and take an active interest in the administration or operations of the firm. Since these individuals will have access to 'managerial' incentives, it may be that their interests conflict in some degree with those of non-director members of the ownership group and also with the interests of shareholders who are not part of this group. In the US McEachern (1975, p. 61) suggested that it is useful to distinguish, within the owner-controlled category, those firms which are dominated by owner-managers from those which are dominated by external stockholders, because 'the dominant external stockholder does not have access to the non-pecuniary benefits which interest the manager, and, consequently, he is interested only in the return on his investment'.

The executive directors will in fact be, to varying degrees, dependent on the voting strength of the non-director members of the group. If so, and if other shareholdings are widely dispersed, it is certain that only these non-director members of the dominant shareholder group will be able to impose an effective *internal* restraint on directors. Indeed, there will always be a certain percentage of shareholders (depending on the performance of the company) who will automatically return their proxy forms in favour of the existing management. Therefore, the probability that disgruntled shareholders outside of the dominant group will be able to mount a credible opposition to the existing management will be lower than in a dispersed ownership company. But the shareholdings of the dominant ownership group itself are often arranged into a complex network of holding companies in which director members hold key shareholdings and positions. Hence, even this restraint is unlikely to be effective.

In relation to external restraints, two factors must be taken into consideration. The first factor concerns the effectiveness of the market for corporate control. Other things being equal, the probability of making a successful unsolicited takeover raid on an owner-controlled firm will be low and will be lower the greater the proportion of voting stock which is held by the owner-group. In fact, if the dominant shareholder group holds more than 51 per cent, this probability will fall to zero and control can be said to be 'absolute'.

Even if the group does not possess an absolute majority of shares, but has more than say 40 per cent, it is almost certain that it will have the resources to reach 51 per cent ownership quickly, if a raider were to enter the market. Consider, for example, the following statement by the president of the US company Dymo Industries (quoted by Holl, 1977, p. 259);

> We have substantial ownership — I'm talking about 40% — that is vested in four or five parties who are all represented on our board and we feel that an unfriendly takeover would not be feasible as long as *these* investors are satisfied. [Our emphasis added]

Thus, ownership groups with absolute control have such a strong threat potential that raiders will not contemplate an aggressive bid for fear of being locked into a minority holding position. However, even groups with less than absolute control will enjoy *some* degree of discretion.

Second, the controlling group's power depends on its maintaining its proportionate interest in the firm. This will be of greatest importance to those ownership groups which can be said to have 'absolute' control. Such firms will, *ceteris paribus*, prefer to finance internally rather than externally. The same can be said of firms with less than absolute control in the hands of the dominant group, but with less force. Once absolute control is lost the necessity to finance mainly (or exclusively) from internal sources can be expected to decline steadily. Hence, any restraint which *could* apply if firms approached the capital market for funds is going to be least effective in absolute owner-controlled firms, but become increasingly more rigorous as the proportionate interest of the ownership group declines.

While owner-managers may have considerable incentive in the form of a large shareholding in the company, restraints from within and outside the firm are likely to be weak. This will leave owner-managers with a considerable range of discretionary power. Since owner-managers will also benefit from non-profit-maximising activities, our model predicts that *ceteris paribus* (e.g. holding constant the incentive effect provided by share ownership) their profitability performance will be lower than that of firms where internal and external restraints are more effective. Owner-managers may desire growth because of the pecuniary and non-pecuniary benefits which can be derived through increased size of the firm. However, rapid growth will require external finance and this will diminish the owner-manager's discretionary power. Hence, he will prefer a higher retention of earnings. But since profitability will be lower and external sources used only infrequently, growth will also be lower. With regard to risk, owner-managers who have strong control will have less to fear from internal and external restraints and may therefore afford to allow greater fluctuations in the rate of return. On the other hand, they may be less well diversified in their investments and this would tend to reduce risk.

Firm maturity can act to modify these effects. If investment opportunities are high the owner-manager may find that it is in his best interests for the firm to expand rapidly. This, in turn will raise the effectiveness of the capital market restraint as more new debt and equity capital is sought. At the same time the market for corporate control will become more effective since the owner group will be diluting its proportionate interest in the firm.

Company Control. Company-controlled firms are those in which another company holds a substantial shareholding. Thus, as in private ownership companies, there is (usually) a single dominant proprietary interest. But unlike private ownership companies, in company-controlled firms the functions of ownership and management are likely to be separated. Control is exercised through the ownership of shares and the effectiveness of this control will depend on the proportion of shares held — i.e. on the number of seats which the firm can secure on the board of directors. Unless the company is a consolidated subsidiary, the controlling firm's representatives are normally non-executive directors. Therefore, they will not have access to 'managerial' incentives and their objective will be to promote the interests of the controlling firm (in which they may hold executive positions).

In an early study Bonbright and Means (1932) investigated the structure and operations of holding companies in the US. The general tenor of their argument was that the holding company device was often used to disenfranchise the large majority of small investors through the pyramiding of control. It was also noted that holding companies were often used as a preliminary to outright fusion of 'subsidiaries'. Several advantages were attributed to this device. Having achieved 'working control' of a company the controlling corporation could practise 'creeping acquisition' by gradually buying up the outstanding stock in the hands of minority interests. Thus, over a number of years a complete takeover could be effected with little opposition and without bidding up the stock price. However, the holding company was also seen as a means to decentralisation of decision-making and was, in that view, an alternative to divisional-isation.

Writing much later, Penrose (1956a, p. 76) was not confident that sufficient integration could be achieved through this form of corp-orate expansion. In her opinion there is an

> important distinction between internal and external growth which lies in the fact that internal growth requires planning, building, organizing, and coordinating each increment of expansion such that the expanded concern remains an administratively integrated organization — an industrial firm in the sense used here. The same planning and integration *may* be involved when growth is by acquisition, but it *need* not and often *is* not.

She saw the danger that firms growing rapidly through acquisition of this type ran the risk of degenerating to the state of a mere financial holding company or loosely connected 'group'. But while this may occur when only a relatively small proportion of shares is owned in each of the 'group' companies, it is much less likely to happen when a large proportion is held. In the latter case, much closer supervision and control can be expected to be exercised by the parent concern.

In their tentative classification of firms, Nyman and Silberston (1978, p. 94) differentiated those 'controlled by outside shareholders such as other firms or financial institutions, severely limiting manage-ment discretion'. It was felt that 'control may pass to industrial capital if the family prefer to have their interests looked after by other industrialists rather than by professional managers who may well have different objectives' or it may do so 'involuntarily as a substitute for a takeover bid'. Finally, the existence of inter-company share-holdings might be indicative of 'collusive practices or simply techni-cal cooperation' (p. 90). However, in a footnote they granted that such shareholdings 'may also be a device by which managers — with or without substantial individual shareholdings — seek to protect their own position against potential interference by other share-holders' and that these cases would work against their argument. In fact companies do arrange allotments and exchanges of shares with 'friendly' firms either in anticipation of a takeover bid or in the course of a bid. Such strategies have the effect of thwarting the market for corporate control and may therefore help to insulate an inefficient management. However, this also is probably true only of companies with a relatively small company shareholding.

Alternatively, a company-controlled firm may be operated with a view to the controlling company (at a later date) offering to purchase the remainder of the outstanding stock. If we were to assume for the moment that the acquiring company was a growth maximiser and already had effective control of the target company, we might ask what its rational approach would be. One theory of conglomerate mergers proposed by Mueller (1969) relied on the proposition that the discount rate of a growth-maximising management is likely to be below that of the marginal stockholders in target firms. Since Mueller (1969, p. 656) took this to imply that managers are faced with a 'seemingly boundless set of merger opportunities', Hindley (1972, p. 7) suggested that an obvious corollary of this hypothesis is that 'ceteris paribus, a growth-maximising firm will always prefer to purchase another growth-maximising firm rather than a stockholder-welfare-maximising firm'. This is because the assets of the growth-maximising firm will always be valued at a lower price than those of an otherwise similar shareholder-welfare-maximising firm. Therefore, if the (growth-maximising) 'parent' of a company-controlled firm actually is in charge, we should expect it to use its power to insist on a growth-maximising strategy in the controlled firm. But profits are required to finance growth, so that it would not be consistent for the management of the growth-maximising parent to tolerate any losses in efficiency in the controlled firm (for example, X-inefficiency in management). This would also be true if the controlling firm were a profit maximiser. Hence, we should expect that managers of firms with a strong company shareholding will be constrained to return some relatively high minimum profit rate and also a high minimum rate of growth.

Compared with domestic companies, foreign-controlled companies might be expected to operate under a slightly different set of circumstances. Some time ago Penrose (1956b) explored the relationships between foreign control and the growth of the firm, and in her view,

> foreign subsidiaries have, for a variety of reasons, a greater degree of independence of the parent than have domestic subsidiaries . . . where foreign subsidiaries are concerned, the area over which a close co-ordination of policy is considered necessarily is often smaller than it is with respect to domestic subsidiaries operating in

a more closely connected national market. For these and similar reasons, a foreign subsidiary once it is established, is, with important exceptions [i.e. finance], more appropriately treated in many ways as a separate firm. (p. 226)

She also made the observation that the organisation which is created takes on a 'life of its own' and is composed of 'men and women who have vested interests in the concern' (p. 229). Like domestic company-controlled firms those with a foreign company shareholding will be insulated from the market for corporate control. The effectiveness of the internal restraint can be expected to vary directly with the size of the foreign company shareholding. However, with a given company shareholding we would expect the internal restraint to be more effective in the case of domestic company-controlled firms.

Company control will also be associated with a degree of independence from the capital market restraint. But this discipline will be replaced by the 'internal capital market' (the visible hand) of the parent company, which can supply new equity capital and debt (in the form of inter-company loans) to the subsidiary. In addition, the parent will be able to regulate dividend payments according to its assessment of the subsidiary's investment opportunities. Since the controlling company will pay a higher rate of marginal tax on dividends than the average investor, we would expect the retention ratio to be generally high.

The managers of company-controlled firms will be in a sensitive position with regard to risk, because they can often be easily replaced if the controlling company's management becomes alarmed by the extent of fluctuations in earnings. However, this is most likely to occur when the management of the controlling company is less involved in the day-to-day operations of the firm. That is, when a small proportion of shares is held, or the parent is a foreign firm, we would expect managers to be more risk averse. Another reason for expecting firms with a low company shareholding to display lower variability in earnings is that management in these firms will feel a greater threat from the market for corporate control. In order to reduce the possibility of a takeover these managers will find it expedient to reduce risk.

Management Control. A recent study examining the performance effects arising from the separation of ownership from control concluded that the increasing dispersion of ownership within many corporations has meant that,

> individual dominant stockholders are becoming rare ... but a few studies have noted the increasing dominance of large financial institutions. Whether these institutions can exercise the control over management that was exercised by the dominant stockholder remains an unresolved issue. (McEachern, 1975, pp. 110-11)

The extent and effectiveness of control by 'finance capital' has in fact been the subject of some debate by protagonists at both ends of the ideological spectrum. Abstracting from the ideological issues, however, we can distinguish three central questions in this debate. First, do financial institutions possess the capacity to control the decision making process in industrial companies? Second, if so, will they be motivated to exercise this potential? Third, if they are, what difference will this make to managerial performance?

One issue bearing on the first of these questions is the extent to which company finance is independent of the support of financial institutions. Galbraith (1967, pp. 81-2) and Baran and Sweezy (1966, p. 16) have held that large companies are largely self-suffi-cient in the provision of funds for investment. That is, given the dispersion of stockholdings, management has complete autonomy over the disposition of retained earnings. Fitch and Oppenheimer (1970, Pt 2, pp. 68-77), on the other hand, have argued that in the US the ratio of external to internal funds has risen dramatically in the 1950s and 1960s and that the 'working capital' and 'quick asset' ratios have fallen to the extent that leading institutions are now in a position to dictate policy to company managements. But the best indicator of potential control by financial institutions is the concen-tration and extent of their shareholdings. In the US, Kotz (1976) con-cluded that a third or more of the largest 200 non-financial cor-porations could be controlled by financial institutions. Briston and Dobbins (1978) estimated that in 1980 half the UK equities market was in the hands of institutions compared with an estimate of 36 per cent for the US (Soldofsky, 1971). However, Nyman and Silberston (1978) were able to identify only ten cases of control by financial institutions in their sample of 225 companies.

If financial institutions, acting alone or as a coalition, could be shown to possess a potential for control, the question of whether they have the motivation and expertise to exercise it would have to be resolved. For instance, Sweezy (1971, p. 160) believed that US bank trust departments,

> not only do not control corporations; they do not even want such responsibility, which would bring all sorts of headaches and open them to expensive damage suits should losses be suffered by trust beneficiaries owing to improper actions by trustees.

In similar fashion, O'Connor (1968, p. 31) felt that although 'non-insurance pension funds hold an increasing share of corporate equities', so that the potential for involvement has risen, 'the top owners and managers of insurance companies, pension funds, etc., not being industrialists, could not conceivably make the important industrial decisions'. To this he added that effective control requires a certain stability of holdings over time and this will inevitably conflict with an optimal investment policy geared to changing conditions in the stock market.

In reply to O'Connor's point that optimal investment policy necessitates liquid holdings, Fitch and Oppenheimer (1970, Pt 2, pp. 61-3) argued that such liquidity may no longer be possible owing to the sheer magnitude of institutional holdings. Since institutions are now 'locked in' to the companies they have invested in, Fitch and Oppenheimer concluded that these institutions will have to take an active interest in the affairs of the companies.

In the UK, Nyman and Silberston (1978) cited specific instances of actual intervention by institutions. For example, in 1969 the merchant bank Hill Samuel together with the Prudential Assurance, Britannic Assurance and Cable and Wireless Investment Trust employed their combined holding of more than 10 per cent of Vickers shares to effect a reshuffle of its top management. However, the examples provided by Nyman and Silberston do not represent a departure from the conventional pattern. The cases of intervention occurred only when companies had approached bankruptcy after prolonged periods of difficulty. It is hard to imagine that the officers of financial institutions will have the expertise to make informed judgements about the direction which a firm's *industrial* (as distinct from financial) strategy should take. At the same time, however, the investment departments of these institutions will have greater knowledge than most other 'outside shareholders' about the relative performances of firms in their portfolios.

Previous writers in the area have placed emphasis on instances of direct intervention by financial institutions in the affairs of industrial companies. Such cases are spectacular or sensational when they occur, but tend to be relatively rare. Probably more important in terms of long-run performance is the continuing influence that large institutional holders can exert on management. Managers will from time to time require the backing of institutions in order to gain support for a major investment programme (such as an acquisition). More importantly, managers will require the backing of institutions in the event of a takeover bid on their own company. One often reads of cases where institutions 'friendly to management' have rallied to stave off an aggressive bidder. In many takeover bids institutions are the first to be approached by a raider, who can by these means very quickly establish a foothold in the firm and greatly enhance his position to bargain with the incumbent management. For reasons such as these we should expect managers in companies with significant institutional ownership to take care in fostering good relations with institutional investors. Thus, the effectiveness of the internal restraint which can be exerted by financial institutions will in large measure depend on the effectiveness of the market for corporate control.

The final issue is what difference institutional dominance will make to corporate performance. Fitch and Oppenheimer (1970, Pt 3, p. 43) were of the opinion that banks, for example, 'have interests opposed to inside management', since if left to 'follow their own self interest, the officers [of industrial companies] seek growth — even relatively unprofitable growth — for its own sake'. In contrast to companies controlled by internal management, they would expect to find companies dominated by financial interests to exhibit a 'higher dividend payout ratio, a low level of working capital, and a high level of external debt' (Pt 3, p. 44). Wheelwright and Miskelly (1967, p. 71) felt that the 'motivations of those in control of financial institutions might be expected to be somewhat different from those of company managers'. However, they added that 'neither is responsible to the shareholders as a whole, or the community at large'.

Certainly we should expect the profitability of firms dominated by institutions to be higher than in otherwise similar firms where managers are free from any sanctions which could be applied by these shareholders. We might also expect managers in firms dominated by institutions to try to dampen the fluctuations in reported profits, since these would be viewed with apprehension by institutions not directly involved in the firms' operations. The reputations of financial institutions are linked to their conservatism and they therefore tend to shun risk.

It would be hasty, however, to conclude that such firms will grow less rapidly or retain a lower fraction of their earnings, as Fitch and Oppenheimer have done. For example, Kotz (1976, p. 141) suggested that as large shareholders with a long time horizon, institutions might be expected to prefer greater retentions. Given the same retention ratio there are two reasons why 'institutionally dominated' firms can be expected to grow at a faster rate. First, we have hypothesised that these firms will be relatively more profitable. Second, proprietorial links with financial institutions can be expected to provide greater access to external sources of finance through placements of new equity and long-term debt facilities. On the other hand, the managers of dispersed ownership companies which are not already dominated by financial institutions can be expected to avoid external finance in order to prevent future incursions on their autonomy. But given the rate of return we should also expect firms with large institutional holdings to retain a higher fraction of earnings.

In sum, dispersed ownership companies *may* be controlled by managers. But if a significant proportion of shares is held by organised and sophisticated investors such as financial institutions, managerial discretion will be somewhat restrained. How effective this restraint is will be dependent on the effectiveness of the market for corporate control. In addition, the need for the company to secure finance from the capital market will have a restraining effect on managerial discretion.

External Restraints

The Product Market

Perhaps the most fundamental of the external restraints on managerial discretion is that imposed by the product market. That is, for there to be any possibility of management deviating from the behaviour implied in the neoclassical profit-maximising model, the firm must be operating in something less than a perfectly competitive market. At various times economists such as Alchian (1950), Friedman (1953) and Becker (1962) have proposed the notion of 'economic natural selection' as a fundamental restraint which drives firms to maximise profits. This position was founded in the belief that the external competitive environment in which the firm operates so constrains its behaviour that mere survival dictates the maximisation of profits. In reply, Winter (1964) has demonstrated that in the imperfect world which forms the environment of 'real' firms — a world of oligopolistic interdependence, barriers to entry and economies of scale — it is more likely that firms pursuing non-profit-maximising goals will be the survivors (also see Marris, 1968, p. 44).

The conventional theoretical view expressed in the industrial organisation literature is that the number and size distribution of firms, *ceteris paribus*, will bear a fairly precise relationship to the extent of market power which is enjoyed. Where a small number of firms accounts for a large fraction of industry output, it is argued, they will come to recognise their mutual interdependence. Although sporadic price wars may break out, in the longer term oligopolists will recognise the futility of this and instead engage in overt or covert collusion. Thus, prices and profits will be higher in more highly concentrated industries. Furthermore, all firms in a given market are expected to share the benefits of the market power which is made available. In the last decade, however, some researchers in the field have challenged the 'shared assets' approach, claiming that the individual firm's market share or its membership in a 'strategic group' within the industry will have important effects on its profitability performance (see Shepherd, 1972, and Porter, 1976, respectively).

In addition, oligopolistic industry structures are often associated with high barriers to the entry of new firms. For example, the products of the existing firms may be highly differentiated, perhaps as a result of intensive advertising. The minimum efficient scale of production in oligopolies is often high and this can create 'capital requirements' barriers. The potential entrants may be able to raise sufficient finance only at prohibitive rates. All these factors allow firms in industries with high entry barriers to raise prices and profitability to some degree before attracting entry, because potential entrants will face higher average cost functions and a limited market.

The extent of market power is positively related to firm size. Firms in concentrated industries tend to be quite large in relative terms[12] and large size is also associated with capital barriers to entry. However, the theoretical relationship between firm size and profitability is by no means one-sided. On the one hand, large firms will benefit from economies of scale in production, marketing, distribution and research and development. Baumol (1967) has argued for a positive relationship between firm size and profitability on the grounds that large firms will have available to them all the opportunities which can be exploited by small firms, but can also take advantage of those opportunities which are denied to small firms. Thus, large firms will have the finance to engage in large-scale projects and will have greater access to new products and technology arising from within the firm and through licensing arrangements with foreign companies. On the other hand, large size may be accompanied by disproportionate increases in organisational complexity (i.e. hierarchical control loss). The market power available to large firms and the consequent lack of competitive pressure may foster the development of X-inefficiency among management. It has also been argued that the separation of ownership from control is likely to be greater within large firms, so that non-profit objectives of managers in these firms will tend to reduce their profitability. In other words, shareholder-oriented incentives of managers in large firms will be less than in small companies.

The relationship between firm size and growth may also be either positive or negative. If profitability were higher in large firms, assuming no external finance and a given retention ratio, their growth rate would also be higher (and vice versa). But large firms will have advantages over smaller companies in the area of external growth. Relative to small firms they will be able to raise debt and equity capital more cheaply and easily and also be in a more favourable position with regard to the acquisition of other firms. Since we would expect the level of retentions to be related to the level of investment opportunities, and therefore to the profitability of the firm, on this account there is no *a priori* justification for predicting either a positive or negative relationship. However, with a given rate of profit large firms, which have greater access to the capital market, could be expected to retain a lower fraction of earnings.

In contrast, with regard to business risk, a negative relationship between firm size and the variability of profits is hypothesised. This is for the familiar reason that large firms tend to be more highly diversified. With operations spread over a number of activities and often in geographically segmented markets, large firms are in a better position to withstand fluctuations in market demand.

As a final point, we should expect the performance-size relationships among company-controlled firms to differ from those experienced by independent firms. Even relatively small company-controlled firms may be able to benefit to some extent from large-scale purchasing organised in conjunction with the parent. Other economies may be reaped in the marketing and research areas, the rationalisation of production and transfers of specialist managerial talent. Hence, the product market restraint will have a lesser influence on company-controlled firms.

Stock Market Restraints

The Capital Market. In Berle and Means's (1932) theoretical framework the need to secure additional funds through the capital market occupied a position of pre-eminence as an external restraint on managerial action. In their view,

> Only one general protection besides the power of active revolt remains to guarantee a measure of equitable treatment to the several classes of security holders. The enterprise may need new capital. The management must, therefore, maintain a situation in which additional capital is forthcoming. (p. 280)

This view has largely been discounted by the 'Managerialist' school (as, for example in Galbraith's *The New Industrial State*) on the basis of evidence which showed that modern industrial concerns are essentially self-financing and that resort to the capital market is attempted only in exceptional circumstances. Indeed it is not unusual, in the light of Donaldson's (1961) research, to find such a view predominating. Donaldson examined the financing arrangements of 20 large US manufacturing corporations over the period 1939 to 1958. Seven of these were found to have generated from internal sources 'more than 100 per cent' of their long-term capital needs, while only in three was this proportion less than 80 per cent. With regard to external sources of funds it was discovered that three companies had never approached the long-term capital market during the period and, of those which had, only four made extensive use of the capital market.

As we suggested in the preceding paragraph the capital market restraint cannot be effective unless firms make new issues and in the US, Baumol (1965) expressed concern about the fact that so few large firms actually *did* approach the market for funds. But two recent UK studies (Whittington, 1971; Meeks and Whittington, 1975b) have questioned whether this is an accurate picture of large firm behaviour.

Other things being equal, private ownership companies will be less willing to engage in external finance, because this will reduce the influence of the controlling shareholders. But simply to demonstrate that companies make use of funds obtained in the capital market is not in itself a sufficient argument. In order to conclude that managerial discretion is effectively restrained by the capital market it must also be shown that this market is *efficient* in allocating funds.That is, efficient in the sense that the market allocates funds under suitable terms to those sectors or firms in the economy which are able to use these funds most beneficially. For example, it has often been alleged that because of capital market imperfections newly established and small enterprises have been allocated funds only at prohibitive rates when compared with large, well-established firms.

Nerlove (1968, p. 318) argued that firms undertaking rapid growth into new markets would be in a disequilibrium position in relation to the capital market. *Ceteris paribus*, he expected higher rates of return in such firms since the market would be slow in supplying capital to them. Writing in a similar vein, Grabowski and Mueller (1975) felt that lagged adjustments in the capital market mechanism helped perpetuate substantial differences in marginal rates of return between mature and non-mature technologies. Thus, the capital market discipline will be more severe in allocating finance to rapidly growing non-mature companies.

The capital market prefers large to small firms. Large firms have a higher marketablity in their shares. This makes the stock of large firms more desirable in the eyes of financial institutions and other investors who wish to trade in large blocks without upsetting prices. More information about the performance and prospects of large firms is available to the market, so that their stock will be in demand by less informed, small investors. Greater information will enable a more perfect market in securities of large firms, making them less subject to over- or under-valuation. Finally, large firms will be seen by the market to be safer. This is not only because large firms will experience lower fluctuations in earnings derived from operations, but also owing to the fact that the probability of failure will be lower. Hence, the capital market will tend to discriminate against small and lesser known companies in the provision of funds, so that, *ceteris paribus*, it will require a higher return on investment from these firms.

The Market for Corporate Control. While Berle and Means (1932, pp. 82-3) dismissed the effectiveness of a market for corporate control, Hindley (1969, p. 431) was moved to write that,

In principle, the market in corporate control is the only external constraint upon the managerial exploitation of the owners. In so far as other constraints are important, they are largely dependent upon the existence of a market in corporate control.

Similarly, Manne (1965, p. 113) felt that since the stock market is the only 'objective standard of managerial efficiency', it must follow that, 'only the take-over scheme provides some assurance of competitive efficiency among corporate managers and thereby affords strong protection to the interests of vast numbers of small, non-controlling shareholders.'[13]

However, the market for corporate control mechanism has its shortcomings. *Ceteris paribus*, the ease with which a successful takeover bid can be mounted will be a decreasing function of the size of the target corporation. A large firm has a more complex organisational structure and is often engaged in activities in a number of markets (which may be geographically dispersed or in foreign countries). These factors raise the information costs, as well as the uncertainties facing a bidder. The larger is the target corporation, the higher will be the capital requirement necessary to secure control. Therefore, the bidder will normally need to be larger than the target or have well-developed financial connections. Most takeover situations see a larger firm bidding for a smaller one. This gives large firms a further advantage in that the number of potential market raiders is reduced. Finally, larger firms will be better placed during a bid because of inter-company shareholdings or interlocking directorships. Consequently, a related company is more likely to enter the market in opposition to a raider.

Holding other things (including firm size) constant, the ease of takeover will also be a function of the distribution of share ownership, that is, of the character of control. Since in private ownership companies the power of the dominant shareholder group rests primarily on its voting strength, such companies will enjoy a considerable degree of freedom from the takeover restraint. The extent of this freedom will depend crucially on the proportion of shares held by the controlling stockholders. Given the proportion of shares held, however, a larger firm can — for the reasons outlined above — be expected to be more effectively insulated from market restraint.

Similarly, a company-controlled firm will have considerable immunity from the external market for corporate control. Under normal circumstances a raider will be wary of contesting a company-controlled firm. In order to secure control it might be necessary to bid for the controlling firm, which is likely to be much larger. Thus, as in private ownership companies the restraint on management must be imposed from within. That is, the dominant company shareholder will have to perform the control function by scrutinising managerial performance. But while the efficacy of this supervision might vary according to the proportion of shares held and depend on whether the 'subsidiary' is domestic or foreign, compared with external scrutiny it will not be as dependent upon the size of the firm. Through its representation on the board of directors the controlling company will have access to inside information and its controlling power may actually increase with firm size as the dispersion of other shareholdings rises.

Thus, the managers of dispersed ownership companies will, *ceteris paribus*, be most vulnerable to a market raid. Increasingly the ownership of equity capital in the Anglo-American economies is being concentrated in the hands of financial institutions. In many instances of 'dispersed ownership', a substantial proportion of shares is now held by a handful of financial institutions. Although these institutions normally wish to avoid the problems associated with involvement in the control of firms in which they hold shares (in contrast to private owners and other companies, which have different objectives), they are generally well informed, responsible and sophisticated investors. Financial institutions and other small shareholders in a dispersed ownership company can play a facilitative role in the market for corporate control. If management's performance has been suboptimal, market raiders will approach institutions, who may collectively account for a high proportion of shares, to assure acceptance before committing themselves to a bid. Managers who are aware of their vulnerability in such an event will therefore strive to perform satisfactorily in order to maintain the confidence of shareholders.

In addition, various institutional factors may affect the efficiency of the market for corporate control. For example foreign takeover legislation designed to restrict foreign control of industry will generally reduce the market's efficiency. The inept or self-seeking management of a domestically owned company may be protected because the only bid for control has come from a foreign company and such a move is outlawed by legislation. Also, takeover rules may increase or decrease the effectiveness of the market for control depending upon the nature of restrictions which are placed on takeover bids. Such legislation may result in a tradeoff between equity and efficiency. For instance, while small shareholders may gain the opportunity for more equal participation, management may gain time for a better defence.

Firm Maturity

The theoretical underpinnings of the life-cycle theory have been considered at some length in Chapter 2 and are not repeated here. Instead we shall outline our expectations regarding the relative performances of mature and non-mature firms.

Non-maturity is associated with a high level of investment opportunities relative to internally generated funds. We have argued that this alters relations with the capital market restraint and also the nature of the incentives confronting managers and shareholders. Non-mature firms are expected to be approaching the capital market more frequently and this imposes a greater restraint on managers. Since a high rate of return is being earned on internally generated funds in non-mature firms, we expect managers and shareholders to agree in preferring a high rate of retentions. Both profitability and growth are expected to be higher in non-mature firms, since both managers and shareholders will wish to exploit all profitable expansion opportunities. However, since non-mature firms will often be engaged in the production and marketing of relatively new products, the demand for which is likely to be more volatile, we should expect that, *ceteris paribus,* non-mature firms will exhibit greater fluctuations in earnings. An additional reason for expecting more variable returns in non-mature firms is that managers may be willing to accept greater risks because the potential pay-off will be greater.

Conclusion

The extended model of industrial organisation presented in this chapter sees potential corporate performance as being determined by the degree of discretion available to the firm. Ultimately this discretion is dependent upon the market power available to the firm, that is, on such factors as market share, concentration and barriers to entry. But the extent to which managers *can* take advantage of the discretion afforded by conditions set in the product market is defined by the effectiveness of internal and external (stock market) restraints on their behaviour. How managers *will* use these residual discretionary powers, however, will depend on their incentive structure.

The internal restraint on managers stems from stockholders. Stockholders can exercise the power to restrain management most effectively if (a) the owner group is cohesive, (b) it has the energy to challenge management, (c) it has the expertise to do so and (d) it is aware that its best interests are being compromised. From this it becomes apparent that the more removed owners are from participation in determining the broad objectives of a company, and the less versed they are in business procedures, the higher will their share of stock have to be to impose an effective constraint on management. On the other hand, if owners are represented on the board of directors, a much lower ownership base will be sufficient to maintain control over managers. Nyman and Silberston (1978) recognised this fact when they lowered the proportion of stock necessary for owner control below the 5 per cent level if one of the ownership group was found to be either chairman or managing director. Thus, if the definition of owner control is centred on the board of directors and the extent of stockholdings they can be shown to represent directly (i.e. directors as a cohesive group), we must surmise that *these* stockholders *can* exercise their potential power and *can* detect that managers are pursuing their own interests. A similar argument would apply in the case of company control, since a large holding by another firm is usually accompanied by representation on the board. In a dispersed ownership company this role may be played by institutional investors.

To summarise, our model provides for three characters of control. Managers in each of these groups of firms are subject to a set of incentives and restraints on their behaviour. However, these incentives and restraints will not be uniform for companies *within* each group. For example, managers' shareholdings will vary and so will the effectiveness of shareholders' power to restrain them. Also, firms of different sizes will be subject to varying degrees of external restraint from stock market influences. Only in those firms which can be shown to be largely independent of internal and external restraints can managers be said to 'control' and this can occur in any of the three groups.

Thus, if the influences of market power and investment opportunities facing firms were accounted for, any differences in performance *between* the three characters of control would merely reflect the *net outcome* of the incentives and restraints acting on their managements. Only by identifying separately the effects on performance which are due to these influences can we uncover the extent of discretion which, at the margin, is available to managers under varying control conditions. Having done so, however, the reasons for any differences which are observed will be obvious. This is the task of the empirical analysis which follows.

Notes

1. Of course this is not always the case. For example, the members of a family which has been associated with the founding or growth of a company may gain utility from the fact of holding shares in it.

2. See, for example, Lintner (1956) and Brittain (1966).

3. On the irrelevance of dividend policy see Modigliani and Miller (1961).

4. It should be mentioned that institutional investors are one group of shareholders who will tend to be long-term shareholders, but will be attracted to the stock of large companies because of their greater marketability.

5. Of course, institutions are likely to be far more knowledgeable than the average investor.

6. Again, institutions will be in contact with one another at a professional level, so that the costs involved in forming a coalition will be greatly reduced.

7. Williamson (1970, p. 94) found that in the top ten industrial corporations listed in the *Fortune 500* list in 1967 the median years served with the same company was 30 for executive vice-presidents and 25 for vice-presidents.

8. The 'moving equilibrium' problem makes a point which is similar to the one expressed by Monsen and Downs, i.e. the gain to managers from diverting resources from discretionary expenditures to profits will be once for all and impose the expectation of that shift being sustained. The 'free-ride' problem recognises the public good characteristics of stock option schemes and the incentive that participants have to cheat.

9. Similarly, Pahl and Winkler (1974) concluded on the basis of interviews with executives that the traditional values of 'hard and unameliorated capitalism' are far from being eclipsed.

10. Hence, if the manager had $250,000 invested in a $500,000 company he would be termed an owner-manager, but if he were manager of a $50 million company we would call him a professional.

11. Note, however, that a large and direct financial interest held by managers may mean that they are more willing to accept risks, since they can internalise more of the benefits arising from a successful but risky venture.

12. For example, in the US Winn (1977) found that the average size in total assets of firms in industries with a four-firm concentration ratio of more than 60 per cent was ten times larger than in firms with a concentration ratio of less than 40 per cent.

13. In fact, Manne (1965) was of the opinion that the market for corporate control was so effective that adoption of a *laissez-faire* approach towards mergers in the US 'at least short of a monopolisation charge under Section 2 of the Sherman Act' (p. 119), would improve the allocation of resources and lessen wasteful bankruptcy proceedings by failing companies.

4 MANAGERIAL INCENTIVES

Introduction

A basic proposition of the model outlined in Chapter 3 was that given the area of discretion enjoyed by managers, company performance will be dependent upon the incentive structure available to them. In fact, concern about the motivation of increasing numbers of professional salaried managers in the US prompted Taussig and Barker (1925) to conduct a study which examined the level and composition of managerial incomes over the period from 1904 to 1914. Since that time there has appeared a number of studies in the US and the UK examining the nature of executive incomes,[1] as well as studies which have sought to examine the relationship between compensation and corporate performance.[2]

In Chapter 2 we noted that owing to the existence of this substantial body of supportive literature researchers have been tempted to proceed directly from the 'establishment' of a separation of ownership from control on the basis of share dispersion (usually distinguishing the two categories of 'owner' and 'management' control), to the consideration of its performance consequences. However, researchers have discovered a considerable range of performances between firms. A major reason for this variability is that there is a considerable range of incentives and restraints *within* control types. For instance we cannot assume that the motivation of managers in management-controlled firms will be invariant to the value of shares held by them (even though these holdings may be small in relation to total issued capital).

In the past the question of managerial incentives has been approached in two ways. The earlier approach was simply to look at the level and composition of executive incomes. The bulk of this research was conducted in the US. The second approach examined the relationships between size, growth, profitability and the level of incomes earned by ranking executives. This evidence is reviewed in the following section. The Australian data on directorial stock-holdings are then presented, and finally the performance effects are examined.

Executive Incomes and Corporate Performance — Previous Research

At the turn of the century the large corporations of the US were still, to a considerable extent, dominated by owner-entrepreneurs, although the professional manager was beginning to make his presence felt. Taussig and Barker (1925) found that between 1904 and 1914 less than 5 per cent of their sample of more than 400 firms had instituted a regular system of extra compensation in the form of a bonus plan. Indeed, this was not surprising in view of the fact that the top executive group in the very largest corporations in the sample accounted for some 18 per cent of total common stock.

Later, Gordon (1940) examined the ownership income and compensation of 264 executives in 149 large US corporations for the year 1935. His data were, as he conceded, somewhat incomplete, because they were based on ownership returns lodged with the SEC and these 'were not required to show proportionate interests in stock held jointly through holding companies, partnerships, and otherwise' (p. 458). The methodology employed was to compare the relative magnitude of executive compensation from salary plus bonus, with income received through the ownership of shares. The major finding of the study was that the 161 executives in 'industrial' corporations earned a median income from salary and bonus of $79,300 and while the median market value of their shareholdings was almost $300,000 the median dividend was only $3,000. Gordon concluded that, on the basis of dividends received, ownership income provides only a minor incentive to executives in the sample.[3]

In more recent years Lewellen (1969, 1971) has presented the results of a painstaking study of 50 top US industrial corporations, spanning the period from 1940 to 1963. Lewellen defined 'earnings from fixed dollar rewards' as the after-tax compensation from salary plus bonus and 'earnings from stock based rewards' as income available from arrangements which use the value of the firm's stock as the compensation medium (i.e. some form of stock option plan). He then compared, for the top executive and the top five executives respectively, the percentage of total after-tax (non-ownership) compensation that these two components constitute. In the 1940s 'earnings from stock-based rewards' averaged only between 1 and 6 per cent of the total for the top executive and 1 and 5 per cent for the top five executives (Lewellen, 1969, p. 312; 1971, p. 50). However, a significant upsurge in the proportion of total compensation accounted for by stock-based rewards appeared after 1950 and this coincided approximately with the favourable changes in tax laws relating to capital gains which were legislated in that year. Between 1950 and 1963, for example, stock-based earnings of the total after-tax compensation of the top executive and top five executives rose from 7 and 5 per cent to 43 and 31 per cent.

Yet the most dramatic results were found when Lewellen (1969, p. 318; 1971, p. 152) compared the sum of after-tax stock-based remuneration, after-tax dividend income and obsolute after-tax capital gains with after-tax fixed dollar remuneration. For top executives this ratio rose from .86 in 1940 to 6.9 in 1963, while for the top five executives group it rose from 1.52 to 6.47 in the same period. With extreme values deleted the ratio for the top five executives group was still found to rise from .757 in 1940 to 2.287 in 1963. Thus, despite Galbraith's (1967, p. 116) assertions that 'stockholdings by management are small and often non-existent', it appears that by the early 1960s the compensation of top executives in large US corp- orations was overwhelmingly dependent on the performance of their stockholdings. This was so even though the *proportion* of total stockholdings for which they accounted had probably fallen since 1940.

But developments in the US towards the end of the 1960s have qualified Lewellen's results. The 1969 Tax Reform Act raised the maximum capital gains tax rate from 25 per cent to 35 per cent, while the maximum rate of 'earned' income fell from 70 per cent to 50 per cent. In addition the US stock market suffered declines in 1969 and early 1970 which persisted. The narrowing of differentials in earned and capital gains tax rates removed much of the advantage previously enjoyed by stock options and, since 93 per cent of large companies in 1969 employed qualified options as their own stock plan, executives came to the close of the maximum five-year term for the exercise of options only to find that they were worthless (Foote, 1973, pp. 212- 13). But while these modifications of the earlier environment must have altered the relative structure of executive compensation away from the capital gains element of stock options, the response was to change the form in which options were offered.

By 1972 only 42 per cent of stock option schemes were qualified and new varieties such as performance shares were being offered.[4] On the whole, the actual implementation of stock-option plans did not seem to suffer greatly, as their employment by such a large proportion of companies had made them a competitive necessity in a package designed to attract and maintain the services of managerial talent. Thus, Baker (1977, p. 52) reported a study of 50 successful industrial companies which he conducted in 1975 showed that, apart from providing substantial cash benefits, 'all 50 had retirement plans; 46 had bonus (incentive) payments; 47 had stock option plans; 29, savings and investment plans; 22, deferred compensation; 22, special executive employment contracts'.

Roberts (1959) was the first to consider the relationship between executive incomes and company performance in the US. For his sample of 77 companies he simply related 1948-50 averages for compensation (defined as salary plus bonus, plus deferred compensation) of executive officers to the average sales and profit levels of that period. He attempted to overcome the problem of collinearity between sales and total profits by including only those cases where the relationship was relatively weak.[5] He concluded that compensation was 'more closely related to sales than to dollar profits' (p. 62). McGuire, Chiu and Elbing (1962) examined the period 1953-9, again using data for 45 large US companies and defining compensation as salary plus bonus. The findings were consistent with those of Roberts in that compensation and sales were found to be statistically significantly related in five of the seven years, while the relationship between compensation and profits was not significant. More recent studies employing US data have cast some doubt on these early results. Lewellen and Huntsman (1970) used data relating to the 50 large companies in Lewellen's earlier work (Lewellen, 1969). Employing the broad definition of compensation (i.e. total after-tax salary plus bonus plus deferred compensation and stock related income) they concluded that 'reported company profits appear to have a strong and persistent influence in executive rewards whereas sales seem to have little, if any, impact' (p. 718). The methodology employed by Lewellen and Huntsman was hailed by some later observers as 'statistically more sophisticated' than those used by earlier researchers (Smyth, Boyes and Peseau, 1975, p. 73), and 'their ability to overcome the problem of multi-collinearity' was credited as the reason for their contrary findings (McEachern, 1975, p. 27).

However, several writers in the UK (Yarrow, 1972; Cosh, 1975; Meeks and Whittington, 1975) have charged that Lewellen and Huntsman functionally misspecified the equation they tested. That is, that their practice of dividing throughout by assets (to overcome problems of heteroscedasticity and multicollinearity) had the effect of eliminating the influence of size on remuneration from the start. Cosh (1975) re-estimated their equation with UK data on a large sample of companies for the period 1969-71 and found that the reciprocal of assets (1/A) explained the bulk of the variance of the dependent variable (R/A), and when (1/A) was replaced by a constant, the coefficient of determination (r^2) fell from its previous value of .68 to .13. Also, the linear form was questioned, since it can credibly be argued that unit increases in, say, the chief executive's remuneration, are likely to be related to *proportionate* rather than absolute increases in size, so that a semi-log form may be more appropriate.[7]

In another US study Masson (1971) provided interesting results on the determinants of changes in executive incomes over the period 1947-66. His conclusion was that stock-oriented incentives were important and that they affected managerial performance much more than did profit or sales incentives. However, the general applicability of Masson's research may be questioned on the grounds that the three industries from which his sample was drawn were the electronics, chemical and aerospace industries, industries whose performance during the study period was highly atypical. The gains to executives from participating in stock-option schemes, for example, will be outstanding if a company is able constantly to better market expectations. The potential of firms in new or technologically progressive industries (i.e. non-mature firms) is often continually underestimated by the stock market.

Meeks and Whittington (1975) reported a study which provided interesting insights into the relationship between directors' pay, growth and profitability in UK companies. We expect that these are more relevant to the Australian situation than are the studies which have recently been conducted in the US because, in the UK as in Australia, the use of stock-option schemes has been far less extensive (Cosh, 1975). In rebuttal of Lewellen and Huntsman's (1970) earlier claims, the effect of size was 'decisively reaffirmed'. However within the bounds of experience which could reasonably be expected in any year, growth (i.e. increasing the company's size) was found to pay no better than raising profits. But the effect on pay of increasing the size of the company was found to be a once-for-all change, increasing remuneration by a constant amount in all future periods, while the effect of raising profitability depended on the increased level of profit being maintained.[8] Hence, the crucial difference between these two variables was shown to rest on the length of management's time horizon.

Only three researchers (Williamson, 1964; Larner, 1970; McEachern, 1975) have considered the question of executive compensation explicitly in relation to the separation of ownership from control. In the earliest of these studies, Williamson (1964) linked executive compensation (defined as salary plus bonus) to various independent variables reflecting seller concentration, administrative and selling expense, barriers to entry and an index of management control. In one of the three time periods executive compensation was significantly higher in management-controlled firms; concentration and barriers-to-entry variables were significant in explaining the variance of compensation received. However, the measure used to identify 'management-controlled' firms was based on the extent to which managers were represented on the board of directors and was highly suspect (see McEachern, 1975, p. 84). Larner's (1970) analysis led to the conclusion that 'the corporation's dollar profit and rate of profit are the major variables explaining the level of executive remuneration and compensation' (p. 61) and that the control condition was not a significant determinant of compensation.

McEachern (1975) examined executive compensation in US corporations on the basis of his threefold classification of control. It was hypothesised that since owner-managers are able to enjoy the same pecuniary and non-pecuniary benefits that professional managers have access to, and because they are able to design the compensation structure with more freedom (i.e. control is strongly rooted), we may find that within the owner-managed firm (depending on the extent to which owner-managers identify primarily as shareholders or as managers) the compensation structure will lie somewhere in between the two extremes of externally controlled (EC) and management-controlled (MC) firms. The procedure employed was basically the same as that used by Lewellen and Huntsman (1970). McEachern concluded that 'the evidence is strong that managers in EC firms are paid more for stockholder welfare variables [accounting rate of profit and market value of the firm] and less (penalised more) for sales than managers in MC firms', and that 'when all sources of pecuniary compensation are included, the owner-managers' pay structure appears more like the EC structure, the structure designed to elicit profit-maximising behaviour from managers' (pp. 80-81). Thus, McEachern's results indicated that

Lewellen and Huntsman's conclusions might have been undermined if the analysis had been extended to account for alternative control patterns.

Executive Remuneration and Directors' Stockholdings

Compared with the US or UK the issue of executive compensation has been virtually ignored in Australia. This has been due, no doubt, to the general inaccessibility of the data. The first attempt to quantify the extent of directors' shareholdings was made by Wheelwright (1957) and in 1971 the Australian Institute of Management (AIM) began its *National Executive Salary Survey*. But even the question posed by Gordon in 1940, whether the gains to executives from stock ownership are comparable to those attributable to salary and bonus, has not been approached.

In this section the major components of Australian executive incomes are considered in three parts: salary and bonus, share ownership income, and executive stock options. The data in the first part are based on the sample of 355 companies used in the AIM Survey (1975), while in the next parts our sample of 226 listed corporations is employed.

Salary and Bonus

The figures showing average income derived from salary plus bonus for four top executive positions as at March 1975 revealed that, the larger the corporation, the higher the average salary which is paid to executives in each position. Since the 'company secretary' position may be regarded as the lower boundary of the top management group, it is probably fair to say that in 1975 the annual average compensation of the top executive group from salary and bonus ranged between $13,000 and $23,000 in the smallest companies to between $19,000 and $42,000 in the largest corporations.

Of the 355 companies contributing to the AIM survey in 1975, only 136, or 38 per cent, reported that they paid *regular* bonuses to executives.[7] Among chief executives the figures were slightly higher, being 39 per cent for those employed by an Australian-owned company and 45 per cent for those managing an overseas-owned concern. In the 136 companies which did implement regular bonus schemes the two most common criteria listed as determining payment were sales (45 companies) and company profits (64 companies). In other words, only 18 per cent of companies in the entire sample of 355 employed bonus schemes which were directly related to company profits. Altogether, then, bonus plans are far less common in Australia than in the US, where even in the mid-1950s Smyth (1959) found them in 75 per cent of manufacturing corporations.

Furthermore, the size of bonuses in relation to salary is far greater in the US. Smyth's study showed that among corporate officers bonuses amounted to 40 per cent to 50 per cent of salary, while for middle managers 20 per cent to 30 per cent of salary was a typical figure. In a more recent US survey Towers, Perrin, Forster and Crosby (1980, p. 9) found that for the chief executive officer of 36 of the largest 100 US firms the median ratio of bonus to salary was 70 per cent in 1979. By contrast, in Australia among chief executives actually receiving bonuses the typical bonus payment constituted only about 13 per cent of salary (the single highest figure being 19.7 per cent for chief executives in companies with annual sales of $5-10 million) while for group general managers and company secretaries an average of 9 per cent of salary was earned from bonus.

Ownership Income

Only the stockholdings of directors of corporations in the sample have been calculated, since members of the top management team who were not also directors could not normally be identified from the data sources. However, it should be noted that the board of directors in Australian corporations is more often than in the US composed of full-time executives. From the examination of directors' share-holdings and their directorships in the sample of 226 listed corporations it became evident that apart from the chairman and deputy chairman, directors who did not possess a title such as those shown in Table 4.1 tended to be outside directors, and were likely to hold a minimum number of shares. Columns 1 to 8 in Table 4.1 display the market value of the stockholdings and dividends received by 463 directors. They accounted for approximately a third of the 1,500 directorships in the 226 corporations.

From the table, which includes the shareholdings of directors in 76 corporations classified as majority or minority ownership controlled, one can gain some impression of the extent to which the personal wealth positions of these men (although there were some women directors not one was a member of this group of 463) is dependent upon the ownership of shares in their employer company. Ten directors held shares with a market value of more than $1 million, but

Table 4.1 : Market Value of Directors' Shareholdings and Income from Dividends, 1974-5.

Market value of shares (M) and dividends (D) in $000s	(1) Chairman		(2) Deputy chairman		(3) Managing director		(4) Chairman and managing director		(5) Deputy chairman and managing director		(6) Deputy managing director		(7) General manager/ chief executive		(8) Company secretary		(9) Average of directors' holdings		(10) Holdings of DCG per director	
	M	D	M	D	M	D	M	D	M	D	M	D	M	D	M	D	M	D	M	D
0	12	19	4	9	8	9		2	1	2	1	1	4	4	3	3	1	25	6	24
> 0 and <1	24	82	7	30	15	58	1	6		2		2	2	12	3	15	15	79	20	45
1 and <5	39	40	15	12	37	24	3	5	1	1	2	2	7	2	8	1	37	93	19	52
5 and <10	19	14	6	9	9	13	3	3	1			1	3	1	3	3	25	21	16	39
10 and <20	19	14	8	4	8	4		7						1	1	2	39	13	17	37
20 and <30	4	6	3	1	11	1	2	1			1		2				28	4	13	15
30 and <40	9	4	1		3	1	3	6	1								18		8	8
40 and <50	9	3	2	1	3		1				1						9	2	20	3
50 and <75	11	1	1		5	2	1	2				1			2		11		18	8
75 and <100	9	2	5		4		1										13		38	2
100 and <200	13	2	8		7	1	5	1			1		1		4		19	1	15	2
200 and <300	6				4		3										6		16	3
300 and <500	7		1		2		7	1									1		10	
500 and <1000	4		1		2		3	3			1						2		8	
1000 and <5000	2		4				3										2		2	
5000 and <10,000																				
≥10,000							1													
Total	187	187	66	66	118	118	37	37	4	4	7	7	20	20	24	24	226	226	226	226

almost all of these were executives in owner-controlled corporations. What is more pertinent is the fact that more than one half of the 'chairmen', 'managing directors' and 'deputy chairmen' held stock with a market value of less than $10,000, while more than three-quarters of the 'general managers' and 'company secretaries' held shares which were worth less then $10,000. Only among men holding the dual title of 'chairman and managing director' is this trend reversed, for in that category more than one-half held shares with a market value of $100,000 or more. However, the majority of these executives were also the heads of owner-controlled corporations.

But the personal holdings of directors may not always disclose the entire picture. In many instances directors represent other interested parties — other members of a director's family, friends and business associates. The last two columns in Table 4.1 are an attempt to capture the effect that these 'outsiders' have. When only the personal holdings of directors are considered (in column 9), the value of the average holding per director is less than $30,000 in half of the 226 corporations. When the holdings of the entire director group (including 'outsiders') is considered in column 10 and divided by the number of directors in a corporation, one finds that in about 40 per cent of the corporations the average value per director is more than $100,000. However, in the lowest quartile the average is still below $20,000 and, of the 89 corporations in which the average exceeds $100,000, 65 have been classified as owner-controlled.

The dividend record for 1974-75 is even more striking. Of the 463 directors included in columns 1-8, only 31 received dividend payments in the $30,000–$40,000 range or above. At the other end of the range 260, or some 56 per cent of these directors, earned less than $1,000 from dividends. Among the 199 men holding positions of 'managing director', 'chairman and managing director', 'general manager' and 'company secretary', those which were most likely to be full-time executives, 115 (57 per cent) received less than $1,000 in dividends, 146 (73 per cent) received less than $5,000 and 166 (83 per cent) received less than $10,000. From these figures it is apparent that the relative value of compensation from dividend payments played only a minor role in the total after-tax remunerations of top executives in Australian corporations in 1975, especially when the marginal tax rate of 65 per cent on incomes above $25,000 is taken into account. In more than half of the companies the dividends received by 'directors as a cohesive group' per director were less than $5,000.

Table 4.2 : Value of Directors' Holdings in 1974-5, by Control Type (Continuing Companies)

Range ($000s)	Number of companies													Total	Mean	Standard deviation
	<2.5	>2.5<5.0	>5<10	>10<20	>20<40	>40<80	>80<160	>160<320	>320<640	>640<1280	>1280<2560	>2560<5120	≥5120			
Control type:																
Private ownership			1	1		4	9	18	15	9	7	3	1	68	721.83	1052.14
Management			1	7	11	16	18	14	5	2	1			75	166.15[a]	236.51
Domestic company*	1		1	1	6	6	6	4		2				27	142.09[a]	199.43
Overseas company	1	1	4	3	7	1	4	2		1				24	103.73[a]	250.63
Company: total	2	1	5	4	13	7	10	6		3				51	124.04[a]	223.49
All companies	2	1	7	12	24	27	37	38	20	14	8	3	1	194	350.85	702.87

skewness: 5.397

Notes: a indicates significance at the .01 level using a two-tail test;
* this category includes firms which were controlled jointly by domestic and overseas companies.

Having thus examined the distribution of shareholdings among individual directors and corporations, we shall look at how the ownership of shares was distributed among control categories which are of central importance to this study.

The results are displayed in Table 4.2. They show that management- and company-controlled firms exhibited a significantly lower value of directors' holdings when compared with private ownership companies, but there were no significant differences between management- and company-controlled firms. The average value of directors' holdings for all companies was $350,854. However, due to the marked positive skewness displayed by the distribution (5.397), in only 42 of the 194 firms was the value of directors' holdings greater than the mean value. From Table 4.2 it is apparent that there was a substantial degree of overlap in the ranges of values observed for each control type and this is especially evident when comparing ownership- and management-controlled companies. Holdings in most firms were clustered in the $20,000–$320,000 range and almost one-half of the owner-controlled firms were in this range. Therefore, in many cases the value of directors' holdings was similar as between owner-controlled and management-controlled firms, which lends support to Lewellen's contentions.

But while in the majority of owner-controlled firms the value of holdings was greater than $320,000, this was the case in only about 10 per cent of management-controlled firms and 6 per cent of company controlled firms. Thus, while all control types were represented in the 'hump' of the distribution, those in its long tail tended to be owner-controlled.

Executive Stock Options

Lewellen (1969) showed that executive stock options became increasingly more important in the US after 1950. Marris (1964, p. 67) noted that during the 1960s about three-quarters of all US listed companies operated some form of plan. Here we find that the Australian situation is markedly different from that observed in the US. In 1975 the AIM survey (1975, p. 42) found that only 25 (7 per cent) of the 355 companies surveyed had a stock option plan whereby executives had 'the right to buy shares to be issued at a specified future date at a nominated price'.[7] A further 20 (6 per cent) companies had plans whereby employees were assisted in purchasing shares on favourable terms.

In our sample of 226 listed corporations it was found that there has, over the ten-year period 1965-6 to 1974-5, been a tendency for greater reliance on the stock option mechanism. But even in 1973-4 only 11 per cent of corporations had options outstanding. One reason for this low proportion (when compared with the US for example) is the traditional mistrust of executive option schemes displayed by Australian shareholders. The Australian Shareholders' Association, for instance, has been active in lobbying the National Companies and Securities Commission (modelled on the SEC) to restrict the issue of options other than on a pro-rata basis to existing shareholders. The tax laws in Australia have also discouraged non-salary executive remuneration schemes.[8]

The option discount (the ratio of the option price is the market price at the time of issue) serves to dilute the interest of existing shareholders and in the case of owner-controlled companies this effect will be felt most strongly by the cohesive ownership group. This may explain why such a small proportion of owner-controlled companies issued stock options. The fact that a slightly higher proportion of management-controlled companies did so is understandable, since stock options are presumably designed to align more closely the interests of professional managers and stockholders. However, it is surprising that in the ten years up to 1974-5, apart from non-mature overseas-controlled companies which were innovators in this area, not a single domestic company-controlled corporation in our sample ever issued stock options. Also, throughout the control categories it is striking to find that the proportion of non-mature corporations issuing stock options was consistently higher than in mature corporations.

Directors' Stockholdings and Corporate Performance

Lewellen (1969) alleged that in the US the compensation package of top executives in large corporations is so closely tied to the performance of the firm that they have a substantial unity of interest with ordinary shareholders. That is, while the proportion of the firm's stock in the hands of managers might be small, the absolute value of these holdings is large relative to their personal wealth positions and the value of earnings from dividends and capital gains (including executive stock options) is large relative to their salary. In the last section we found that most executive directors in Australian corporations still earn most of their income from salary. However, in some of the large corporations directors do have substantial stockholdings, even though these are small in proportionate terms. The question we shall address now is whether directorial holdings do provide sufficient incentive to make a difference to corporate behaviour and performance.

The point regarding substantial shareholdings in large managerial corporations was later raised by Nyman and Silberston (1978, p. 93) who were critical of studies which 'infer managerial motivation from statistics of controlling ownership'. Nyman (1974) had examined the relationship between directors' holdings in the top 100 UK companies and their profitability, growth and retention records. Profitability, growth and the retention ratio were all positively and significantly related to the value of shareholdings, but ownership was found to explain only a small part of the total variances of these variables.

In Chapter 3 it was hypothesised that positive relationships should be observed between profitability, growth and the retention ratio and directors' shareholdings, but that risk should be negatively related to directors' shareholdings. These hypotheses can be treated in a model of the form,

$$P = \beta_0 + \beta_1 \, VDH + \beta_2 \, NMAT + \beta_3 \, SIZE + \varepsilon \qquad (4.1)$$

where,

P   is performance, measured by RNA, GNA, SDRNA and RET

VDH   is the value of directors' shareholdings

NMAT   is a dummy variable with a value of 1 if the firm is non-mature and zero otherwise

SIZE   is a measure of firm size, calculated as the reciprocal of net assets

ε is the stochastic error term

Specifically, we will be testing the null hypothesis that $\beta_1 = 0$ (i.e. $H_0: \beta_1 = 0$) against the following one-sided alternative hypotheses:

if P is,   RNA $H_1: \beta_1 > 0$

REA $H_1: \beta_1 > 0$
GNA $H_1: \beta_1 > 0$
SDRNA $H_1: \beta_1 < 0$
RET $H_1: \beta_1 < 0$

There are several reasons for expecting a curvilinear relationship between profitability and the absolute value of directors' holdings.[9] The higher the value of shares held the more wealthy directors will be, so that after-tax earnings from dividends will rise more slowly owing to a higher marginal tax rate. Also, as the directors become more wealthy their valuation of a marginal dollar in dividends or capital gains will fall. Finally, the process of raising profitability, either through greater attention to cost minimisation or more effort being expended in the search for profitable avenues for investment, will be subject to diminishing marginal returns. We should also expect a curvilinear relationship between growth and the value of directors' holdings. This is partly because profitability and growth are expected to be highly correlated.

Simple regression analysis employing both linear and logarithmic forms of the VDH variable were tried first. Using the entire continuing company sample, VDH and ln VDH were unimportant in determining performance, except for operating risk (SDRNA) and the retention ratio (RET). However, all coefficients had the predicted signs. When maturity and firm size variables were included, the value of directors' holdings (ln VDH) was found to be positively and significantly (at the .05 level) related to the rate of return on equity assets (REA). The coefficient of .00357 indicated that increasing the value of directors' holdings from, say, $5,000 to $50,000 or $50,000 to $500,000 would raise profitability by .82 of a percentage point. Thus, when employing the entire sample the effect of directorial holdings did not appear to be quantitatively important and whatever effect there was appeared to diminish rapidly with higher values of directors' holdings. The effect on pre-tax return on net assets (RNA) was even less pronounced and neither was it statistically significant.

A major problem with the analysis just described is that differences in the nature of incentives and restraints acting on managers of companies with a different character of control can distort the results achieved. That is, according to the model of firm behaviour outlined in Chapter 3, there will be interaction effects between control type and the influence of shareholdings by company directors on performance. One way of accounting for this would be to include control-type dummy variables and additional variables to capture any interaction effects. There is also reason to expect significant interaction effects between control type and maturity and between control type and firm size. To include these effects in the regression equation would require another four explanatory variables. But an alternative treatment and one which is suitable within our framework — that is, to examine first the determinants of corporate performance *within* control groups — is to run a separate series of regressions on each control-type sample. The results of this approach are shown in Table 4.3, where OC, MC and CC refer to owner-, management- and company-controlled firms respectively.

The coefficients on ln VDH in the first three equations in Table 4.3 indicate that in OC and MC firms the response of RNA to increases in directors' holdings was about the same and the coefficients are significant at the .01 level. But there is no relationship between the value of directors' holdings and RNA in company-controlled firms. In equations 4.3.4, 4.3.5 and 4.3.6 it can be seen that the effect on REA of increases in VDH was positive and again significant at the .01 level in OC and MC firms. Moreover, the effect of directors' holdings on the rate of return on equity is now significant in absolute terms. For example, in MC firms a ten-fold increase in VDH was associated with an increase of 2.53 percentage points in the rate of return on equity assets. In company-controlled firms the coefficient on ln VDH is about three-quarters of that in OC and MC firms, but is significant at only the .10 level.

From the coefficients relating to ln VDH in equations 4.3.7, 4.3.8 and 4.3.9 it is apparent that only in OC firms does the value of directors' holdings have a very strong influence on growth. Indeed, the size of the coefficient in OC firms (.022) was two and half times greater than in MC firms, while in CC firms the coefficient was negligible in size. Although in all three equations relating the value of directors' holdings to operating risk the sign on VDH is negative as predicted, none of these coefficients is either statistically or economically significant. Thus far it would seem (at least in MC and OC firms) that firm size, or product market considerations, have the most important influence on exposure to business risk. However, it would be premature to conclude that internal factors have no implications at all.

In equations 4.3.13, 4.3.14 and 4.3.15 the coefficient on VDH is positive for OC and MC firms, but negative in CC firms. The negative sign found on the coefficient in CC firms is caused by the fact that

Table 4.3: Directors' Holdings and Corporate Performance,
by Control Type

Equation number	n	Control type	Dependent variable	Constant	*In VDH*
4.3.1	68	OC	RNA	.025	.018 (3.193)[a]
4.3.2	75	MC	RNA	.074	.017 (3.341)[a]
4.3.3	51	CC	RNA	.157	.287E-3 (.044)
4.3.4	68	OC	REA	.015	.010 (3.113)[a]
4.3.5	75	MC	REA	.034	.011 (4.118)[a]
4.3.6	51	CC	REA	.056	.008 (1.372)[c]
4.3.7	68	OC	GNA	—.058	.022 (5.696)[a]
4.3.8	75	MC	GNA	.051	.009 (1.597)[c]
4.3.9	51	CC	GNA	.111	.891E-3 (.141)
4.3.10	68	OC	SDRNA	.031	
4.3.11	75	MC	SDRNA	.026	
4.3.12	51	CC	SDRNA	.041	
4.3.13	64	OC	RET	.398	
4.3.14	75	MC	RET	.376	
4.3.15	49	CC	RET	.458	

VDH	NMAT	SIZE (1/NAo)	R^2	$\bar{R}^2$	F-ratio
	—.023 (.950)	.129 (5.186)^d	.388	.360	13.540^a
	.014 (.892)	.218 (7.695)^d	.490	.468	22.727^a
	.065 (3.066)^a	.043 (1.919)^f	.282	.236	6.157^a
	—.003 (.247)	.056 (4.017)^d	.320	.288	10.052^a
	.018 (2.160)^b	.094 (6.342)^d	.460	.437	20.181^a
	.067 (3.424)^a	—.353E-3 (.010)	.227	.177	4.595^a
	.014 (.859)	.137 (8.187)^d	.685	.670	46.470^a
	.019 (1.040)	.123 (3.739)^d	.198	.164	5.850^a
	.009 (.386)	.052 (2.232)^e	.118	.061	2.087
—.246E-5 (.812)	—.008 (.691)	.024 (2.099)^b	.088	.045	2.061
—.629E-5 (.744)	.012 (2.113)^b	.032 (3.229)^a	.205	.171	6.091^a
—.172E-4 (1.007)	.009 (.942)	.004 (.437)	.061	.001	1.019
.361E-4 (1.949)^b	.006 (.089)	.102 (1.493)	.095	.050	2.095
.649E-4 (1.105)	.023 (.605)	.190 (2.715)^e	.108	.070	2.861^b
—.407E-4 (.508)	.136 (3.304)^a	.008 (.195)	.241	.190	4.757^a

Notes: a, b and c denote significance at the .01, .05 and .10 levels respectively using a one-tail test; d, e and f denote significance at the .01, .05 and .10 levels respectively using a two-tail test.

VDH is negatively correlated with firm (non)maturity ($r = -.210$), and maturity in turn has a strong positive influence on the retention ratio ($r = .466$) in these firms. Again, the sizes of the coefficients relative to the mean values observed make them insignificant in quantitative terms.

To summarise the main points, our findings indicate that the value of directors' shareholdings has a significant impact on the rates of return earned by OC and MC firms. With regard to the rate of return on equity assets this finding certainly provides support for the notion that, other things being equal, a greater equity participation by top management may elicit performance which more closely maximises shareholder welfare. However, the strength of the relationship is weaker in company-controlled firms. In these firms the stage of maturity has by far the largest impact on profitability. One explanation for this is that the discretion available to executives in CC firms is severely limited by the controlling corporation. This limit to discretion may have taken the form of an imposed minimum performance constraint. Thus, even where shareholdings of directors are very small this minimum performance is achieved.

It appears that maturity and firm size also have differential impacts on the performance variables. Statistical confirmation of this observation is presented in Appendix Table A.4.1 which shows the F-values obtained on the application of a Chow test.[10]

The generally high F-values indicate that the explanatory variables as a group affected performance differently with each control-type category, especially in the case of profitability of growth. These results provide further support for our contention that the nature of incentives and restraints varies according to the character of control.

Both theoretical arguments and econometric evidence have supported a curvilinear relationship between the rate of return and the value of shares held by directors. Indeed, within the range of coefficients observed, it would seem that the effect of greater equity participation on the rate of return tapers off quite rapidly. For instance, they suggest that increasing the value of shares held by directors in management-controlled firms from $1,000 to the average for all firms (of $350,000) would be associated with an increase of 6.4 percentage points in the return on equity assets. Yet raising the value of shareholdings to twice that amount (i.e. to $700,000) would result in only a .07 percentage point increase. Therefore, while the welfare of shareholders might be substantially improved were directors and executives with small shareholdings to increase these to, say, $300,000 to $400,000, further rises would not make too much difference to the profitability performance which could be expected.[11] Since in most owner-controlled firms the directors already held more than $300,000 worth of shares in their company, but this was the case in only a small minority of MC and CC firms, it appears that the largest gains from such a move would have been made by the shareholders in the latter groups of companies. The relationship between control type, profitability and directorial holdings is shown in Figure 4.1, which is drawn for mature firms with net assets of $10 million, which is close to the median size of firms in the sample. This visual representation gives an impression that the responsiveness of profitability to directorial holdings was much the same for management- as for owner-controlled firms, with slightly less responsiveness in the case of company control. However, it must

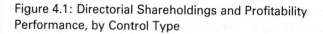

Figure 4.1: Directorial Shareholdings and Profitability Performance, by Control Type

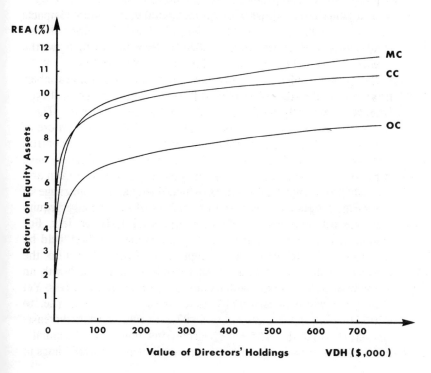

be borne in mind that the CC curve is a rather weak relationship. The vertical distances between the curves are of particular importance. They indicate, for example, that an owner-controlled firm of that size needs more than $600,000 worth of directors' equity to exceed the profitability of a similar-sized management- or company-controlled firm with $25,000 worth of directors' equity. This appears unlikely, given the range of values displayed in Table 4.2.

A possible criticism of these results relates to the problems of direction of causation. For instance, it could be argued that the positive association between value of directors' holdings and profitability is due to access to confidential internal information on the future prospects of their company. This viewpoint would see directors, acting on inside information, adjust their holdings to own a greater share of firms which will be more profitable in the future. Hence, the direction of causation would run from the anticipation of future success (or failure) to the purchase (or sale) of shares in the company. However, there are several arguments which could be offered in opposition to that viewpoint. First, directorial shareholdings are closely monitored for evidence of insider trading.[12] Second, the shareholdings of directors tended to be quite stable over time. Third, if the value of shareholdings had no influence on profitability, but rather the opposite was true, there would be no reason to expect a curvilinear relationship between the two variables. Fourth, such a view could not explain the wide discrepancies in the *levels* of profitability attained with a given value of directors' shareholdings, in OC, MC and CC firms.

Summary

The weight of empirical research which has examined managerial incentives suggests that size and the pursuit of size through growth will be a primary concern of the professional manager. It is also apparent, however, that this preference may be modified to some degree by schemes which are designed more closely to align the interests of managers and outside shareholders. In the US, during the 1920s and 1930s, as professional managers became more widespread various bonus schemes were devised. These proved to be insufficiently flexible and open to abuse, but have nevertheless survived as an important element of executive compensation.

In 1940 the stock option was being implemented by only a small number of US corporations. This situation changed when new tax laws in 1950 initiated a trend which progressed to the point that by the late 1960s about one-third of managers' after-tax income (not including dividends and capital gains) was accounted for by profits from the exercise of stock options (Lewellen, 1972, p. 119). During the 1970s a falling stock market and the effect of the 1969 Tax Reform Act have again served to modify the picture. But, while the proportion of after-tax compensation represented by the exercise of stock options has no doubt declined, most companies still offer some form of plan based on the market price of shares. Thus, although the absolute number of shares held by executives may still be a small proportion of all shares on issue, and does not provide grounds for control in the traditional entrepreneurial sense, when combined with the holdings of their immediate family it may in many cases bulk large in comparison with the executives' personal wealth.

The Australian experience contrasts sharply with that of the US and appears more like the UK situation. A relatively large number of Australian corporations are still dominated by owner-managers, but non-private-owner-controlled corporations account for a majority of the output of listed companies. However, it has been established that only a small proportion of Australian companies use bonuses as an incentive for management and where they are present they represent only a small fraction of executives' salaries. Except in owner-controlled companies, it was found that the shareholdings of most directors were small in relation to their wealth positions during the study period. Also, the income derived from dividends and capital gains was likely to be small in relation to income from fixed salary and bonus. In 1965-6 executive stock options were virtually non-existent and, while a trend towards greater use of this incentive may be developing, particularly after the tax changes effected in 1974, it is fair to say that in comparison with the US this form of compensation is (and was, during the study period) still embryonic. It was no surprise to find that the 23 firms in our continuing sample which issued stock options were twice as large as non-issuing companies.

When the influence of directors' shareholdings on performance was examined it was found that they had their greatest effect on the profitability and growth rates of firms. The relationships were curvi-linear, however, so that increments to profitability and growth diminished rapidly with further increases in directors' shareholdings. Thus, on the basis of shareholdings *alone* we could not expect owner-controlled firms to perform very much better, in terms of profitability, than management-controlled firms. In company-controlled firms the responsiveness of profitability and growth to directors' holdings was less pronounced. It was suggested that this may be due to the presence of a strong external shareholder — the dominant company — imposing a minimum performance constraint on management in these firms.

Directorial shareholdings had a negative effect on risk, but this was quite small and was not statistically significant. Retentions were positively related to directors' holdings in owner- and management-controlled firms, although the effect was statistically significant only in owner-controlled firms. On the other hand, in company-controlled firms the relationship was negative, weak and non-significant.

The most intriguing aspect of these findings is the presence of substantial gaps between the performance of owner-, management- and company-controlled firms given any *level* of directors' share-holdings, maturity and firm size. These results have indicated that the existence of a dominant shareholder (whether a person or another corporation) does not necessarily mean that small shareholders' interests will be protected. Dominant shareholders may have objectives which conflict with those of small non-controlling shareholders and, as we will demonstrate in the following chapters, they have considerable discretionary powers. Finally, the varying effects of the explanatory variables employed in separate regressions on the control-type sub-samples have indicated that different sets of restraints act on managers of firms in each group. In the next chapter we examine the 'internal' stockholder restraint. Chapter 6 will then investigate the relationships between these internal restraints and the external market restraints.

Notes

1. See, for example, Baker (1938), Gordon (1940) and Lewellen (1969).
2. These include studies by Roberts (1959), McGuire, Chiu and Elbing (1962), Lewellen and Huntsman (1970), Masson (1971), Cosh (1975), Meeks and Whittington (1975a), McEachern (1975) and Smyth, Boyes and Peseau (1975).
3. However, it should be noted that the generality of Gordon's results was limited by the fact that (a) there was an understatement of the real extent of stock ownership, (b) 1935 was a year of depressed economic conditions and (c) gains from capital appreciation and stock options were ignored (although these may well have been negative).
4. Performance shares are allocated to executives at the beginning of a period to be earned out over the length of the period subject to the attainment of specified performance goals which need not be associated with the behaviour of the market price of the firm's stock. However, the value of the pay-out at the end of the

period is dependent upon the market price of the shares allocated.

5. This collinearity among independent variables was later noted by Ciscel (1974), who felt that it 'permanently obscures the identification of the hypothesised relationship' (p. 617).

6. By ranking alternative specifications according to correlation coefficients and Durbin-Watson statistics, Baker (1969) made a claim that a log-linear relation is most appropriate, although Smyth, Boyes and Peseau (1975, p. 72) discounted his methodology.

7. Meeks and Whittington (1975, p. 2) argued this on the basis of the frequency distributions displayed by the three variables. The frequency distribution of size showed marked positive skewness, while those of profitability and compensation were only slightly positively skewed.

8. It is interesting to note that in a study examining the profitability of mergers in the UK, Meeks (1977, p. 32) found that the average merger represented a one-third increase in size. This meant an increase of £1,198 in the remuneration of the highest paid director. On the other hand, the typical loss in profitability of 1.05 percentage points which was associated with a typical merger resulted in a loss of only £93 in pay, making the net gain £1,105.

9. For example, see 'Aust tax laws stop US-style executive perks', *Australian Financial Review*, 7 January 1979, p. 11, which compares the Carter wage guidelines with Australian legislation.

10. For example, Clark and Wilson (1961, p. 133) reasoned that all incentives will 'have a diminishing marginal utility'.

11. See Chow (1960).

12. Of course if the shareholdings (and therefore, the incentive) of directors in all companies were to rise, the overall gain in profitability would depend on how far the gains of particular firms were made at the expense of competitors relative to gains in internal efficiency (e.g. by the elimination of some X-inefficiency). Also, higher shareholdings by managers could increase their control over the firm and wider discretionary powers could result in lower profits.

13. In fact the Senate Select Committee on Securities and Exchange (the Rae Report, 1974) uncovered several instances of insider trading during the minerals boom, although these were, in the main, confined to mining rather than industrial companies.

5 Owners and Managers

Introduction

In this chapter it is argued that the nature of *internal restraints*, i.e. restraints on managers which can be imposed by current shareholders in the company, will depend on its 'character of control'. Our model distinguishes three control types: private ownership, company and management. The third category is residual in the sense that it is defined by the absence of a dominant private or company stockholder. Previous studies have taken for granted that a dispersed ownership structure can be immediately equated with managerial fiat. Thus, for example, the often important holdings by financial institutions have been assumed to lie in passive hands, giving managers free reign over the affairs of these companies.

Similarly, it has almost without exception been assumed that the behaviour of 'owner-controlled' firms can automatically be identified with the interests of all shareholders. In the US McEachern (1975) has proposed that this need not be the case — especially where the dominant shareholder is also part of management. But in many owner-controlled firms there is no *single* dominant shareholder. Control is normally in the hands of a 'cohesive group' of shareholders who have direct links with, or are represented on, the board of directors. Since these shareholders are not a part of management their interests may be closer to those of other shareholders who are not part of the controlling group. Indeed, given the strength of their shareholdings and their unified position only this group will be able to make directors heed their demands. Shareholders who are not part of this group, however, will have even less opportunity to influence management decisions than those with similarly small proportionate holdings in a dispersed-ownership company.

In previous research 'company-controlled' firms have either been assigned to the owner control category or to the control type occupied by the dominant company shareholder. Neither of these procedures can be justified, since the nature of internal and external restraints will differ as between owner- and company-controlled firms, and between the controlling firm and the controlled firm. Furthermore, the degree of restraint which can be imposed by the controlling firm may depend on whether it is domestic or foreign.

The first objective of the present chapter is to identify the nature of internal restraints imposed on the managements of companies according to their character of control. Second, we shall be seeking to assess the effects that these internal restraints have on company performance.

The Structure of Stockholdings

The 'separation of ownership from control' thesis is founded on the proposition that, owing to widely dispersed ownership, professional managers in the large modern corporation are a self-perpetuating group unconstrained by proprietary interests. Thus, it is essential that any discussion of the constraints faced by managers should begin (at the very least) with the establishment of *prima facie* evidence that managers are indeed relatively free from the exercise of control by stockholders. The most commonly used approach, and one which stems from that originally applied by Berle and Means (1932), has been to examine the ownership sources and dispersion of voting stocks. This is because the party controlling the majority of votes actually cast at the annual general meeting will presumably be in a position to control a majority of the seats on the board of directors. If stockholdings are found to be widely dispersed it is held that directors and managers will take advantage of the proxy mechanism to ensure their reinstatement.

Using this broad framework, but relying on 'street knowledge' and information on stockholdings derived from various trade publications, Berle and Means (1932) concluded that as many as 44 per cent of the 200 largest US corporations could be classified as being under the control of management.[1] They defined stockholder control to be in evidence if 20 per cent or more of the common stock of a corporation was in the hands of a single party. A later investigation by the Securities and Exchange Commission (1940) dropped the stock ownership requirement for owner control to the 10 per cent level and calculated the largest 20 stockholders in the largest 200 non-financial corporations. The results reported that two-thirds of these corporations were dominated by family or other outside interests, although this was challenged by Gordon (1945) who claimed that only in a third of these did a 'small compact group of individuals exercise control'. Subsequent US studies by Villarejo (1961, 1962),

Larner (1970) and Palmer (1972) served to illustrate an increasing trend toward managerial dominance. Using a 10 per cent cut-off point Larner showed that in 1963 the degree of management control within the largest 500 corporations had risen to 84 per cent, while Palmer calculated a figure of 88 per cent for 1969.

Apart from some isolated work by Florence (1961) and Nyman and Silberston (1978) in the UK, and Wheelwright (1957) and Wheelwright and Miskelly (1967) in Australia, UK and Australian researchers showed surprisingly little interest in the apparent development taking place in the US. Moreover, recently researchers in the US and UK have brought new evidence to light which casts some doubt on the conclusion that 'the managerial revolution is all but complete'. In the US Burch (1972) objected that relying on available information on stockholdings would understate the actual stock ownership of the dominant groups. On information drawn from journals and newspapers he concluded that the control of the 500 largest non-financial corporations in 1965 was markedly different from that reported by Larner: he claimed to have found almost twice the number of owner-controlled corporations. Later still, Pedersen and Tabb (1976) used previously unavailable data[2] which inflated the proportion of stock visibly in the hands of important stockholder interests (although they felt that this would still represent an underestimate) and dropped the requirement for stockholder control to 5 per cent. On this basis they could classify only 36 per cent of 597 corporations in their sample as being subject to management control. In addition, they produced evidence regarding mergers which indicated that owner interests were predominating in the acquisition process, so that there may in fact be a tendency for the degree of management control to be reduced over time.

In the UK Nyman and Silberston (1978) estimated that in 1975 only 100 (44 per cent) of the top 225 corporations were of 'no known control'. Of the 125 companies classified as 'owner-controlled', however, in only 53 was the control exercised by directors and their families through the ownership of more than 5 per cent of stock; and only seventeen more were deemed to be under ownership control because a family chairman or managing director was in evidence (even though the stockholding of an individual or group was less than 5 per cent). Nyman and Silberston contended that the 'conventional wisdom' that the proportion of large companies controlled by ownership interests is declining may therefore be somewhat misleading.

In Australia Wheelwright (1957) examined the ownership and control of the largest 102 public companies for 1954. Excluding foreign-controlled firms and those companies which were unclassified owing to data deficiencies, 37 per cent of the remaining companies were deemed to be under management control (using a 10 per cent ownership cut-off point). However, these management-controlled firms accounted for 51 per cent of total shareholders' funds. It was concluded that the 'divorce between ownership and control may not have proceeded quite so far in these Australian companies', but that the observed pattern was 'not substantially different from that existing in large British and American companies' (p. 5).

Ten years later Wheelwright and Miskelly (1967) published the results of a wider study based on a 200-firm sample which included many large non-listed as well as public companies. On the definitions used in the earlier study, by number the proportion of management-controlled firms remained constant, but they now accounted for 71 per cent of total assets. Since this sample included many firms which were not in the top 100 (where the separation of ownership from control is likely to be most advanced) these results indicated a considerable dispersion of shareholdings in the intervening period. However, financial institutions were coming to dominate the registers of many large companies. It was conjectured that if these institutions were to become interested in exercising their potential for control, 'the result would be to virtually eliminate the managerial classification, and to substitute for it a new category of control by financial institutions' (p. 8).

As might be expected from Wheelwright and Miskelly's data for 1962-4, stock ownership in our sample is heavily concentrated. If we take the largest 20 'cohesive groups' in each company, more than half the market value of ordinary shares in our 226 companies is accounted for. (A 'cohesive group' may of course be an individual, a group of individuals which could include directors, a single company or financial institution, or a group of such companies or institutions.) From Table 5.1 it can be seen that the small shareholdings excluded from the 'largest 20 cohesive groups' in each company — altogether hundreds of thousands of holdings in the 226 companies — accounted for only 48.3 per cent of the market value of the companies' total ordinary shares.[3]

In Australian listed companies the most significant shareholders in the 'largest 20 cohesive groups' are the financial institutions, which

Table 5.1: The Ownership Structure (226 Companies*)

	Market value of shares ($ million)	% of value of total shares
'Largest 20 cohesive groups' in each company		
Persons	450	10.3
Financial institutions	801	18.2
Companies	756	17.2
Nominees	263	6.0
Total, 4,500 'cohesive groups'	2,270	51.7
Other shareholders	2,117	48.3
Total	4,387	100.0

*Average 1974-5 prices

held shares with a market value of $801 million, or 18.2 per cent of the total. Companies, both domestic and overseas, were next in importance with holdings valued at $756 million.

It will be seen that shares held in the category 'persons' are calculated to have been worth $450 million. In 1974-5 the directors of our 226 companies held (either as individuals or as members of actual groups) shares with an estimated market value of $79.2 million, while the remaining members of the director-linked groups held shares valued at $265.2 million. The sum of these holdings, almost $345 million, accounted for some 77 per cent of the total value of shares designated as owned by 'persons' within the holdings of the 'largest 20 cohesive groups'. Thus, ownership within the 'persons' category was heavily concentrated in the hands of a relatively small number of individuals. Though ownership by nominees accounted for only 6 per cent of the total value of shares, this unidentified group is not strategically insignificant.

Foreign ownership was largely contained in the 'companies' category, although all three of the other categories also incorporated elements of foreign ownership which could not always easily be distinguished. While Australian-owned companies exhibited ownership in all industries, the extent of overseas ownership was varied: in some industries there was a complete absence of identifiable foreign company ownership. Most selective appeared to be the American multinationals, whose holdings were concentrated in two industries — food, beverages and tobacco (concentration being highest in tobacco) and chemical, petroleum and coal products. Holdings by UK companies were also concentrated in these industries, but the spread of ownership was greater. The specialisation of overseas investment in industries which have offered profitable investment opportunities since the Second World War has sometimes been proposed as a reason for their performing better than Australian-owned companies;[4] this forms the basis of a set of hypotheses which will be tested later in the chapter.

Table 5.2 suggests that management-controlled companies accounted for almost half the total tangible assets of the sample. The other half was reasonably equally distributed between company and private ownership control. Within the private ownership control sector only eleven firms, or 4.9 per cent of the total, were deemed to be controlled by private kinship units owning a majority of ordinary shares. Somewhat surprisingly, these companies were on average only slightly smaller than companies controlled by private kinship units owning between 10 and 50 per cent of ordinary shares. Thus it appears that a small number of family-dominated corporations have managed to grow to a reasonably large size without much dilution of ownership. However, the growth has usually been slow: most of these firms are long-established, several having their origins in the last century.

Table 5.2 shows that overseas companies, the dominant element in the 'companies' sector, controlled in whole or in part $3,774 million

Table 5.2: The Control Structure, 1974-5 (226 Companies)

Control classification	Number of companies	%	Total tangible assets ($ millions)		%
			Mean	Total	
Majority ownership	11	4.9	40.0	439.7	3.3
Minority ownership	65	28.7	41.3	2,683	19.9
Management	79	35.0	83.7	6,612.1	48.9
Companies					
— Domestic	28	12.4	44.7	1,250.7	9.2
— Overseas	39	17.3	51.6	2,013.8	14.9
— Joint Domestic/					
Overseas	4	1.8	127.5	509.8	3.8
Total	226	100.0	59.8	13,509.7	100.0

(28 per cent) of the total assets in the sample. In contrast the total market value of ordinary shares held by overseas companies was only about $496 million, indicating a substantial degree of leverage in control. Only four companies were found to be jointly controlled by domestic and overseas companies. This is not surprising in view of the problems which can arise under joint control. Brash (1966, p. 68) cited conflict over dividend policies as the main reason for the collapse of two 50/50 ventures.

Table 5.3 provides further data on ownership, notably by institutions. Hall (1958, p. 375) made the observation that, while in Western Europe and the US institutional investors had come to occupy a dominant position in the new issue market, in Australia 'the bulk of finance obtained by companies by the issue of securities is supplied by private investors'. Until 1956-7 persons and unincorporated businesses remained the largest net purchasers of stocks in Australian companies. Institutional investors were supplying only 20 per cent of injections of new money into the corporate sector through security issues. Nevertheless, by extrapolating the underlying trends into the future, Hall predicted an increasingly important role for institutional investors. By the early 1960s precedence had clearly passed to financial institutions and net purchases by overseas investors had also risen significantly. In the latter half of the 1960s, when Australian private investors were making massive net sales of corporate securities, net purchases by institutions and overseas investors soared. A recent comparative study by Davies (1982) showed that the Australian trends mirror those in the US and UK. However, share ownership by persons is still much more widespread in the US: 15 per cent of the US population owned shares in 1970, although the percentage fell to 11.9 per cent in 1975. In the UK, only about 3.7 per cent of the population own shares, similar to the estimate of 4.2 per cent for Australia (Davies, 1982, p. 320).

Thus, a large proportion of private investment in listed companies in Australia is now indirect, being channelled through life offices, pension funds and the trust departments of major banks. The increased concentration of such holdings, together with a rising number of interlocking directorships between financial and industrial entities, necessitates an enquiry into how these may act to constrain managerial discretion. This question will be left to a later section. At this stage, however, it is important to analyse strategic ownership by financial institutions relative to other shareholder groups. This relationship is shown by control-type category in Table 5.3. We find

Table 5.3: Ownership Structure by Control Structure, 1974-5

Control classification / Ownership class	Majority private ownership				Minority private ownership				Management				Companies Domestic				Companies Overseas				Companies Joint domestic-overseas			
	P	I	C	N	P	I	C	N	P	I	C	N	P	I	C	N	P	I	C	N	P	I	C	N
Percentage																								
0			9	2		1	33	6	5		35	4				4					1			
0<1				1			8	6	6		11	7				6	7	3		9	2			2
1<10		8	2	8		12	18	44	48	2	23	54	18	12	2	16	23	17		23	1	3		2
10<20		3			8	21	4	7	15	22	10	11	9	6	2	2	4	13	1	3		1		
20<50					48	31	2	2	5	54		3	1	8	14		4	6	12					
50<75	11				9										8				23				2	
75<100										1					4				3				2	
Total 0–100	11	11	11	11	65	65	65	65	79	79	79	79	28	28	28	28	39	39	39	39	4	4	4	4

Note: the letters P, I, C, N stand for persons, financial institutions, companies and nominees.

that holdings by financial institutions were least important in company-controlled and majority private-ownership-controlled firms where other companies and private holders were clearly dominant. Institutional holdings were most impressive among what we have classified as management-controlled firms. Here 55 (71 per cent) of the 79 management-controlled firms had institutional holders among the largest 20 cohesive groups with more than 20 per cent of issued shares. Moreover, what made these holdings all the more important was the fact that no other group of shareholders had a similar concentation of voting power in such a large proportion of management-controlled firms. Thus, while in minority ownership-controlled companies the institutions held more than 20 per cent of shares in 31 (48 per cent) of the 65 companies it would have been strategically significant in only a small number of these. This is because private owners, the majority of whom were members of a directors' cohesive group, unquestionably held the balance of power in most of these companies. On the basis of size and distribution of shareholdings then, we can conclude that institutions had their greatest potential influence within 'management-controlled' firms. Furthermore, it would appear that this influence was of far greater potential importance than in either the US or the UK, though nowhere near the levels of financial control experienced in Germany, where it has been estimated that 60 per cent of industry is controlled by banks (Dobbins and McRae, 1975, p. 390).

In the UK, Prais (1976, p. 116) estimated that financial institutions accounted for more than 40 per cent of ordinary shares. We would expect the majority of these to be concentrated in holdings in the largest companies. Yet Nyman and Silberston (1978, p. 86) were surprised at the relative lack of ownership by financial institutions among the top 250 UK companies. They could identify only 9 cases of control by financial institutions (4.4 per cent of the sample). In the US, however, Chevalier (1969) found 15.5 per cent of his sample to be controlled by institutions. In a more recent US study, Kotz (1978) concluded that between 30 and 40 per cent of the top 200 were under the control of financial institutions. By way of comparison, among the 79 companies in our sample which have provisionally been classified as 'management-controlled', there were 13 companies in which the largest shareholder was an institution owning more than 10 per cent of shares and another 30 companies in which the largest shareholder was an institution holding between 5 and 10 per cent of share capital.

In proportionate terms the extent of dominance by financial

institutions is considerably greater in Australia than in the US. For instance Crough's (1980) study has found that a single institution, the Australian Mutual Provident Society (AMP), was among the five largest shareholders in 66 of the top 98 companies. In 40 of the companies it held more than 5 per cent of shares and in 21 of these it was the largest shareholder. Indeed, it is the concentration evident in the Australian financial community which, through its shareholdings in and financing of business, holds implications for the future direction of Australian industry.

Private Ownership Control

Choosing the 'Correct' Cut-off Point

Up to this point it has been assumed that the existence of 10 per cent of ordinary shares in the hands of a cohesive group of private individuals who are members of, or can be linked with, the board of directors is sufficient for the exercise of control. One means of testing whether this is indeed a critical value is to examine the frequency distribution of companies according to the percentage of ordinary shares which is held by directors as a cohesive group.

On *a priori* grounds, if we believe 10 per cent to be the critical value for a transition from owner to management control and 50 per cent to be critical for distinction of majority from minority ownership control, we should expect the frequency distribution to behave as follows: as companies move from majority control to minority control a preference will be shown for the maintenance of absolute control, so that we would expect to see a clustering of companies just above the 50 per cent level, but once absolute control is lost (and retaining effective control is the only question of importance) we should expect to see a gradual rise in the frequency distribution starting from just below the 50 per cent level and peaking at the 10 per cent level, the minimum 'safe' level for control. Below the 10 per cent level this process should be repeated; as control based on voting power is lost the rationale for holding a large but ineffective block of shares in one company disappears. Since there are more companies in each successive category as we move from majority ownership to management control, the local peaks at 50 per cent, 10 per cent and 0 per cent should become progressively higher. A diagrammatical representation of this hypothesised relationship is presented in Figure 5.1.

Figure 5.1: Hypothetical Distribution of Shares Held by Directors'
Groups

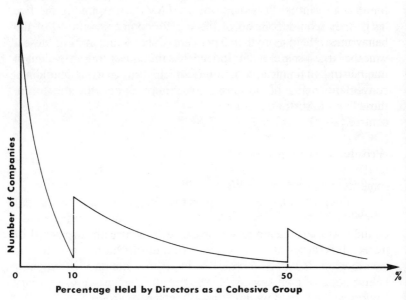

The histogram based on actual data from our sample appears in
Figure 5.2, with companies grouped at 2 per cent intervals. Moving
from 0-2 per cent towards the 8-10 per cent interval the distribution
displayed accords fairly closely with the one appearing in Figure 5.1.[5]
At just above the 10 per cent level a concentration of companies is
encountered, indicating that a 10 per cent cut-off point may well be
perceived as the critical value for delineating minority ownership
from management control. But instead of falling away gradually
towards the 50 per cent level, the distribution falls sharply until a
second, lesser, peak is encountered at the 18-20 per cent level. This
process is then repeated and a lesser peak is once again found at the
28-30 per cent level. However, unlike the hypothesised relationship,
there is no evidence of a peak at the 50 per cent level, with the nearest
peak occurring at the 42-4 per cent level.

The fact that three distinct concentrations of companies are found
at levels of ownership which are roughly ten percentage points apart
suggests that in owner-controlled companies the dominant cohesive
group aims at achieving *target* levels of ownership. The relinquish-
ment of a higher level of ownership for a lower one is associated with
the surrender of a degree of discretion. Thus, the existence of a final

peak at 42-4 per cent may be of crucial importance in that at this level of ownership the maximum level of discretion is attainable. That is, for all practical purposes the dominating director group can behave 'as if' they have majority control. We might, therefore, expect the behaviour of private owner-controlled firms to vary depending on which of the four groups they happen to be in. Owing to the small number of observations falling within each group it may be more convenient for empirical purposes to make a distinction between those firms in which the director group can be said to have absolute control (DCG ⩾ 42 per cent) and those where control is weaker (DCG ⩾ 10 per cent and < 42 per cent). However, at the same time it needs to be recognised that even 'weak' control by a group of share-holders centred around the board of directors will be associated with some discretionary powers.

Strength of Private Ownership Control and Firm Performance

Of the previous researchers who have sought to test the 'separation thesis', Palmer (1973a) was first to make a distinction between 'owner-controlled' companies based on the strength of control. Palmer separated 'strong owner-controlled firms' where one 'party'

Figure 5.2: Shares Held by Directors' Groups

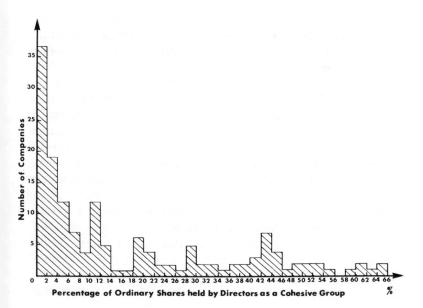

Percentage of Ordinary Shares held by Directors as a Cohesive Group   %

owned 30 per cent or more of voting stock, from 'weak owner-controlled firms', where the dominant party owned between 10 per cent and 29.9 per cent of stock. However, the rationale behind the employment of a 30 per cent cut-off was not made clear.[6]

Palmer (1973a) argued that only in industries with high entry barriers should we expect to find that control type makes a difference to performance. His results showed that where barriers were high, owner-controlled firms returned higher profits than management-controlled firms. Whether firms were 'weak' or 'strong' owner-controlled did not seem to make a difference. But where barriers were of 'medium' height, strong owner-controlled firms appeared somewhat less profitable than weak owner-controlled firms.[7] More recently Qualls (1976) employed Palmer's control-type classification in a model designed to test the concentration-profits hypothesis. Using the 'excess economic profit margin'[8] as the dependent variable, Qualls found that both in firms with medium and high (Shepherd (1972) individual firm weighted average) four-firm concentration ratios and medium and high barriers to entry, weak owner-controlled firms had a higher average margin than strong owner-controlled firms. Qualls (1976, p. 97) concluded that this finding 'seem[ed] contradictory to the managerial hypothesis'. In another US study, Bothwell (1980) achieved similar results.

This apparent 'paradox' is not surprising when the facts are viewed in the context of the model being developed here. Our view is that a dominant private ownership group has a substantial range of discretion when no effective internal restraint exists. That is, when there is no strong opposition from other voting shareholders. The dominant shareholder group is almost invariably structured around the board of directors. Since the discretionary power of these cohesive ownership groups derives largely from the votes attached to their shareholding, the extent of discretion varies directly with the proportion of votes held. We have identified two categories of private ownership control, 'absolute owner control' and 'weak owner control'. Thus, internal restraints deriving from outside the dominant ownership group are highest in weak owner-controlled firms and lowest in absolute owner-controlled firms. We must now consider how this is linked with external restraints.

Two factors must be taken into consideration. First, the controlling group's power depends on maintaining its proportionate interest in the company. This will be of greatest importance to those ownership groups which can be said to have 'absolute' control. Such firms will, *ceteris paribus,* prefer to finance internally rather than externally. The same can be said of firms with less than absolute control in the hands of the dominant group, but with less force. Once absolute control is lost, the necessity to finance mainly (or exclusively) from internal sources can be expected to decline steadily. Hence, any restraint which *could* apply if firms approached the capital market for funds is going to be least effective in absolute owner-controlled firms.

The second factor concerns the effectiveness of the market for corporate control. By definition, the ownership group which has 'absolute control', need not fear a takeover bid. It is almost certain that the group with more than 40 per cent will have the resources to reach 51 per cent ownership quickly if a raider were to enter the market. This fact gives groups with absolute control such a strong threat potential that raiders will not contemplate an aggressive bid for fear of being locked into a minority holding position. As the proportionate shareholding of the group declines, however, the probability that a determined raider will be able to win control rises. Whether the incumbent ownership groups in these firms will be able to retain control depends on the financial resources at their disposal and on the effectiveness of their defensive strategy.[9] But even if an outside bid for control fails, the experience will probably stir directors to institute some reforms in management in order to raise the future share price of the company. In that event the market for corporate control will have partially fulfilled its function. However, the higher is the proportionate holding of the existing private ownership group, the lower is the probability that the firm *will* experience a bid.

In order to test these propositions we shall employ a model of the form,

$$P = \beta_0 + \beta_1 \, \text{WOC} + \beta_2 \, (\ln) \, \text{VDH} + \beta_3 \, \text{NMAT} + \beta_4 \, \text{SIZE} + \varepsilon$$

$$(5.1)$$

where,

P   is company performance measured by RNA, REA, GNA, SDRNA and RET

WOC   is a dummy variable taking a value of 1 if private ownership control is weak and zero if control is absolute (ln) VDH   is (the natural logarithm of) the value of directors' shareholdings

NMAT   is a dummy variable with a value of 1 if the firm is non-mature and zero otherwise

SIZE   is a measure of firm size, calculated as the reciprocal of net assets

ε is the stochastic error term

The specification of our model allows us to test the performance effects of the strength of control when the influences of managerial incentives (VDH), firm maturity (NMAT) and the size of the firm (SIZE) are taken into account. The strength of control dummy will indicate how the performance of companies dominated by ownership groups with weak control differs from the performance of firms where the groups have absolute control. Our original hypotheses regarding the signs on the coefficients of (ln) VDH, NMAT and SIZE are unchanged.

Since firms where directors have less than absolute control will be making more frequent use of the capital market in obtaining finance and will be more vulnerable to the discipline of the market for corporate control, we should expect that their profitability will, *ceteris paribus*, be higher than that exhibited by firms where directors have absolute control. Hence, we hypothesise that in the profitability equations $\beta_1 > 0$. Because firms with less than absolute control will be using new debt and equity issues more in financing expansion, they should be growing faster. Therefore, we predict that in the growth equation $\beta_1 > 0$. Directors with absolute control will have less to fear from other shareholders or the stock market if their operating profits are variable, so that in the risk equation we expect $\beta_1 < 0$. Finally, since directors who have absolute control will prefer to finance internally we should expect a low dividend pay-out in these firms. Thus, in the retentions equation our expectation is $\beta_1 < 0$.

The results are displayed in Table 5.4. In both profitability equations (5.4.1 and 5.4.2) the coefficients of WOC have the predicted positive sign, but are not statistically significant. Firms where control was weak had returns on net assets and equity assets which were respectively only .8 and .6 of a percentage point higher than firms where control was absolute. However, in the growth equation the coefficient on the weak owner-controlled dummy has the correct

Table 5.4: Performance Effects of Strength of Ownership Control

Equation number	n	Dependent variable	Constant	WOC	ln VDH	VDH	NMAT	SIZE (1/NAo)	R^2	$\bar{R}^2$	F-ratio
5.4.1	68	RNA	.020	.008 (.489)	.018 (3.164)[a]		−.024 (.983)	.128 (5.103)[d]	.392	.353	10.135[a]
5.4.2	68	REA	.011	.006 (.599)	.010 (3.085)[a]		−.004 (.293)	.056 (3.936)[d]	.325	.282	7.575[a]
5.4.3	68	GNA	−.071	.021 (1.960)[b]	.022 (5.770)[a]		.012 (.744)	.134 (8.156)[d]	.703	.685	37.366[a]
5.4.4	68	SDRNA	.031	−.703E-4 (.022)		−.246E-5 (.806)	−.008 (.683)	.024 (2.075)[b]	.088	.030	1.522
5.4.5	64	RET	.439	−.058 (1.251)		.358E-4 (1.943)[b]	.011 (.167)	.109 (1.597)	.118	.059	1.979

Notes: a and b denote significance at the .01 and .05 levels respectively using a two-tail test; d denotes significance at the .01 level using a one-tail test.

positive sign and is significant at the .05 level. Moreover, this growth effect is highly significant in absolute terms since, other things being equal, the coefficient indicates that firms with weak ownership control grew at a rate 2.1 percentage points higher than those with absolute ownership control. This would tend to depress the reported profits of weak owner-controlled firms since higher depreciation charges would be incurred on their younger asset mix.

From equation 5.4.4 it can be seen that the strength of control (even though the coefficient on WOC is negative) apparently had little effect on the operating risk of firms. In equation 5.4.5 we find that in weak owner-controlled firms that the retention ratio was 5.8 points lower than in firms where the director group had absolute control. While the coefficient is not statistically significant, its size is quite large.

In conclusion it is apparent that weak ownership control had a slight positive effect on profitability. The effects on operating risk and retentions were also broadly consistent with expectations but statistically insignificant. The most striking effect, however, was on the growth rates of firms. Firms in which the dominant owner had absolute control were reluctant to lessen their controlling interest. As a result external finance was avoided and the growth rate of these firms was very low. Since, if anything, the profitability of these firms was slightly depressed relative to other owner-controlled firms, while the retention ratio was somewhat higher, it is not unreasonable to conclude that small shareholders outside of the director groups had suffered in the process. The overall results are consistent with the implications of Reder's (1947) model discussed in Chapter 2.

Company Control

Company Control and Managerial Discretion

In her study of the growth and profitability performance of Australian firms Sheridan (1974, pp. 122-3) noted, on the basis of Wheelwright and Miskelly's (1967) classification, that eleven of the 19 fastest-growing firms in her sample were 'company-controlled'. In addition, the rate of profit of several of these firms was depressed relative to more slowly growing firms, but because of the concentration of ownership she concluded that the possibility of takeover in these firms was 'probably minimal or even nonexistent in some cases'.

This was an interesting proposition, but the full implications were not pursued. However, it is important to do so since almost one-third of the firms in our sample were classified as being controlled by other companies.

In Chapter 3 we considered various motives for inter-company holdings. Penrose (1956a, p. 75), it was noted, was sceptical of the holding company form of organisation, because she believed that proper co-ordination and control of activities in the subsidiaries might not be achieved. Moreover, with specific reference to Australia, she felt it 'significant that the term "group" is so widely used in Australia to characterize some of the largest industrial organisations'. Bushnell (1961, p. 71) has argued that purely financial groups of the type alluded to by Penrose are not in fact common in Australia. While some companies have acquired and disposed of subsidiaries as though they were simply financial assets, the majority of mergers, he observed, had the aim of integrating 'an additional enterprise into the operational unit', but there were cases where this goal was 'only partially realized because of the shortage of skilled management personnel'. In sum, it was proposed that, while there were many cases of pure holding companies in Australia, the subsidiaries were often in closely related fields and operated in a reasonably integrated manner, akin to the divisions of US companies.

It was also mentioned in Chapter 3 that inter-company shareholdings could arise because of defensive tactics employed during a takeover bid. It appears that such cases are not unknown in fact. An Australian Senate committee (Rae *et al.*, 1974, p. 10.5) investigating the operations of securities markets condemned the trend towards private placement of shares, noting cases where 'two companies have made large private issues to each other ... in order to avoid one or both of the companies being taken over by an outside group'. Intercorporate shareholdings of this kind must be perceived by managements as a strategy designed to increase, rather than diminish, their discretion. However, this is probably true only of firms with a relatively small company shareholding.

Thus, the discretion available to managers in a company-controlled firm is likely to be higher the lower is the company shareholding. First, because it is more probable that the company shareholder will issue directives on strategic policy when it holds a large proportion of the shares. Second, because small shareholdings by another company are more likely to be there simply as a defence against future takeover threats.

Figure 5.3: Shares Held by Dominant Company Shareholders

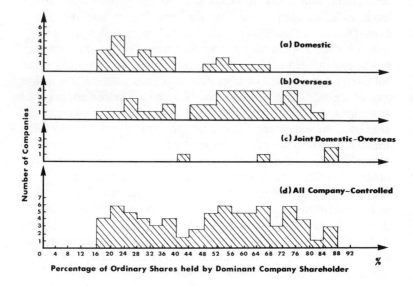

Strength of Company Control and Firm Performance

We have already employed an analysis of the frequency distribution
of firms in choosing the 'correct' cut-off point to denote 'private
ownership control'. Similar frequency distributions are drawn in
Figure 5.3 for company-controlled firms in our continuing firm
sample, except that 4 per cent intervals for the percentage of shares
owned by the dominant company stockholder(s) are used. The
distributions for domestic company, overseas company, and joint
domestic/overseas company controlled firms are shown in Figures
5.3(a), 5.3(b) and 5.3(c) respectively. Figure 5.3(d), the distribution
for all company-controlled firms, is the vertical summation of the
other three distributions.

The small number of observations in each of the company-control
categories makes it difficult to distinguish 'weak', from what might be
termed 'strong' company control. Even the 'all company-controlled
firms' distribution in Figure 5.3 (d) is multi-modal. However, the
most critical minimum point in the total distribution appears to lie
within the 40-4 per cent range which, as we saw in Figure 5.2, was also
the critical percentage at which directors of absolute owner-
controlled firms were argued to enjoy the maximum degree of
discretion.

It has already been pointed out that there may be several motives underlying such inter-company holdings and that the degree of managerial discretion within such companies may vary considerably. For example, if these holdings are low they might imply a buffer against potential takeover bidders. However, once the company holding is high, or consolidation has taken place (in which case a new subsidiary, or quasi-division, will have been 'internalised'), we might expect greater constraints to be imposed on the performance of the company-controlled 'firm's' management. It would be of considerable interest, then, to test the hypothesis that company-controlled firms with a dominant stockholding of less than, say, 40 per cent, will have a higher potential degree of management discretion than will otherwise similar firms in which the stake of the controlling company is greater than 40 per cent.

If managerial discretion is less, and the control exercised by the dominant stockholder greater, in 'strong' company-controlled firms there should be less X-inefficiency in these firms. That is, strong company-controlled firms should be operating closer to their 'efficiency frontier' in the profitability-growth plane. Hence, we would predict that both profitability and growth will be higher in strong company-controlled firms.

It is difficult to predict, *a priori*, whether managers in strong or weak company-controlled firms will be more risk averse. Greater fluctuations in the earnings of weak company-controlled firms will be subject to closer scrutiny by the external market. In contrast, the managers of strong company-controlled firms will be more wary of internal restraints. Since retained earnings are a source of discretion for management, we might expect that retentions will be higher in weak company-controlled firms. On the other hand, if the controlling firm has strong control and wishes to raise the growth rate of its subsidiary a higher retention ratio might go with strong company control.

The strength of company holdings (COH) is defined as the proportion of shares on issue held by the controlling company or companies. To distinguish between strong and weak company control, a dummy variable, CHD, is defined as,

$$\text{CHD} \begin{cases} = & 1 \text{ if the firm is under strong company control,} \\ & \text{i.e. COH} \geqslant .40 \\ = & 0 \text{ otherwise} \end{cases}$$

The model tested is specified as,

$$P = \beta_o + \beta_1 \text{ CHD} + \beta_2 \ln \text{VDH} + \beta_3 \text{ NMAT} + \beta_4 \text{ SIZE} + \varepsilon \quad (5.2)$$

but the continuous variable, COH, is also employed for comparative purposes. The coefficients on COH and CHD achieved in the regression analysis are displayed in Table 5.5.

Although profitability appeared to be slightly higher in strong company-controlled firms, none of the coefficients is statistically significant. Yet the growth rate of strong company-controlled firms was 3.4 percentage points higher than in weak company-controlled firms. The coefficient on the continuous variable (COH) is significant at the .05 level and the coefficient on CHD is just short of significance at the .05 level. It is important to note, moreover, that the finding of a higher growth rate among strong company-controlled firms implies that their profitability may have been understated relative to the more slow-growing weak company-controlled firms.

Positive signs are found on the company-control variables in the operating risk equations, implying that controlling firms were willing to tolerate higher variability in earnings. However, the coefficients

Table 5.5: Effects of Company Control on Firm Performance

Dependent variable	COH	CHD	FOR	FOR*
RNA	.035	.017	.017	—0.22
	(.713)	(.836)	(1.179)	(1.052)
REA	.028	.010	—.256E-3	—.041
	(.620)	(.519)	(.032)	(2.172)[b]
GNA	.087	.034	.014	—.009
	(1.746)[b]	(1.635)[c]	(1.054)	(.421)
SDRNA	.025	.011	.002	—.017
	(1.336)	(1.396)	(.470)	(2.093)[e]
RET	—.039	—.022	.061	—.039
	(.434)	(.590)	(2.060)[a]	(.986)

Notes: figures in brackets are t-ratios; a and b indicate significance at the .01 and .05 levels respectively using a one-tail test; e and f indicate significance at the .05 and .10 levels respectively using a two-tail test.

are not significant when a two-tail test is performed. Company control has a negative sign in the retentions equations, suggesting that weak control was associated with higher retentions, but these coefficients also are not significant. On statistical grounds there is not much to choose between the continuous and discrete versions of the strength of company control variables. On theoretical grounds, however, we should prefer the discrete variable (CHD) since this will indicate when internal (as opposed to external) restraints become more important in the determination of firm conduct.

In contrast to the situation observed in private owner-controlled firms, maturity tends to be a highly significant determinant of firm performance, while firm size does not. We can suggest several reasons for this. First, only a small number (three) of domestic company-controlled firms could be classified as being non-mature and this is not due purely to chance. The high investment opportunities available in a non-mature firm, since they may be undervalued by the market, mean that the controlling firm (with access to inside information) will see the purchase of all the stock in such a company as a good investment. Hence, there will be relatively few non-mature company-controlled firms (which are listed) operating at any one time and the distinction between mature and non-mature firms will be much sharper than in private owner-controlled firms.

In overseas-controlled companies we should also expect greater disparities between the performance of mature and non-mature firms, because in order to establish operations in a different country (in the face of uncertainty and withholding taxes on dividends remitted to the home country) the expected returns must be quite significant. In addition, direct foreign investment often flows in a spasmodic manner in response to economic influences; during the post-war period, import restrictions and state government subsidies to overseas firms for example. However, while the non-mature firms had significantly higher rates of return (whether related to net assets or to equity assets) and a significantly higher retention ratio, they grew at about the same rate as mature firms. Since the non-mature firms would have been situated on a higher 'demand growth curve', this suggests that mature firms were trading more potential profits for faster growth.

Finally, there was a difference in performances not only between non-mature owner-controlled and company-controlled firms, but between mature owner- and company-controlled firms. Since these differences worked in opposite directions they accentuated the difference due to maturity between company-controlled firms and owner-controlled firms. For example, while the profitability of non-mature company-controlled firms of a given size was *higher* than that of non-mature owner-controlled firms, the profitability of mature company-controlled firms was *lower* than that of mature owner-controlled firms.

Foreign Company Control and Managerial Discretion. An important sub-set of company-controlled firms are those firms, operating in Australia, which may be classified as being under the control of foreign corporations. Sheridan (1975) studied the profitability and growth performances of Australian firms, as opposed to those with American and British affiliations, over the period 1950-73. Briefly, her findings were that *both* foreign affiliated groups exhibited a performance superior to that of Australian-owned companies over most of the period, but in terms of profitability fell short of Australian companies in the latest sub-period (1968-73). However, the foreign affilitates exhibited greater rates of growth throughout the period, even though during the last sub-period their profitability was depressed relative to that of Australian-owned companies. In terms of both profitability and growth, American affiliates out-performed the British ones. In viewing these results we are left with the impression that foreign affiliates were unwilling to accept correspondingly lower rates of growth despite the lower profit rates earned towards the end of the period.

The general superiority of performance displayed by foreign affiliates led Sheridan to search for its causes. One explanation was that foreign affiliates have better access to new technology and capital resources.[10] Another explanation was that foreign affiliates might have been mostly large, and operating in oligopolistic market structures.[11] A third possibility was based on Hymer and Rowthorn's (1970) hypothesis that a firm must be aware of the inherent advantages it will possess in producing in a foreign country before embarking upon such a course. Finally, it was suggested that only 'dynamic' or 'enterprising' firms will be bold enough to establish subsidiaries in foreign countries and these characteristics will be carried over to the subsidiaries.

We believe there is no reason to suppose that the motivation of executives in foreign-controlled companies in Australia should be any different, given the same incentive structures, to that of executives in Australian-owned companies. If this is granted, in order to demonstrate our argument it is necessary only to show that these executives (in foreign-controlled firms) are largely unconstrained. In Chapter 3 it was suggested that, *ceteris paribus*, managers of foreign subsidiaries will have a greater area of discretion than will managers of domestic subsidiaries. This notion has been corroborated by Brash (1966, p. 104). He found that the executives of several US affiliated companies, and these were companies in which the interest of the parent exceeded 25 per cent, 'felt themselves completely free of American "control", while almost all felt themselves to be independent in at least some areas of policy'. More recently, to assess independence of 'parental domination', and hence the possibility of conflicts with Australian policy goals, North (1976) attempted to ascertain the role played by the boards of directors of foreign-controlled companies. His finding was that in two-thirds of the respondent firms the board could be classified either as an 'executive committee board' dominated by executive directors, or merely as a 'board of review' composed of outside directors playing the role of moderators and not providing the initiative in many areas.[12] Another third of the companies had a board whose role was thought to be 'largely comparable to the fullest role likely to be played by the board of an Australian company which has a major corporate shareholder, in that it formally considers, and exercises substantial influence over, the planning, progress and decision-making of the company' (p. 139).

Many of the products and processes introduced by foreign firms in the post-war period, although perhaps not 'immature' in their country of origin, were certainly immature in the Australian market environment. A number of these foreign companies established subsidiaries or affiliates in Australia in preference to paying the high duties imposed on imports. Yet there are also a number of foreign-controlled firms (the majority of them, we suspect, of British origin) which were established in Australia well before 1939, whose product structures have gradually matured.

Sheridan's (1975) sample was composed of (by today's standards) reasonably well-established firms which may have been, in the 1950s, still non-mature; this may account for their superior profitability and growth during that period.[13] The maturing of their activities by the late 1960s could partially explain their lower *absolute* average profitability in 1968-73. Sheridan (1975, p. 562) suggested that by increasing the effectiveness of the market for corporate control (that is, providing a greater number of potential takeover bidders in

Australia) foreign-affiliated companies had the effect of raising the efficiency of Australian-owned companies. A consideration she overlooked was that by the same token the 'efficiency' of these foreign-affiliated companies may have suffered because of the lack of a market, in Australia, for the control of foreign-owned companies. This absence of an external restraint, combined with relative freedom from internal restraints, could have accounted for the declining profitability of foreign-controlled companies *relative* to Australian-owned companies in the period 1968-73.

Foreign Control and Company Performance: Empirical Evidence.
In a recent (four-digit) industry level study Phillips (1978) reasoned that there should exist a positive association between foreign control, measured by FCD,[14] and profitability, measured as the ratio of operating profits to funds employed (OP/FE).[15] In a simple regression the coefficient on FCD was positive but non-significant. When this variable was included in a more fully specified structure-profitability model significance was found at the .05 level. The sample was then split into high concentration (CR4 $\geqslant$ 65 per cent) and low concentration industries. In high concentration industries FCD was insignificant, which led Phillips (1978, p. 311) to conclude that 'foreign controlled industries in a high concentration group do not earn significantly higher profit rates than other highly concentrated industries'. In the low concentration industries sample FCD was again positive, but either weakly significant (at the .10 level using a one-tail test) or insignificant depending upon model specification.

Our own view is that if foreign-controlled firms are more profitable than domestic firms this is likely to be due to a larger proportion of these firms being non-mature than in a random sample of domestic firms. Thus, *ceteris paribus*, when the maturity factor is taken into account much of the previously observed differential in profitability should disappear. A similar line of reasoning would also apply to growth rates. Except, that is, for the fact that foreign-controlled firms may prefer higher retention ratios in order to defer payment of withholding taxes on dividends and may have advantages in raising capital internationally to finance expansion. However, it is difficult to say whether operating risk will be higher in foreign-controlled firms, whether, that is, multinational companies attach a premium to stability of earnings.

To test our hypotheses a dummy variable representing foreign control is defined as follows:

$$\text{FOR} \begin{cases} = & 1 \text{ if the company is overseas-controlled} \\ = & 0 \text{ otherwise} \end{cases}$$

and the model is specified as,

$$P = \beta_o + \beta_1 \text{ FOR} + \beta_2 \ln \text{VDH} + \beta_3 \text{ NMAT} + \beta4 \text{ SIZE} + \varepsilon \tag{5.3}$$

The third column of Table 5.5 shows the coefficients yielded by simple regressions of FOR against the performance variables using the 'all companies' sample. In general the signs of the coefficients on FOR are as predicted, but the negative sign in the REA equation is puzzling. Only the coefficient in the retentions equation is statistically significant. In the RET equation the coefficient on FOR implies that foreign-controlled firms had a retention ratio 6.1 points higher than in domestically controlled firms. This is highly significant, but foreign ownership only explains a small proportion of the variance of retentions.

Estimating equation 5.3 on the basis of the 'all companies' sample would not isolate some important factors which have a bearing on performance. For example, it would not take into account that, as stressed earlier, overseas-controlled firms are generally not subject to the domestic market for corporate control. Furthermore, in Chapter 4 we found that in company-controlled firms maturity and firm size have different impacts on performance than in management- or owner-controlled firms. Within the framework of our model these interrelationships between internal and external restraints are of crucial importance in determining firm performance. Hence, the more appropriate comparison — and one which corrects for these interaction effects — is between domestic and foreign company-controlled firms.

Our hypothesis, it will be recalled, is that when all other factors have been taken into consideration, the managers of foreign-controlled subsidiaries will have more discretion to pursue their own interests than will managers in domestic company-controlled firms. Following this line of reasoning, our prediction is that the profitability and growth rates of overseas-controlled firms will be lower, and the retention ratio higher, than in domestic companies. However, no predictions can be made regarding the variability of earnings. The coefficients achieved in regressions run on the company-controlled sample appear in the last two columns of Table 5.5. FOR denotes the foreign-control dummy in the simple regressions, while FOR* denotes foreign control in the multiple regressions. The foreign-control dummy is not significant in any of the simple regressions. In the multiple regressions the sign on FOR is uniformly negative. In the first of the profitability equations we find that the rate of return on net assets (RNA) in foreign-controlled firms was 2.2 percentage points lower than in domestic company-controlled firms. On its own this finding supports our contention that managers of domestic company-controlled firms are subject to closer scrutiny by the dominant company shareholder, but the coefficient is not significant. However, the return on equity assets was 4.1 percentage points lower in overseas-controlled firms and this coefficient is statistically significant at the .05 level. This would hold interesting implications if it were found that foreign companies were heavily capitalised on debt commitments to their overseas parents. Since interest repayments overseas are not taxable (as dividends are), such a finding would suggest that domestic investors in these companies (not to mention the Australian balance of payments) had suffered to the benefit of the multinationals. But a redeeming feature of the results is that operating risk was also significantly lower in overseas-controlled firms. Hence, the fact that the rate of return tended to be lower in foreign-controlled firms may have been compensated for by the fact that there was less variability in their earnings stream. Finally, the non-significance of the coefficient on FOR* in the retentions equation suggests that both foreign and domestic parent companies preferred a high retentions policy.

In sum, the results do not provide strong support for the contention that managers of foreign-controlled companies are less restrained by their parent than are their counterparts in domestic company-controlled firms. While the absolute sizes of coefficients were respectable, there appeared to be a good deal of 'noise' in the data. It is probably more accurate to conclude that the differences in performance which have been shown are a reflection of the different conditions facing domestic and overseas parents.

Management Control

The Role of Financial Institutions

Within the context of our model, the behaviour of managers in 'dispersed ownership' companies will be conditioned by the incentives and restraints which confront them. In these companies institutional investors are expected to play a central role in determining the internal restraint on management. However, the effectiveness of this restraint will, in turn, depend on the strength of the external restraints imposed by the stock market. Thus, Dobbins and McRae (1975, p. 388) felt that 'the foremost reason of all for the increasing power of financial institutions is that corporate management is aware of the need for institutional support in takeover situations'. Prais (1976) has suggested that institutional behaviour has also sharpened the market for corporate control in the UK through the provision of cheap debenture finance to large companies growing by takeovers. However, this has had the effect of accentuating the concentration process and raising corporate debt/equity ratios. Furthermore, the capital market constraint may actually have been weakened by uncritical provision of takeover finance to the larger corporations without strong evidence of real benefits from the takeovers.

But as Kotz (1978, p. 127) points out, between takeovers the main mechanism of institutional control is 'informal pressure on the non-financial corporation's management'. This power, in turn, will be related to the voting power of institutions, the presence of institutional representatives on the company's board and the financial dependence of the company on particular institutions. Crucial to this power relation is the possession of superior knowledge by financial institutions — they must know if their interests are being compromised. A development in that direction is the increasing use of private-placement share issue, whereby institutions are invited to subscribe directly to large blocks of newly issued shares. During these exchanges institutions are often allowed access to confidential information which is not disclosed to the market as a whole. Also, the high proportion of old shares in the hands of institutions means that the success of rights issues depends heavily on their support.

Despite several descriptions of the increasing dominance of institutions in the Anglo-American economies relatively few hypotheses have been proposed regarding the performance effects of such dominance. Even less bi-variate and multi-variate testing of hypotheses has emerged. For instance, Dobbins and McRae (1975) recalled that US evidence has shown that individual institutions have been unable to distinguish the most profitable investments. Having said that they hypothesised that it is in the larger companies, where institutional shareholdings are concentrated, that the greatest influence will be exercised. Second, they hypothesised that for institutions the cash flows from dividends will be of great concern (i.e. retentions will be lower). Third, they proposed that the buying and selling of shares by expert portfolio managers is likely to stabilise share prices at their intrinsic values. An opposing view holds that institutions are subject to 'herd-like' behaviour which only accentuates share price movements. There is no strong evidence for either view.[16]

Though the recent extensive US study by Kotz (1978) was largely descriptive, a number of hypotheses were advanced. First, Kotz expected that as financial control took hold, banks would use their influence to channel business to themselves. This opinion runs counter to the normal managerial hypothesis that the dispersion of stockholdings will result in greater management control and, therefore, avoidance of external debt capital. Kotz's hypothesis is consistent with the fact that debt/equity ratios have been rising in the US over the past few decades (also see the Australian evidence presented in Chapter 6 below).

Second, Kotz felt that institutions would be interested in eliminating market competition in order to reap the benefits of monopoly profits. Shepherd (1976) has similarly proposed the hypothesis that institutions would be keen to promote anti-competitive mergers. Third, in contrast to Dobbins and McRae, Kotz (p. 141) hypothesised that financial institutions, as large investors, would have a longer time-horizon than the average investor, and prefer greater retentions. Looking in the longer term Drucker (1976) speculates that while in the current growth phase pension funds will prefer reinvestment, as many policies mature towards the end of the century, dividends will be preferred.

Kotz also noted that different types of institutions will follow different goals. Banks, for instance, will be torn between their interest in profits as shareholders and their interest in solvency as creditors. A life insurance company, on the other hand, is expected to follow 'cautious profit maximisation', while an investment company is 'an investor pure and simple'. However, it betrays a simplistic view of 'owner-control' to conclude from all this that 'the goal of the financially-controlled corporation is similar to that of the owner-controlled corporation' (p. 143). The 'owner-controlled corporation' is controlled by people whose incentive structures, time-horizons and tax regimes differ from those of financial institutions, which will also differ among themselves in these respects. However, it seems reasonable to conclude that firms under financial control will, *ceteris paribus*, be constrained to a close approximation to profit maximising. It is also highly likely, as Kotz suggests, that by ignoring financial control past studies of the performance effects of separation of ownership and control have yielded 'results of questionable value'.

Institutional Control and Corporate Performance

Although direct intervention by Australian institutions in the affairs of operating companies is not unknown, little publicity has been given to it (Rolfe, 1967, p. 6). Rather, if the price has been right institutions have chosen to sell their holdings. Since significant unanticipated sales by financial institutions could herald the beginning of a market raid, security conscious managers will try to avoid the dissatisfaction of these key shareholders. As in the UK the major Australian institutional shareholders are insurance companies and superannuation funds. The banks are not major shareholders.

In Chapter 3 it was hypothesised that both profitability and growth should be higher, and risk lower, in dispersed-ownership companies where shareholdings are concentrated in the hands of institutions. Because institutions have long time-horizons it was suggested that they will also prefer higher retention of earnings. In addition, certain capital market imperfections in Australia can be expected to influence institutions further towards retentions. Institutional investors in Australia are highly concentrated, there are impediments to the listing of overseas companies on Australian exchanges and institutions are restricted to investing only $2 million annually overseas. At home, participation by such institutions is denied in the financing of the considerable portion of Australia's industry which is wholly foreign-owned. In the decades since the Second World War Australian financial institutions have expanded much faster than listed companies and the growth of their cash flow has outpaced the available investment opportunities in manufacturing industries. With such a limited range of possible applications relative to the size of funds available there is considerable reason to expect that institutions will prefer higher retentions by the industrial companies in which they have a strong influence.

Furthermore, in Australia superannuation funds and the investments of life offices relating to superannuation are generally free of tax if they invest 30 per cent of their funds in government securities. However, any capital surplus on other funds is taxed at the company rate and this has two effects. First, if the price of a company being taken over results in a surplus a cash bid will be discouraged by the institutions. In such cases institutions will press for share-exchange deals and Stewart (1977) has presented evidence that share exchanges gained in popularity during the 1960s. A second implication is that if the company's share price has slipped below that originally paid by an institution it may wish to use the deficit as a taxation offset, in which case a cash bid will probably be welcomed (Craig, 1979).

Having outlined the expected effects of a strong institutional influence, our task now becomes one of defining what is meant by a 'strong influence'. It has been suggested that major institutional holders will have more power if their shareholdings are high relative to other groups of shareholders. In addition, it would be necessary for a small number of institutions together to hold a significant proportion of total shares on issue. The precise magnitudes which fulfil these conditions will vary from company to company. They will also depend on such factors as interlocking directorships and the personalities, abilities and business/political connections of the key characters — elements it would be impossible accurately to quantify. Therefore, we have had to opt for a set of (admittedly) rather arbitrary criteria which nevertheless give some indication of situations in which institutions have a good deal of *potential* power. Specifically, firms with a strong institutional influence have been defined as those in which institutions among the largest 20 cohesive groups held more than half of the 20 groups' shareholdings *and* more than 15 per cent of shares on issue. This influence is represented by a dummy variable (INST), i.e.

$$
\text{INST} \begin{cases} 1 & \text{if institutional holdings among the largest 20} \\ & \text{cohesive groups accounted for more than 50 per} \\ & \text{cent of the groups' holdings, } and \text{ institutional} \\ & \text{holdings accounted for more than 15 per cent of} \\ & \text{shares on issue} \\ \\ = 0 & \text{otherwise} \end{cases}
$$

Of the 194 firms listed continuously during 1965-75, 59 could, on these grounds, be considered to have a strong institutional influence. Out of these 59 firms, 53 were classified as 'management-controlled' and six as 'minority ownership-controlled'. It is particularly noteworthy that in 70 per cent of the firms which were classified as being

Table 5.6: Influence of Strong Institutional Shareholdings on the Performance of Management- and Owner-Controlled Firms

Dependent variable	Coefficient on INST	
	Management-controlled	Owner-controlled
RNA	.011	.055
	(.862)	(2.458)[a]
REA	.007	.010
	(1.021)	(.762)
GNA	.026	.018
	(1.831)[b]	(.502)
SDRNA	—.005	.017
	(1.234)	(1.675)[b]
RET	.094	.041
	(3.326)[a]	(.591)

Notes: figures in brackets are t-ratios; a and b indicate significance at the .01 and .05 levels respectively using a one-tail test.

under management-control, institutions had considerable potential to impose an internal restraint on managers. But for this fact to be significant it must be shown that performance did differ depending on whether institutions were, or were not, significant shareholders. Hence we shall test the model,

$$P = \beta_0 + \beta_1 \text{ INST} + \beta_2 \text{ lnVDH} + \beta_3 \text{ NMAT} + \beta_4 \text{ SIZE} + \varepsilon$$

$$(5.4)$$

The first column of Table 5.6 presents the coefficients on INST for our 'management-controlled' sample. A first feature to be noted is that each coefficient is of the 'correct' sign. Strong institutional holdings were associated with higher rates of return, whether measured pre-tax on net assets or post-tax on equity assets, and risk tended to be lower. But institutional holdings had a statistically significant (and positive) impact on only the growth rate and the retention ratio. On this evidence one might be tempted to conclude that the objectives of institutions and professional managers were not too far removed, or that institutions were not exercising a restraint. Higher growth and retentions would be welcomed by utility-maximising managers. However, there are two reasons for rejecting such conclusions.

First, since their growth was significantly greater it is likely that the reported profitability of firms with strong institutional holdings was relatively understated. Second, and more important, within the framework of the model outlined in Chapter 3 we should expect the effectiveness of restraint imposed by institutions to be dependent on the strength of external stock market restraints. Indeed, there is ample evidence available to suggest that the efficiency of these restraints diminishes with firm size. This issue will receive more extended consideration in Chapter 6.

As mentioned earlier, by applying the same share-ownership criteria to owner-controlled firms it was found that only six could be considered to have a strong institutional holding. In five of these firms between 10 and 14 per cent of shares were held by directors as a cohesive group. These firms were therefore classified as being subject to 'weak' owner control and were probably in the process of transition from owner to 'management' control — or rather, from owner to 'institutional' control. In the sixth firm, McEwans Ltd, the directors' group held 19.8 per cent of ordinary shares, but the largest five institutional holders together held 23.7 per cent. With large institutional shareholdings providing a further check on managerial discretion we might expect that the performance of these firms would be somehow improved. The results shown in the second column of Table 5.6 show that, while the presence of strong institutional holders was positively associated with profitability and growth, only the rate of return on net assets was significantly higher. Yet these higher returns were also accompanied by significantly higher operating risks, which is puzzling. Perhaps these results mean that in owner-controlled firms institutions were confronted by a more powerful and unified ownership group centred around the board of directors. For example, in a recent takeover bid for McEwans, sales by institutions paved the way for Repco to establish a 32 per cent stake in the company. But this was not before the family-dominated board at McEwans had secured a friendly majority in the company.

It may be objected that some of the firms classified as management-controlled might have retained some characteristics of ownership control. In several of the firms in which the director group held less than 10 per cent of shares, the founders (or family heirs) still retained key positions on the board and had a substantial financial interest in the firm. We have argued that the power of these directors stems not from the ownership of shares, but from the inertia generated by their long associations with the company. Furthermore, the ownership structure of these firms was often dominated by institutions. Therefore, the discretion available to directors in these firms would have been less than in owner-controlled firms.

Examinations of firms in the management-controlled category indicated that a 4 per cent cut-off point (for shareholdings by directors as a cohesive group) was appropriate in identifying firms with elements of 'family control'.[17] This was represented by a dummy variable, FAM (1 if family-dominated, 0 otherwise). The regression results are shown in Appendix Table A.5.1 and will only be briefly summarised. The simple regressions show that the profitability of family-dominated firms was (at the .01 level) significantly higher, while growth was not significantly greater. Also, operating risk was slightly higher and the retention ratio was significantly greater in family-dominated concerns. However, when firm maturity and differences in size are taken into account much of the disparity in rates of profitability, risk and retentions disappears. Finally, when differences in directors' shareholdings are also considered, there remain no significant differences in the performance of family- and non-family-dominated management-controlled firms. In other words the 'control' variables are capable of explaining any disparities in the performance of family- and non-family-dominated companies.

Summary

Our analysis of the distribution of ownership has shown that the ownership of strategic blocks of shares in most of the listed companies in our sample was highly concentrated. The vast majority of small shareholders therefore had little chance of consolidating their votes in order to impose an effective internal restraint on corporate decision-makers. Any internally generated opposition would have to come from the large shareholders. But the objectives and goals of these large shareholders need not — indeed, will rarely — reflect the views of smaller shareholders.

In approximately one-third of the companies private 'kinship units' aligned with the board of directors appeared to exert control through their voting capacity. That is, more than 10 per cent of ordinary shares was held by the directors' group. These directors wielded considerable discretionary powers. First, because the ownership of a large block of shares in the company gave some immunity from the market for corporate control. Second, there was generally no powerful internal opposition to challenge the incumbent management group. Third, the position of the dominant ownership group depended on the persistence of its relative voting strength and external finance was avoided. This was especially visible in firms where the director group could be considered to have absolute power. As a consequence owner-managers with 'absolute control' seemed inordinately conservative and this was reflected in lower profitability and rates of growth and higher retention ratios than in firms where less discretion was available to directors.

The company-controlled sector also accounted for approximately one-third of the firms in the sample. Here the dominant stockholder was another company, either domestic or foreign. Since this character of control also entailed the ownership of a significant portion of shares by a single party, the market for corporate control could not be expected to restrain managers — restraint would have to come from the dominant shareholding company. However, the form and effectiveness of this internal restraint would depend on the knowledge, power and objectives of the 'parent' concern. The knowledge possessed by a domestic parent, for example, would be greater than that available to an overseas parent, so that managerial discretion could be expected to be greater in a foreign subsidiary. In fact, domestic company-controlled firms earned somewhat higher rates of return than otherwise similar overseas company-controlled firms. However, since firms with foreign affiliations also tended to be less risky this difference may have been due to multinationals' preference for stable performances. Also, the proportionate ownership by the parent concern could be taken as an indicator of its power. Thus, higher ownership tended to have a positive effect on performance, but this was only significant in equations explaining firm growth. However, since growth was higher profitability may have been understated relative to firms where company control was weaker.

A significant factor to emerge from our examination of the structure of shareholdings was the significant proportion of shares which have come to be owned by financial institutions. This situation parallels similar developments in the US and UK. However, given the high concentration of Australian institutional investors, restrictions on overseas investment and high incidence of foreign ownership of manufacturing industry, this development holds even greater implications for Australia. Our evidence provided only limited support for the contention that firms with a strong institutional holding earned higher rates of return than firms which had no similar internal restraint. On the other hand, growth and retentions were significantly higher in companies dominated by institutional holdings. However, it was suggested that the efficacy of the restraint posed by institutions will depend on the operation of external restraints, in particular, the market for corporate control and the capital market.

In sum, given the functioning of internal restraints, the degree of discretion available to management will ultimately depend on the effectiveness of external restraints. The nature of these restraints, and how they vary in relation to control type, firm size and maturity are the subject of Chapter 6.

Notes

1. However, Lundberg (1937) claimed that in most of the corporations denoted management-controlled in Berle and Means's samples the management was actually installed by the dominant stockholding family who were usually represented on the board of directors.
2. This included data on bank control due to their trust activities and information (made available through changes in the SEC insider disclosure rules) on the stock held by the immediate family of officers and directors.
3. It follows of course that not more than 4520 (20 × 226) 'groups' controlled 51.7 per cent (by market value) of the companies' shares.
4. See, for example, Brash (1966), Johns (1967) and Sheridan (1975).
5. Note that recent Scottish (Scott and Hughes, 1976) and English (Nyman and Silberston, 1978) data also tend to conform to this basic pattern.
6. Furthermore, Palmer's (1972) classification lumped together, under the 'owner-controlled' category, firms which were dominated by private owners and firms which were controlled by other companies (which were 'ultimately' controlled by private owners). Since many dominant private owners are also managers (having access to the same pecuniary and non-pecuniary benefits as 'unpropertied' managers) while their discretion is likely to be greater than that enjoyed by managers in 'company-controlled' firms, Palmer's (1973a) results should be viewed with some caution.
7. This difference was not statistically significant. However, Palmer did not consider growth rates and if weak owner-controlled firms were growing faster this would have biased their profitability downwards relative to strong owner-controlled firms.
8. Qualls's measure is defined as,

$$\frac{\text{net after-tax profit} - \text{normal return on owners' equity}}{\text{net sales revenue}}$$

where the normal return is calculated as 6 per cent times stockholders' equity. See Qualls (1972).

9. Defensive tactics which may be applied during a takeover bid are extensively discussed by Hayes and Taussig (1967). Recently, two owner-controlled firms in our sample have experienced takeover bids. Pharmaceuticals producer F.H. Faulding Ltd, where the director group held about 22 per cent of shares, was contested by Kiwi International Ltd. The Faulding board, led by chairman and managing director W.F. Scammell, responded by making a share placement to a 'friendly' company (G-Chem Cooperative), and purchasing shares on the market to maintain the share price above the Kiwi bid price. Hardware retailer McEwens Ltd experienced a determined bid from Repco Ltd. The Luxton family and associates, which before the bid held some 20 per cent of McEwens, spent $2 million to retain control. In addition the board issued convertible notes, which when converted to ordinary shares would account for 9 per cent of capital, to the Canadian Tyre Corporation. Thus 51 per cent of the expanded capital was placed in friendly hands. The W.R. Carpenter Ltd board, which is dominated by the Carpenter family (who however own only 12 per cent of shares) responded to recent market activity in its shares by issuing another 5 per cent of shares to its executive superannuation fund.

10. See Johns (1967) and North (1975).

11. However, this explanation was rejected since the foreign affiliates were (on average) only slightly larger than Australian firms and did not appear to be especially concentrated in oligopolistic markets.

12. The necessity of an independent role was summed up by one of North's respondents in the following words: 'You ought to try sometimes making decisions about a large company that is 12,000 miles away in a country you don't visit more than once a year' (p. 196).

13. Sheridan (1975, p. 552) pointed out that 'of the total of 61 foreign affiliates, 50 were established before 1950 and the remaining 11 between 1951 and 1960'.

14. This was a dummy variable assigned the value of unity when an industry was more than 50 per cent foreign-controlled and zero otherwise.

15. Phillips also employed the net price-cost margin as a measure of profitability, but OP/FE is more comparable with our RNA variable.

16. A study by Dobbins and Greenwood (1975) could not find the negative correlations between institutional purchases and the share price index which would be consistent with the price stability hypothesis.

17. Some of the more obvious cases of firms with family links were: Sydney Cooke Ltd where L.W. Cooke was managing director and DCG held 4.4 per cent of shares; Edwards Dunlop and Co. Ltd where Sir J. Dunlop was chairman and DCG held 4.9 per cent of shares; and, Gibson Chemical Industries Ltd where V. Gibson was chairman and managing director and DCG held 6.3 per cent of issued ordinary shares. In all, 21 of the 75 continuing management-controlled firms were classified as being dominated by families associated with the board of directors.

6 MANAGERS AND MARKETS

Introduction

Palmer (1974) felt strongly that although the absence of an effective internal (dominant stockholder) restraint is a necessary condition for managers to be able to pursue other than profit-maximising goals, by itself it is not a sufficient condition. A sufficient condition, it was argued, would require that in addition managers must be 'relatively free from product market constraints' and 'the threat of takeover from outside the corporation' (p. 147).

However, Palmer did not formally incorporate the restraint imposed by the market for corporate control in his model. Nor did he give consideration to the possible restraint imposed by the need to secure a constant flow of funds from the capital market. These constraining elements are fundamental considerations in the model being developed in this book. Thus, if a company does not rely solely on internally generated funds (i.e. retained profits and depreciation provisions) it must demonstrate a capacity to return profits on newly acquired funds which will be regarded favourably by the capital market. Furthermore, such an appraisal will, in the first instance, be weighted heavily by the company's past and present performance.

The market for corporate control is essentially a manifestation of the capital market's assessment of the profitability of past and present investments projected into the future. Thus, if managers entertain non-profit objectives the price of their company's stock will become depressed relative to its potential value. This, in turn, causes a fall in the ratio of the market value of the firm to the book value of its net assets (the valuation ratio), making it more profitable for a corporate raider to take over control of the company, institute reforms in management and thereby secure capital gains.

While the product market restraint has received a good deal of attention in industrial organisation literature, capital market restraints have been given scant attention. In the following three sections of the present chapter we examine these market restraints in turn, emphasising how they relate to one another and to the other elements of our model.

137

The Product Market

Theory and Evidence

The discretion which a firm has over its product market is governed by a number of factors. Prominent among them are the ease with which collusive agreements can be reached (and policed) and what may be termed 'the condition of entry' faced by new competitors. The first factor will depend on the number and size distribution of firms and the industry growth rate. Where a small number of firms accounts for a significant proportion of industry output the costs of collusion are reduced, but if the industry is growing rapidly there is more incentive for members of the collusive group to cheat and increase their market share. The condition of entry depends partly on the cost advantages which established producers have over potential entrants. However it will depend also on how current producers conduct their pricing, diversification and advertising strategies. Thus, setting price below the maximum entry forestalling price, increased diversification (which allows cross-subsidisation between products) and higher advertising outlays will all raise costs for newcomers.

This traditional line of reasoning suggests that firms in highly concentrated industries should earn higher profits in the long run than firms in less concentrated industries. It has also been argued (by Caves and Yamey, 1971) that we should expect firms in high-concentration industries to exhibit wider fluctuations in profit rates. First, because in a cartel situation there may be periodic breakdowns in collusion; second, because of specific risk-creating on the part of surviving producers which are designed to deter entry. Since higher profits will be earned by firms in concentrated industries we would also expect them to be able to grow faster. Growth in the base industry may only proceed apace with industry growth since output may be restricted to raise profits. However, growth through diversification and vertical integration can serve to increase corporate power. Finally, since firms in concentrated industries have the means as well as the motivation to grow rapidly, and even though they would be well placed in attracting external finance, we should expect to find them retaining a higher proportion of earnings.[1]

In Chapter 3 it was noted that the *a priori* hypothesised relationships between firm size and performance are not clear cut, except that large firms are expected to exhibit lower variability in earnings. Several writers have noted that in Australia there is a particularly close association between large absolute size and positions of market dominance (Sheridan, 1974, pp. 36-8). Thus, large firms would be expected to earn higher rates of return. On the other hand, a connection between large size and higher costs may be imposed by organisational complexity. But it is possible to argue, like Phillips (1978, p. 164), that costs of complexity would not be of great significance in Australia because the 'large' firms are still relatively small by US and European standards. In the framework of our model it has been suggested that large size will also be associated with freedom from internal and stock market restraints on managerial discretion. If this were true we should expect that whatever the 'potential' relationship between firm size and profitability, the observed relationship would be lower.

We expect a connection between firm size, concentration and profitability, particularly where size and concentration are related positively. If firm size and profitability are negatively associated, we should expect the association between concentration and profitability to be at best only weak and possibly negative. On the other hand, if firm size and profitability are positively related, the same result should prevail in the relationship between concentration and profitability.

On a broad international basis these relationships do, in fact, appear to move together. For example, in the US over the past 30 years researchers using a variety of data sources, definitions and statistical techniques have in the great majority uncovered a positive association between concentration and profitability.[2] In the main, studies of the firm size — profitability relation have also revealed a positive relationship (e.g. Hall and Weiss, 1967), although a negative association has been found on occasions (e.g. Shepherd, 1972). However, in the UK empirical tests of the concentration — profits hypothesis have shown it to be either statistically insignificant (Shepherd, 1972; Holterman, 1973; Kalilzadeh, 1974; Hart and Morgan, 1977), economically insignificant (Phillips, 1972), or negative (Holtermann, 1973). A similar inconclusive result has been achieved regarding firm size and profit. Singh and Whittington (1968) and Whittington (1971) found a negative but statistically insignificant relationship and this finding has received more recent confirmation in Whittington (1980). A break in the pattern emerges in Jenny's (1974) study of 187 French manufacturing firms which concluded that concentration had a positive and significant impact on profitability while between asset size and profitability there was a negative and significant relationship. However, Jenny, like Shepherd

(1972), was picking up the independent influences of concentration and firm size.

Round (1975) and Norman (1976) were the first Australian researchers to provide evidence on the association between concentration and industry profitability. Neither could find a significant relationship. However, Round also put to test Demsetz's (1973) hypothesis that any higher rates of return observed in concentrated US industries are due more to greater efficiency in large firms than to collusive practices. Ideally, firm-level data would be required in order rigorously to test such a hypothesis. That is, it would need to be shown that as concentration rises the difference between small and large firms' profit rates widens, with large firms becoming relatively more and more profitable.

Round's data were aggregated industry statistics compiled by the Tariff Board (now the Industries Assistance Commission), but first, second and third quartile rates of return for a group of large firms in each industry were available. Round found no relationship between first or second quartile profitability and concentration, but a highly significant positive relationship between concentration and third quartile profitability. It was concluded that 'collusion, if present, does not affect all large firms equally, and ... some other factors need to be found in order to explain increasing profitability as concentration rises [above 50 per cent]. Some large firms may become more efficient than others, or management slack may develop in some firms as competitive pressures ease' (p. 278). Without knowledge of the actual relationship between firm size and profitability, however, it was not possible to provide real evidence to support either of these alternative hypotheses. Later investigations by Round (1976b, 1976d) and Parry (1978) also revealed relatively weak associations between concentration and profitability, although Round (1979a) found that 'structurally bad' four-digit industries in Australia incurred higher welfare losses calculated from Harberger's (1954) formula.

Phillips (1978) provided the first Australian study to employ four-digit industry data in testing the concentration-profits hypothesis. Like Round (1976b), Phillips found a weak positive relationship between concentration and a sales-based profitability measure, but he also found a negative and significant (at the 1 per cent level) relationship between concentration and his capital-based measure of profitability. It was his intention to show that part of the strong negative association between concentration and profitability was due

to the fact that there was a positive association between high concentration and large absolute size and a negative association between
size and profitability. The turnover of the largest four firms in each
industry was used as an index of firm size. Phillips's belief was borne
out when, with size included in logarithmic and reciprocal formula-
tions, the inverse association between concentration and profit rates
on capital employed was reduced, while the significance level of the
coefficient on the concentration measure fell from 1 per cent to 5 per
cent. It was concluded that

> The failure of the absolute size variable to emerge as significant (in
> either direction) in the sales-based regressions, and the stronger
> evidence of an inverse rather than a positive association in the
> capital-based regression would tend to suggest that X-inefficiency
> factors are outweighing the potential competitive advantages of
> large firms. (p. 168)

In Australia Sheridan (1974) is the only researcher to have
examined the concentration-profitability and size-profitability
relationships at the firm level. Her methodology was to calculate
mean rates of return by the degree of concentration for each year
between 1950 and 1967. Since eleven of the rank correlation
coefficients between concentration and profitability were negative
(one significant at the 10 per cent level) and seven were positive (five
significant at the 10 per cent level) she felt that 'there is little
association between profit rates and degrees of concentration' (p.
67). With regard to size and profitability, rank correlation coefficients were calculated for the same 18 year period, and for three sub-
periods within that time. In general it was found that as firm size
increased profitability fell. Thus, Sheridan found that in her 'eight
major industrial groups, there are 81 negative relations out of a total
of 96, and 43 of these are statistically significant (significant at or less
than the 10 per cent level)' (p. 54). Firm growth rates appeared to be
positively related to size and a strong negative association between
risk and firm size was discovered.

As a rationale for the observed negative association between firm
size and profitability, Sheridan proposed that

> the separation of ownership and control is more common in larger
> firms and thus the maximization goal(s) of larger firms is likely to
> be diverted away from 'profit' towards other objects such as fast
> growth. (pp. 67-8)

In a similar vein, Phillips (1978) was drawn to the conclusion that

our findings ... suggest that whatever association there is between large absolute size and profitability is negative rather than positive. The close association between large absolute size and relative size, coupled with the likelihood that the separation of ownership and control is more prevalent among large firms, combine to suggest that firms in high concentration industries will generally possess wide discretionary power to pursue non-profit maximization objectives. (p. 367)

Thus, both of these researchers suggested that size is associated with discretion and, because ownership is more likely to be separated from control in large firms, managers in these firms choose to utilise their discretion to pursue alternative objectives. However, this interesting hypothesis was not formally tested.

Absolute Size and Firm Performance

In the first instance we shall examine the relationships between firm size and performance. The observed relationships for the 'all companies' sample and the three control-type sub-samples, are displayed in Table 6.1. Since we have no *a priori* hypotheses regarding the directions of the relationships between firm size and profitability, growth and retentions, in these equations the significance of coefficients is established by a two-tail test. Since we have proposed that greater size will result in lower risk, in this respect a one-tail test is applied. Various functional forms were experimented with, but the one explaining the greatest proportion of the variance in performance, particularly of profitability and growth, is the reciprocal of opening net assets (i.e. $SIZE = 1/NAo$).

Examination of the residuals from the equations testing for size-performance relationships revealed heteroscedasticity, with the size of the residuals decreasing as size increased. This was confirmed by a test procedure devised by Goldfeld and Quandt (1965).[3] Hence, while the coefficients on SIZE are statistically unbiased estimates of the true parameters, they are inefficient (i.e. the variance was not being minimised). However, it will be observed that in the 'all companies' sample each coefficient is highly significant. The positive coefficients on SIZE indicate that firm size was negatively associated with each performance variable. Thus, while profitability declined with firm size, so did the risk involved in operations. Large firm profit rates may have been lower, but in this sense they were of a 'higher quality' (i.e. more certain). The negative relationship held at the two-digit industry level, even though it was stronger in manufacturing than in service industries.

That retentions fell as size increased probably reflects large firms' ability to attract proportionately more external finance. But while our results suggest that small firms were growing significantly faster than large firms we cannot conclude — like Smyth, Boyes and Peseau (1975, p. 89) who achieved a similar result using UK and US data — that concentration is decreasing. This is because our sample consists only of continuing companies and small firms are more likely to be taken over or merged into larger ones.

From the point of view of our central hypotheses, however, it is most interesting to find that firm size had a differential impact on performance depending on control type. If control type has a significant bearing on the relation between size and profitability, the reasons must probably be related to differences in the association between size and internal and external restraints. We find, for example, that the relation between size and profitability is much steeper in management-controlled firms. Thus, if managerial discretion is a cause of this negative relationship it appears that in management-controlled firms the extent of discretion available to managers is more highly correlated with firm size.

Another feature of the results is that only in management-controlled firms was there a highly significant negative relationship between firm size and retentions. We have already proposed as a reason for this that large size is associated with freer access to the capital market. However, it would appear that in owner- and company-controlled firms this consideration was not an important determinant of the level of retentions. In these firms other factors were more important. For example, in Chapter 4, we saw that a significant determinant of the extent to which earnings were being retained within owner-controlled firms was the value of directors' shareholdings. In company-controlled firms, however, non-maturity provided the single most important explanation of high retentions.

The observation that in company-controlled firms performance in general did not show the same variability in relation to size as in other firms may simply indicate that the concept of 'the firm' has less meaning here. Many economies of firm size, as distinct from economies of scale, might be reaped by company-controlled firms irrespective of their own size. That is, the resources of the wider

Table 6.1: Relationship between Firm Size and Performance, by Control Type

Dependent variable	All companies, n = 194*				Owner-controlled, n = 68			
	Constant	$SIZE$ $(1/NAo)$	r^2	$\bar{r}^2$	Constant	$SIZE$ $(1/NAo)$	r^2	$\bar{r}^2$
RNA	.158	.095 (6.979)[a]	.202	.198	.135	.109 (5.132)[a]	.285	.274
REA	.089	.040 (4.143)[a]	.082	.077	.075	.051 (4.285)[a]	.281	.20
GNA	.097	.094 (7.469)[a]	.225	.221	.073	.138 (8.452)[a]	.520	.51
SDRNA	.032	.017 (3.366)[d]	.056	.051	.029	.020 (2.268)[e]	.072	.05
RET	.431	.092 (3.028)[a]	.047	.042	.430	.087 (1.557)	.038	.02

Notes: figures in brackets are t-ratios; * in the retentions equations the sample sizes are: all companies (188), owner-controlled (64), company-controlled (49); a, b and c denote significance at the .01, .05 and .10 levels respectively using a two-tail test; d and e denote significance at the .01 and .05 levels respectively using a one-tail test.

Table 6.2: Relationship between Concentration and Performance, by Control Type

Dependent variable	All companies, n = 147*				Owner-controlled, n = 47*			
	Constant	$CR4$	r^2	$\bar{r}^2$	Constant	$CR4$	r^2	$\bar{r}^2$
RNA	.159	.105 (2.142)[b]	.031	.024	.150	.075 (.700)	.011	<
REA	.087	.043 (1.691)[b]	.019	.013	.078	.054 (1.003)	.022	.00
GNA	.106	.052 (1.206)	.010	.003	.090	.095 (.860)	.016	<
SDRNA	.033	.009 (.610)	.003	< 0	.042	−.043 (1.205)	.031	.01
RET	.413	.191 (1.989)[b]	.027	.020	.380	.445 (1.802)[b]	.071	.05

Notes: figures in brackets are t-ratios; * in the retentions equations the sample sizes are: all companies (143), owner-controlled (44), company-controlled (40); b and c denote significance at the .05 and .10 levels respectively using a one-tail test.

Management-controlled, n = 75				Company-controlled, n = 51*			
Constant	*SIZE* (1/NAo)	r^2	$\bar{r}^2$	Constant	*SIZE* (1/NAo)	r^2	$\bar{r}^2$
.154	.207 (6.972)[a]	.400	.391	.173	.063 (2.782)[a]	.136	.119
.086	.089 (5.378)[a]	.284	.274	.100	.021 (.997)	.020	< 0
.097	.120 (3.645)[a]	.154	.142	.117	.005 (2.514)[b]	.114	.096
.026	.036 (3.548)[d]	.147	.135	.410	.007 (.816)	.013	< 0
.392	.182 (2.654)[a]	.088	.076	.484	.053 (1.204)	.030	.009

Management-controlled, n = 59				Company-controlled, n = 41*			
Constant	*CR4*	r^2	$\bar{r}^2$	Constant	*CR4*	r^2	$\bar{r}^2$
.157	.152 (2.299)[b]	.085	.069	.191	−.021 (.141)	.001	< 0
.092	.048 (1.403)[c]	.033	.016	.096	−.001 (.032)	.000	< 0
.117	.005 (.095)	.000	< 0	.111	.072 (.837)	.018	< 0
.027	.018 (1.024)	.018	.001	.034	.030 (1.047)	.027	.002
.403	.108 (.975)	.016	< 0	.450	.164 (.829)	.018	< 0

parent organisation could be employed to gain economies in research and development, marketing, purchasing, etc. In addition, through its association with a larger parent corporation the financial resources at the disposal of a company-controlled firm can be expected to be greater than for another similar-size company. The observed relationship may also indicate that internal restraints (in terms of required performance) imposed by parent companies are related more to factors which are independent of firm size.

An alternative explanation of the lower responsiveness of performance to size in company-controlled firms (in particular, profitability and growth performance) rests on the assumption that many of these firms were previously independent companies which had recently experienced a partial takeover bid. Among the reasons for their being subject to takeover may have been slow growth and below-average rates of return, reasons which might have continued during the study period. The relationships between firm size and performance would be less pronounced than if the small companies had not been distinguished by the poor performance which caused them to come under company control in the first place. It is true that several domestic company-controlled firms fell into this category, but almost all of the overseas-controlled firms had originally been established by a foreign corporation. A comparison of the coefficients for each of these groups of firms (see Appendix Table A.6.1) indicates that there is little merit in the argument. That is, the values of the coefficients on the firm size variable are generally *higher* in the domestic companies group, which is the opposite to what we would expect on the basis of this alternative hypothesis.

Seller Concentration and Firm Performance

The results, showing simple regressions of performance on the four-firm concentration ratio (CR4), are shown in Table 6.2. However, the sample is restricted to firms which were involved in manufacturing. Also, the concentration ratios have been calculated at the two-digit level of aggregation, are averaged over the two years 1968-9 and 1972-3 and are not adjusted for the influences of regionally segmented markets and import competition. For these reasons the results must be viewed with caution.

In the 'all companies' sample each coefficient has the predicted positive sign, although only in the profitability and retentions equations are the coefficients on CR4 statistically significant. The coefficient of .105 in the RNA equation, for example, indicates that a ten-point increase in the four-firm concentration ratio of an industry is associated with a 1.05 percentage points higher pre-tax rate of return on net assets. Since most of the two-digit industries had a four-firm concentration ratio in the range .10-.30, firms in industries at the top end of this range earned profit rates which were some two percentage points higher than at the bottom of the range. The post-tax rate of return on equity assets was slightly less responsive to changes in concentration, but since this measure reflects financial decisions as well as operating decisions this is not surprising.

Retentions show a very slight response to increasing concentration. In terms of our previous example, firms in high concentration industries (i.e. CR4 $\simeq$ .30) had retention ratios which were on average 3.8 points higher than those operating in low concentration industries (i.e. CR4 $\simeq$ .10). Moreover, it should be noted that concentration 'explains' only a very small proportion of the total variance in performance.

When the sample is split we find that concentration had different effects depending on type of control. Only in management-controlled firms was the rate of profit significantly related to the level of industry concentration. This would seem to cast some doubt on the hypothesis that separation of ownership from control is of itself responsible for weak positive or negative relations between concentration and profitability. On the other hand, the effects of concentration on growth appear stronger (though statistically insignificant) in owner- and company-controlled firms. In the risk equations concentration has a positive coefficient in the management- and company-controlled samples, but in owner-controlled firms it is negative. Finally, while in management- and company-controlled firms the effects of concentration on retentions are weak and insignificant, in owner-controlled firms the effect is strong and significant at the .05 level. Although the highly aggregated nature of these data on concentration must be kept in mind, these results suggest that, depending on their character of control, firms choose to utilise the discretionary power afforded by high concentration in different ways.

We can gain some impression of the relations between concentration, firm size and profitability by stratifying firms by size category and running separate regressions of profitability on concentration for each group. The results displayed in Table 6.3 indicate that as firm size increases the size of the coefficient on CR4 declines and the proportion of the variance in profitability explained by the concen-

Table 6.3: Effects of Firm Size on the Relationship between Concentration and Profitability

Dependent variable	n	Constant	CR4	r^2	$\bar{r}^2$
Small firms:					
RNA	44	.188	.178 (1.792)[b]	.071	.049
REA	44	.103	.064 (1.247)	.036	.013
Medium-sized firms:					
RNA	65	.144	.117 (1.821)[b]	.050	.035
REA	65	.077	.053 (1.538)[c]	.036	.021
Large firms:					
RNA	38	.149	.025 (.349)	.003	< 0
REA	38	.083	.017 (.453)	.006	< 0

Notes: figures in brackets are t-ratios; b and c denote significance at the .05 and .10 levels respectively using a one-tail test.

tration ratio (i.e. r^2) also declines. This negative relationship is clearly strongest in relation to the pre-tax rate of return on net assets, which we have argued gives a better indication of the rate of return on the firm's operations in the product market. These findings are at odds with Demsetz's (1973) hypothesis, but do provide some tentative support for Round's (1975) alternative hypothesis that managerial slack develops in some large firms because of the easing of competitive pressures. However, such behaviour is not the exclusive preserve of management-controlled companies.

In addition, the results shown in Table 6.3 provide support for Phillips's (1978) contention that managerial discretion associated with firm size is a primary cause of the observed negative association between *industry* rates of return on capital and industry concentration in Australia and suggest that a similar relation might be observed in the UK. Since industry profitability is calculated from aggregate revenues and costs, the actual rates of return earned by the largest firms in the industry will be weighted most heavily in the final figure. Thus, the higher the concentration ratio, the greater the weighting attached to large-firm rates of return, and if there is a negative association between firm size and profitability within industries, it is not surprising to find a negative or weakly positive relation between industry concentration and industry rates of return emerges.

The Capital Market

Theoretical Expectations

The capital market restraint cannot be effective unless firms actually make new issues. Baumol (1965) outlined a number of reasons why managers would wish to avoid external finance. These include transactions costs, information costs and losses in autonomy. He expressed concern about the fact that few large US firms approached the market for funds. But two UK studies have questioned whether this is an accurate picture of large firms' behaviour. In the first study Whittington (1971, p. 126) concluded that 'more of the larger firms raised external finance [and this] suggests that size is not associated with independence from the capital market ... possibly because [large firms] can make new issues more cheaply than small companies'. In the second study Meeks and Whittington (1975, p. 827) showed that in 'giant' companies (i.e. those which were among the largest 100 quoted UK companies in 1964) the capital market supplied 70 per cent of growth in long-term finance as compared with a figure of 56 per cent for smaller companies.

Lintner and Butters (1955) and Benishay (1961) in the US and Meeks and Whittington (1975) in the UK all concluded that the capital market prefers large to small firms. With its greater market-ability the stock of large firms is more desirable in the eyes of financial institutions and other investors who wish to trade large blocks without upsetting prices. More information about them is generally available to the market, so they will be demanded by less informed, small investors. Finally, large firms experience lower fluctuations in earnings derived from operations and the probability of failure is lower. Hence, *ceteris paribus*, the capital market will require a higher return on investment from small firms.

A less widely canvassed view is that some part of the 'equity' of owner-managers derives from their ability to *control*. Reder (1947,

p. 455) speculated that 'in order to keep his control the entrepreneur will fight reorganizations to the bitter end and will reject outside funds which might bring annoying restraints on his freedom of action'. Kamerschen (1970, p. 670) also noted that 'fear of loss of control could . . . influence owners to prefer internal over external financing'. Hence, a conflict with 'outside' shareholder interests may develop if owner-managers fail to take advantage of profitable expansion opportunities which often require external finance, and, after a point, loss of control. Dominant shareholders will be wealthier than the average shareholder and would therefore prefer a high retentions policy which will result in under-taxation. The agency theory literature proposes that internal agents will seek to maximise their welfare at the expense of external shareholders (Jensen and Meckling, 1976); however, labour market forces (Fama, 1980) and capital market mechanisms (Fama and Jensen, 1983) are seen as efficient market responses to agency problems.

It is difficult to make predictions about company-controlled firms because of the variety of motivations lying behind inter-corporate shareholdings. Bonbright and Means (1932) argued that the holding company device is often used to disenfranchise the large majority of small shareholders and as a preliminary to outright fusion of subsidiaries. Over a number of years 'creeping acquisition' could be practised in order to effect a complete takeover without bidding up the stock price. Nyman and Silberston (1978) felt that the discretion of a company-controlled firm's management would be severely limited. Thus, while we can expect company control to be associated with a degree of independence from the capital market restraint, this discipline may be replaced by the 'internal capital market' of the parent company, which can supply new equity capital and debt finance to the subsidiary.

It has often been alleged that because of capital market imperfections newly established enterprises have been allocated funds only at prohibitive rates when compared with well-established firms. Nerlove (1968, p. 318) argued that firms undertaking rapid growth into new markets would be in a disequilibrium position in relation to the capital market. He expected higher rates of return in such firms, since the market would be slow in supplying capital to them. Grabowski and Mueller (1975) also felt that lagged adjustments in the capital market helped perpetuate substantial differences in marginal rates of return between mature and non-mature technologies. Thus, the capital market discipline is expected to be more

Table 6.4: Percentage of Growth in Net Assets Financed
Externally, by Firm Size, Control Type and Maturity

Classification scheme		Percentage of growth financed externally
a By firm size:		
1. Small	63	42.9
2. Medium	82	41.4
3. Large	49	50.7
b By control type:		
4. Owner	68	36.4
5. Management	65	48.7
6. Company	51	48.1
c By maturity:		
7. Non-mature	36	46.2
8. Mature	158	43.8

Statistically significant differences:

$3 > 2^b, 3 > 1^c, 5 > 4^a, 6 > 4^b$

Note: a, b and c denote significance at the .01, .05 and .10 levels respectively using a two-tail test.

severe in allocating finance to rapidly growing non-mature companies.

The main point, however, is that it is not sufficient merely to
demonstrate that companies make use of funds obtained in the
capital market. In order to conclude that managerial discretion is
curbed by the capital market it must also be shown that this market is
effective. That is, effective in the sense that the market allocates funds
under suitable terms to those sectors or firms in the economy which
are able to use these funds most beneficially.

The Extent of Capital Market Scrutiny

One measure of capital market scrutiny of growth is the proportion of
growth in net assets financed externally. How did this proportion vary
according to the particularly relevant characteristics of firms in our
sample, i.e. by size, control type and maturity? These figures are

shown in Table 6.4. Part (a) shows that while small and medium-sized firms financed roughly the same percentage of their growth through new issues, in large firms (i.e. those with opening net assets in 1966 of more than $20 million) a statistically significantly higher percentage of growth was externally financed. From part (b) it is apparent that management- and company-controlled firms achieved a statistically significantly higher proportion of their growth externally than did private ownership companies. Non-mature firms did not display a significantly higher proportion of external finance than mature firms. However, since non-mature firms also grew much faster than mature firms, in absolute terms (i.e. in relation to opening size) the use of external sources of finance was more important to them.

Appendix Table A.6.2 analyses the structure of new equity issues over the study period by control type and maturity. Compared with mature firms, total new equity issues as a percentage of opening net assets were three times as great in non-mature firms. Within the non-mature group minority ownership and management-controlled firms made greatest use of new equity issues, with rights issues and issues in the course of acquisitions being the most important sources. However, private placements and allotments were also used frequently. Domestic company-controlled firms made only rights issues. This is consistent with a desire by the controlling companies to maintain their ownership stake in these firms (two of these were already 60 per cent owned subsidiaries). Overseas company-controlled firms, on the other hand, made most of their new issues in the course of takeover offers. Since Stewart (1977) has found that such companies tended to finance 70 per cent of their takeovers with 'mainly cash', this indicates that takeovers were an important means of expansion for them.

Among the mature firms only two of the seven companies which were majority ownership-controlled made new issues. In minority ownership companies rights issues and issues in the course of takeovers were quantitatively most important, but the extent of financing through new issues was much less than in management- and company-controlled firms. In those groups, issues made in connection with acquisitions were most important. Furthermore, in company-controlled firms private placements and allotments were quantitatively much more important than in management- and private ownership-controlled companies. In many cases these issues were made to the dominant shareholder company, increasing its control over the firm. Public placements, which involve the greatest degree of capital market scrutiny (because a prospectus needs to be issued and all investors may participate), were relatively unimportant.

The figures in Appendix Table A.6.3 show that as a rule, the proportional reliance on new equity issues tended to be inversely related to firm size. Larger firms made greater use of debentures, long-term loans and preference shares in their capital structure. Proportional reliance on rights issues also increased with firm size while reliance on private placements and allotments fell. Perhaps this reflects a desire on the part of top managements in larger firms not to upset existing ownership and control relations.

The Effectiveness of Capital Market Scrutiny

The discipline of the capital market, as an allocator of funds, should work in two ways. First, the market should allocate funds to those companies with what it considers to be projects capable of returning 'satisfactory' profits in the future. That is, it *selects* those companies with good future prospects and denies funds to those who would use them in unworthy ventures. Second, the market's discipline will extend not only to those funds which are derived directly from it, but also to funds already invested in the company. This is because the returns to subscribers to new equity issues or debentures will be dependent on the *overall* profitability of the company, not only on those funds contributed by them.[4] Thus, new issues are normally accompanied by optimistic reports of prospective returns on total funds. Whittington (1971, p. 124) felt that,

> The simplest hypothesis arising from this is that companies which raise external finance tend to have higher future profitability than companies with similar past profitability which do not go to the market ... A more complex hypothesis ... is that, more specifically, amongst those companies which had below-average past profitability, those which raised external finance would tend to have higher future profitability than those which did not go to the market.

That is, the discipline of the market was expected to be greatest among companies with below-average past profitability. It was conjectured that the second hypothesis would give an indication of how well the market performed another duty — the provision of funds to companies with a poor current profitability record (and therefore unable to make use of retained earnings) but good future prospects.

These models may be summarised as,

$$RNA_t = \beta_0 + \beta_1 GNA_{t-1} + \beta_2 RNA_{t-1} + \beta_3 EXF_{t-1} + \varepsilon \tag{6.1}$$

$$RNA_t = \beta_0 + \beta_1 GNA_{t-1} + \beta_2 RNA_{t-1} + \beta_3 EXG_{t-1} + \varepsilon \tag{6.2}$$

$$RNA_t = \beta_0 + \beta_1 GNA_{t-1} + \beta_2 RNA_{t-1} + \beta_3 EXFB_{t-1} + \varepsilon \tag{6.3}$$

where,

RNA_t	is the pre-tax rate of return on net assets in period t.
RNA_{t-1}	is the pre-tax rate of return on net assets in period t−1.
GNA_{t-1}	is the growth rate of net assets in period t−1.
EXG_{t-1}	is the external growth rate in period t−1.
EXF_{t-1}	is a dummy variable which reflects the *fact* that a company made significant use of external finance during period t−1

i.e.

$$EXF_{t-1} \begin{cases} = & 1 \text{ if a company had an external growth rate of more than 1 per cent per annum in period } t-1^5 \\ = & 0 \text{ otherwise} \end{cases}$$

$EXFB_{t-1}$ is a dummy variable which reflects the *fact* that a company had *below average* past profitability (RNA_{t-1}) but made significant use of external finance in period t−1.

i.e.

$$EXFB_{t-1} \begin{cases} = & 1 \text{ if a company had an external growth rate of more than 1 per cent per annum in period } t-1 \text{ and its past profitability } (RNA_{t-1}) \text{ was below the average for } all \text{ companies} \\ = & 0 \text{ otherwise} \end{cases}$$

ε is the stochastic error term.

The average time lag considered by Whittington was of six years' duration. In order that our results may be directly comparable with Whittington's we have estimated identically specified equations. However, while the average time lag between the dependent and independent variables is six years, these are only three-year averages (as compared with Whittington's six-year averages). Thus, in this study t refers to the period 1972-3 to 1974-5, while t−1 refers to the period 1966-7 to 1968-9.

We are interested in what is happening to the rate of return on net assets, which reflects the earnings of all long-term capital. The discipline of the market will be operating not only through new share issues, but also through debenture issues, mortgage loans and other long-term borrowings undertaken by the firm. Since profitability has been found to be a persistent characteristic of firms[6] we should expect that past profitability will be positively related to future profitability, i.e. $\beta_2 > 0$. We also have the one-sided expectation that the discipline of the capital market will be associated with higher future profitability, i.e. $\beta_3 > 0$.

Since past growth is expected to be related to future profitability, and should be positively correlated with external finance, it is possible that in an equation relating past profitability and external finance to future profitability the external finance variable will yield a biased estimate of its independent influence on future profitability. For this reason, past growth is included as an additional explanatory variable. If 'Penrose Effects' arise, so that faster growth consumes an inordinate proportion of managerial resources and depresses current profitability, future profitability might also be affected adversely. Thus, our expectation is that $\beta_1 < 0$.

The regression results from fitting equations (6.1), (6.2), and (6.3) to the sample are shown in Table 6.5 In a number of respects the results are similar to those obtained by Whittington using UK data — but there are also differences. The signs of all coefficients are identical to those obtained in the UK study, but the R^2 values are only half as large. The coefficient on the external finance dummy variable (EXF_{t-1}), which is significant at the .05 level, indicates that externally financed companies had a rate of return in 1972-3 to 1974-5 which was 2.18 percentage points higher than firms which relied exclusively on internally generated funds. This figure is somewhat higher than the 1.40 percentage points for externally financed UK firms which was estimated by Whittington. Equation 6.5.2 includes the continuous variable (EXG_{t-1}) measuring past external growth. The

Table 6.5: Effects of External Financing on Future Profitability

Equation number	n	GNA_{t-1}	RNA_{t-1}	EXF_{t-1}	EXG_{t-1}	$EXFB_{t-1}$	R^2	$\bar{R}^2$
6.5.1	194	−.090 (1.683)[b]	.505 (6.728)[a]	2.18 (1.797)[b]			.197	.185
6.5.2	194	−.095 (1.063)	.509 (6.163)[a]		.057 (.576)		.185	.172
6.5.3	194	−.070 (1.385)[c]	.556 (6.552)[a]			2.05 (1.619)[c]	.195	.182

Notes: the dependent variable is RNA_t; figures in brackets are t-ratios; a, b and c indicate significance at the .01, .05 and .10 levels respectively using a one-tail test; the regression coefficients relating to the dummy variables EXF_{t-1} and $EXFB_{t-1}$ are expressed as percentage points.

coefficient is small in relation of the UK finding (.057 as compared with .177) and is statistically insignificant. When coupled with the fact that equation 6.5.2 explains a lower proportion of the variance in future profitability than equation 6.5.1, this finding supports Whittington's claim that it is the *fact* of going to the capital market and not the *extent* of funds raised which is most important.

In equation 6.5.3 the size of the estimated coefficient for the $EXFB_{t-1}$ variable of 2.05 per cent is remarkably similar to the value of 1.92 per cent obtained by Whittington, but is significant only at the .10 level. Thus, while in the UK the capital market appeared to impose a greater discipline on firms with below-average past profitability — compelling them to raise their future profitability by a greater amount than firms in general — this did not seem to be the case in Australia. Even so, on the basis of his results Whittington's conclusion was that while 'the companies which did go to the capital market did seem, on average, to achieve slightly higher future profitability than internally financed companies . . . the difference was not quantitatively important' (p. 245). That is, not important in relation to the average rate of return for all companies over the period under consideration. Whittington was comparing the *greatest* difference in future profitability attributable to external finance (1.92 per cent) with the average profit rate for all firms of 15.2 per cent. In our sample this claim could be put forward with equal conviction, for we should be comparing figures of 2.18 per cent and 17.9 per cent respectively.

Whittington's study did not explicitly consider the effects that alternative ownership patterns can have on relations with the capital market. In particular, company-controlled firms are likely to be in a unique situation. On the one hand, subsidiaries of larger companies may be able to raise external finance on more favourable terms than otherwise similar independent firms because of the protection afforded by the reputation and greater resources of the parent concern. On the other hand, the parent is likely to adopt many of the attributes and responsibilities normally associated with the external capital market. For example, Williamson (1973) has stated a case that the central offices of conglomerates take on the role of an internal 'capital market' — one which allocates resources among divisions and subsidiaries in an optimal fashion. It was argued that this 'market' will have more information, thereby allowing 'fine tuning' adjustments in investment. Furthermore, the managers of subsidiaries will need to justify retained earnings. Hence, the scrutiny which accompanies new issues may not exceed that on retained earnings. Since Whittington excluded listed subsidiaries of the 1,955 firms in his sample (in order to eliminate 'double counting') it is possible that some part of the weaker results in Table 6.5 can be accounted for by these considerations.

The effects of external financing on the future profitability of firms in the individual control-type categories are displayed in Table 6.6. The propriety of this refinement is indicated by the $\bar{R}^2$ values which are higher than those obtained when the entire sample was used.[7] The results indicate that external finance had no positive effect on the future profitability of company-controlled firms, since all three external finance coefficients are non-significant. This does not necessarily mean that the capital market did not exert any discipline over the uses to which funds supplied by it were put. Rather, it shows that company-controlled firms financed entirely from retained earnings were no less profitable than those which had approached the market. However, it could also indicate that company-controlled firms were receiving external finance on more favourable terms than independent companies.

In the management- and owner-controlled categories externally financed companies earned 1.07 percentage points higher rates of return, but neither of these coefficients is statistically or economically significant. This merely means that *some* internally financed firms in these categories had high future profit rates. In accordance with the UK results the market appeared to apply greater restraints on firms with sub-average profitability. These firms earned future rates of profit which were 4.45 (2.52) percentage points higher than otherwise similar internally financed owner- (management-)controlled firms.

The coefficients on the external growth variable in equations 6.6.2 and 6.6.5 are roughly twice the value obtained by Whittington. In management-controlled firms the coefficient of .448 suggests that other things being equal a firm with a 10 percentage points higher external growth rate in 1966-7 to 1968-9 had a rate of return on net assets which was 4.48 percentage points higher in 1972-3 to 1974-5. The corresponding coefficient on EXG_{t-1} estimated for owner-controlled firms is somewhat lower at .289, but is still considerably greater than the .170 which was obtained in the UK study. Thus, when all company-controlled firms are excluded we cannot conclude, as Whittington did, that the fact of going to the capital market was more important than the extent of new funds raised. However, the capital market exerted a significant restraint on the

Table 6.6: Effects of External Financing on Future Profitability, by Control Type

Equation number	n	GNA_{t-1}	RNA_{t-1}	EXF_{t-1}	EXG_{t-1}	$EXFB_{t-1}$	R^2	$\hat{R}^2$
a) Owner-controlled:								
6.6.1	68	−.112 (.933)	.689 (3.689)[a]	1.07 (.466)			.186	.147
6.6.2	68	−.223 (1.527)[c]	.687 (3.730)[a]		.289 (1.384)[c]		.207	.169
6.6.3	68	−.182 (1.505)[c]	.884 (4.269)[a]			4.45 (1.931)[b]	.228	.192
b) Management-controlled								
6.6.4	75	.003 (.032)	.650 (6.676)[a]	1.07 (.548)			.411	.386
6.6.5	75	−.134 (1.668)[c]	.634 (7.021)[a]		.448 (3.036)[a]		.476	.454
6.6.6	75	−.010 (.141)	.727 (6.851)[a]			2.52 (1.755)[b]	.433	.409
c) Company-controlled*:								
6.6.7	48	−.048 (.505)	.441 (14.860)[a]	−1.96 (.469)			.257	.207
6.6.8	48	−.018 (.042)	.449 (15.085)[a]		−.168 (.544)		.259	.208
6.6.9	48	−.055 (.630)	.408 (8.836)[a]			−.88 (.121)	.252	.201

Notes: *this excludes three non-mature company-controlled firms; the dependent variable is RNA_t; figures in brackets are t-ratios; a, b and c indicate significance at the .01, .05 and .10 levels respectively using a one-tail test; the regression coefficients relating to the dummy variables EXF_{t-1} and $EXFB_{t-1}$ are expressed as percentage points.

profitable application of new share and loan capital by non-company-controlled firms.

Since management-controlled firms on average had a higher external growth rate *and* a higher coefficient on EXG_{t-1} than owner-controlled firms, this suggests that the degree of capital market scrutiny may increase at an increasing rate the greater the extent of external financing. However, empirical support for a curvilinear relationship could not be found. Experiments with cubic and logarithmic variants of EXG_{t-1} failed to improve on the explanation achieved with the linear form. Therefore, other reasons should be sought to account for the lower coefficient on EXG_{t-1} for owner-controlled firms. One possibility is that owner-controlled firms, in spite of good future prospects, chose to finance a lower proportion of their growth externally.

The life-cycle hypothesis proposes that managers in mature corporations will tend to avoid the discipline of the capital market. In an earlier section we found that non-mature firms had a significantly faster rate of growth and external sources were more important in relation to their size. Also, since non-mature firms were smaller and less well established, it is likely that they would be subject to greater capital market discipline. This hypothesis is tested in Table 6.7. Comparing the coefficients on EXF_{t-1} in equations 6.7.1 and 6.7.4 we find that there was a greater positive differential in the future profitability of externally financed non-mature firms. Although this supports our hypothesis, both coefficients are non-significant. Stronger support is found in a comparison of the coefficients on the external growth rate variable, EXG_{t-1}. In the mature firms sample its value is small (.099) and non-significant, while in the non-mature firms sample the coefficient is almost seven times greater. Other things being equal, in non-mature firms a 10 percentage points rise in the external growth rate in 1966-7 to 1968-9 was associated with a 6.72 percentage points rise in the rate of return on net assets in 1972-3 to 1974-5. This suggests that compared with mature firms the capital market was quite selective in allocating funds to non-mature companies. That is, only those firms with very good future prospects could raise large amounts of capital market funds. In equation 6.7.6 we find that non-mature companies with below-average past profitability which *did* obtain funds achieved a future profit rate which was 11.5 percentage points higher than that of companies which had similar (below average) past performance, but did not obtain funds in the market.

Table 6.7: Effects of External Financing on Future Profitability, by Maturity

Equation Number	n	GNA_{t-1}	RNA_{t-1}	EXF_{t-1}	EXG_{t-1}	$EXFB_{t-1}$	R^2	$\bar{R}^2$
a) Mature firms:								
6.7.1	122	−.099	.811	.80			.342	.326
		(1.346)[c]	(7.715)[a]	(.547)				
6.7.2	122	−.138	.835		.099		.345	.328
		(1.507)[c]	(7.744)[a]		(.841)			
6.7.3	122	−.136	.931			2.81	.370	.354
		(1.859)[b]	(8.146)[a]			(2.341)[b]		
b) Non-mature firms:								
6.7.4	21	.037	.451	2.10			.174	.028
		(.197)	(1.694)	(.318)				
6.7.5	21	−.514	.667		.672		.261	.130
		(1.204)	(2.291)[b]		(1.452)[c]			
6.7.6	21	−.098	.671			11.50	.343	.228
		(.635)	(2.655)[a]			(2.126)[b]		

Notes: the dependent variable is RNA_t; figures in brackets are t-ratios; a, b and c indicate significance at the .01, .05 and .10 levels respectively using a one-tail test; the regression coefficients relating to the dummy variables EXF_{t-1} and $EXFB_{t-1}$ are expressed as percentage points.

It appears that the only group of mature firms which was closely scrutinised by the market was the group of firms with below-average performance. These externally financed companies achieved a 2.81 percentage points higher future rate of return. Thus, among mature firms at least, it is clear that the market operated — as Whittington has suggested — in a way which tended to eradicate below average performance without compelling 'good' performers to raise their profitability.

Another dimension which was not explored by Whittington is the relationship between firm size and capital market scrutiny. It is generally recognised that large firms can make new issues more cheaply than small firms and have a wider range of sources of capital market finance. At various times it has been suggested that dichotomisation of the Australian market has proceeded to such a degree that it closely parallels the 'two-tier' market which is said to exist in the US.[8] Domestic institutions seeking liquidity tend to concentrate their activities on the largest 100 listed corporations; however, institutions do seek out the stock of promising small companies (Davies, 1982).

In these circumstances it is likely that the most severe capital market discipline will fall on small and medium-sized firms. That is, if these firms are to attract funds in the market they will need to provide good reasons (i.e. potentially highly profitable investment proposals) for doing so. Similar pressures could not be applied to large firms. In the UK Meeks and Whittington (1975) provided evidence to support this hypothesis. Their study showed that the capital market supplied 'giant companies' — those among the top 100 — with proportionately more external finance despite their lower return on net assets. This apparent anomaly was rationalised by (a) the smaller risks to which giants were subject and (b) their higher gearing, which meant a rate of return on equity assets less unfavourable compared with smaller firms.

Our regression results are displayed in Table 6.8. We have excluded non-mature firms from the sample in order to separate the effects of size *per se.* In general the results conform to our expectations. Neither the discrete external finance variable (EXF_{t-1}) nor the continuous external growth rate variable (EXG_{t-1}) is statistically significant in any size category. However, the magnitudes of these coefficients diminish with firm size. The differential impact of capital market discipline can be seen most clearly where its effects were strongest, i.e. in eliminating below-average performance. Relatively

Table 6.8: External Finance and Future Profitability, by Firm Size (Excluding Non-Mature and Company-Controlled Firms)

Equation number	n	GNA_{t-1}	RNA_{t-1}	EXF_{t-1}	EXG_{t-1}	$EXFB_{t-1}$	R^2	$\bar{R}^2$
a) Small firms:								
6.8.1	36	−.043 (.373)	.647 (3.004)[a]	2.84 (.908)			.247	.176
6.8.2	36	−.102 (.686)	.708 (3.196)[a]		.176 (.843)		.244	.173
6.8.3	36	−.058 (.540)	.931 (3.827)[a]			6.73 (2.036)[b]	.316	.252
b) Medium-sized firms:								
6.8.4	50	−.360 (1.993)[b]	.912 (4.577)[a]	1.10 (.497)			.321	.277
6.8.5	50	−.385 (1.789)[b]	.936 (4.551)[a]		.093 (.414)		.320	.276
6.8.6	50	−.492 (2.757)[a]	1.089 (5.301)[a]			4.46 (2.211)[b]	.383	.343
c) Large firms:								
6.8.7	36	−.119 (1.202)	.883 (6.613)[a]	.52 (.316)			.585	.547
6.8.8	36	−.122 (1.118)	.874 (6.678)[a]		−.014 (.095)		.584	.545
6.8.9	36	−.194 (1.820)	.927 (6.960)[a]			1.41 (1.338)[c]	.606	.569

Notes: the dependent variable is RNA_t; figures in brackets are t-ratios; a, b and c indicate significance at the .01, .05 and .10 levels respectively using a one-tail test; the regression coefficient relating to the dummy variables EXF_{t-1} and $EXFB_{t-1}$ are expressed as percentage points.

unprofitable small firms seeking external finance raised their future profitability by 6.73 percentage points compared with otherwise similar internally financed firms. In medium and large firms the corresponding figures were 4.46 and 1.41 percentage points respectively. Thus, the market appeared to require a greater improvement in the profitability of small and medium-sized firms which had below-average profitability and sought external finance.

A closer look at the underlying relationships reveal that the market's behaviour was rational. Within each size category the operating risk of externally financed firms with below-average past profitability was generally higher than that of similar internally financed firms. Also externally financed companies were exposed to considerably higher financial risks, i.e. they had higher gearing ratios. Between size categories we find that, although the rates of return on net assets were roughly comparable, the operating risks declined as firm size increased. Furthermore, the average rate of return on equity assets increased with size. Larger firms were able (essentially because of their less risky nature) to raise proportionately more, and cheaper, external finance. Hence, pressures on large firms to raise future profitability to finance new equity and loan capital were much less severe than on smaller companies.

Another point is the persistence of profitability, as indicated by the value of the coefficient on RNA_{t-1}. Generally it was high and statistically significant. In the 'all companies' sample about half of above-or-below-average profitability persisted, which is close to the figure for the UK estimated by Whittington. If, as the results have suggested, the main function of capital market restraint is to raise the profitability of hitherto relatively unprofitable companies, we should expect to find the persistence of profitability to be lowest where this market discipline has been shown to be most effective. For example, we find that persistence of profitability was lower in non-mature firms than in mature firms and lowest in small firms. However, the company-controlled group showed the lowest persistence among the three control-type categories. A larger proportion of company-controlled firms with below-average profitability in 1966-7 to 1968-9 had significantly improved their profitability by 1972-3 to 1974-5, and this was regardless of whether external finance had been raised or not. Hence disciplinary action seemed to originate from within and not from outside these firms. The final issue concerns the relationship between past growth and future profitability. In the UK Whittington found that growth had a highly significant negative effect on future profitability, suggesting that some firms, at least, were investing beyond the margin of profitability. In our tests a much weaker negative relationship was found in the 'all companies' sample. However, the extent of the effect appeared to be more pronounced among owner-controlled firms, mature firms and in medium-sized firms.

The Market for Corporate Control

Theoretical Expectations

While Berle and Means (1932, pp. 82-3) dismissed the effectiveness of a market for corporate control, Hindley (1969, p. 431) and Manne (1965, p. 113) regarded it as the ultimate external restraint protecting the interests of shareholders. There is a substantial body of theories regarding the motivations and logic behind the buying and selling of corporate control.[9] There have also been a number of studies examining the efficiency of the market for corporate control (Kuehn, 1969; Hindley, 1969; Singh, 1971; Kuehn, 1975). A relatively recent US study (Holl, 1977) was aimed at identifying which large management-controlled firms had evaded market discipline and comparing the profitability performance of these firms with that of a matched sample of all owner-controlled firms. However, very little effort has been directed at the question of how the character of control affects the working of this market mechanism.

If there existed a frictionless and perfect market in corporate control, resources would be allocated in an optimal manner as far as stockholders and the capital market are concerned. That is, internally inefficient managers would be displaced through takeovers. But this requires, *inter alia*, that the market be able to determine whether the observed performance of a firm is indeed due to sub-optimal performance by management, which in turn requires intimate knowledge of internal operations in a target company. Information costs, transactions costs and the rationalisation costs will be non-negligible. Considering these costs Williamson (1969, p. 317) concluded that 'the market for corporate control would appear to be imperfect'.

Ceteris paribus, the ease with which a successful takeover bid can be mounted will be a function of the size of the target corporation. A large firm has more complex organisational structure, which raises the capital and information costs facing a bidder. The bidder will normally need to be larger than the target, which for large firms reduces the number of potential market raiders. Finally, larger firms will have greater resources with which to organise a defence.

Holding other things (including firm size) constant, the ease of takeover will also be a function of the distribution of share ownership, that is, of the character of control.[10] This factor is often mentioned by researchers (for example, see Hannah, 1974; Kuehn, 1975), but is seldom expanded upon.[11] In unlisted private ownership companies takeovers often arise out of changes in family circumstances. By selling control owners can capitalise their future earnings stream as capital gains rather than as dividends, which are taxed at a higher rate. Family circumstances may also have some bearing on closely held listed companies — especially those in which first-generation owners are still active in management — although a takeover bid would be conditional upon family acceptances. Hence, the attitude of the board would be crucial and, if it were known in advance to be hostile, a bid might not be considered.

Reporting the results of a major study of UK takeovers Kuehn (1975, p. 40) found that over 90 per cent of offers were successful. There is no doubt that bidders were being careful to approach only those firms where they felt their chances to be best. However, it is interesting that three-quarters of the 44 unsuccessful offers were for firms with net assets of less than £5 million. The reason was that in these firms voting control was firmly in the hands of the directors. Hence, in private ownership companies vulnerability to an uninvited market raid will depend more on the structure of shareholdings than on firm size. However, given the level of shareholdings controlled by incumbent directors, the ease of takeover would still diminish with size.

In a dispersed ownership (or management-controlled) company top management will be composed either of true professionals with a relatively small ownership stake, or of former owner-controllers who may have retained a substantial but proportionately small equity interest. Furthermore, the wealth of this latter group is likely to be much more highly diversified than that of owner-controllers. Since financial institutions often make up the bulk of holdings in such companies and may be willing to sell their holdings if an attractive offer is made, these firms will be more vulnerable to a takeover bid. Small firms are most vulnerable because the dispersion of share-holdings is lower than in large firms. Generally speaking, protection is afforded only by size and this realisation must place a good deal of pressure to perform on those managements of smaller companies which value their independence.

In the company-controlled sector the *market* mechanism, of itself, will be ineffective in disciplining management through the threat of a takeover bid. Here the corrective discipline must come from *within*, either at the initiative of the board or the dominant stockholder company. Once it has a dominant shareholding the parent company has considerable discretion over the firm's future. If difficulties are encountered it can institute reforms in management, increase its control by buying out minority shareholdings or divest itself of the subsidiary's assets. In these circumstances the market may act as a barometer in notifying the parent that action is required. Also, since the parent already has effective control over the firm, size considerations will not play the same role that they do in, say, management-controlled firms.

Testing the Effectiveness of Corrective Discipline

Holl (1977) devised a test of the effectiveness of the corrective discipline of the market for corporate control in which it was argued that in the longer period a firm's management will take corrective action in order to avert takeover. Such action will eventually translate into a rising valuation ratio, so that if the market operates efficiently it will ensure that a firm 'pursue policies which result in its valuation ratio moving towards the long run industry average'. Hence, the basic relationship proposed by Holl was of the form,

$$VAL_{i,t} = \beta_0 + \beta_1 VAL_{i,t-1} + \varepsilon_{i,t} \qquad (6.4)$$

where,

$VAL_{i,t}$	is the valuation ratio of the ith firm, in time period t
$VAL_{i,t-1}$	is the valuation ratio of the ith firm, in time period t−1
β_0 β_1	are constants
ε	is the stochastic error term

A value of $0 > \beta_1 < 1$ would indicate that there is a movement towards the long-run average for all firms over time periods t−1 and t. In other words, the corrective discipline of the market has succeeded *partially* in motivating policies designed to move firms' valuation ratios closer to the industry average. If $\beta_1 = 0$, the constraint is fully effective because firms with below-average valuation ratios in period t—1 would have raised their valuation ratios to equal the industry average in period t. On the other hand, if $\beta_1 > 1$, the constraint is non-existent.

There are at least two problems with this formulation. The first is that the calculations were based on the movements of individual company valuation ratios relative to the average for the entire sample. In the UK Kuehn (1975, p. 53) has argued that 'since the vast majority of takeovers occur within the same or similar industries, it is the performance of the firm with respect to similar firms in the same industry which will single it out as takeover candidate'. Therefore it may be irrelevant to ask how a firm is valued in relation to all firms in the quoted industrial population.[12] This observation may not be particularly valid in the case of the US, where a large proportion of mergers have been of the conglomerate variety, but this is not the case in Australia (Stewart, 1977).

The second problem is that raw values of the valuation ratios in both periods were employed and these will be sensitive to fluctuations in the stock market. Consider the case in which a representative company has a valuation ratio which is two-thirds of the industry (or population) average in period t—1. If the stockmarket is depressed in period t by a factor of .5 in relation to what it was in period t—1, but the representative company nevertheless maintains a valuation ratio in t which is two-thirds of the average valuation ratio in t, using raw values of VAL the slope coefficient would be .5 and indicate a functioning constraint when in effect the relativities of all companies have not changed. Under these circumstances then, if the industry averages in periods t—1 and t were set equal to unity and the positions of individual firms were calculated as proportions of these averages the resultant slope coefficient would also assume a value of unity, indicating that a corrective restraint was non-existent.

An alternative approach is to specify the relationship in the following manner,

$$\frac{VAL_{i,j,t}}{\overline{VAL}_{j,t}} = \beta_0 + \beta_1 \frac{VAL_{i,j,t-1}}{\overline{VAL}_{j,t-1}} + \varepsilon_{i,j} \qquad (6.5)$$

where,

is the valuation ratio of the ith firm in industry j in period t

$\overline{VAL}_{j,t}$	is the average valuation ratio for all firms in industry j in period t
$VAL_{i,j,t-1}$	is the valuation ratio of the ith firm in industry j in period t−1
$\overline{VAL}_{j,t-1}$	is the average valuation ratio for all firms in industry j in period t−1
β_0 β_1	are constants
ε	is the stochastic error term
t	refers to the years 1972-3 to 1974-5
t−1	refers to the years 1966-7 to 1968-9

This formulation allows us to take into account both the industry effects and general stock market effects which were not considered by Holl. To recapitulate, if we show that β_1 is not significantly different from unity, or that it is significantly greater than unity for a group of companies arranged by control type, this is tantamount to showing that this control group was free to ignore the corrective discipline of the market for corporate control. Conversely, if we obtain an estimate of β_1 which is significantly less than unity we may conclude that the constraint is operating in some degree. However, to conclude that the constraint is *fully* effective we must be able to show that β_1 is significantly less than one and not significantly different from zero. Following Holl, our *a priori* hypothesis would be that the coefficient β_1 should increase with firm size. However, the results which are shown in Table 6.9 do not appear to support his hypothesis. Rather, in each size category the market was at least partially ineffective and, contrary to expectations, the value of the β_1 coefficient falls marginally as we move from the small to the large firm category.

The analysis is repeated in part (b) of Table 6.9, where firms are grouped according to control type. Here, Holl's hypothesis that the market is more effective in restraining owner-controlled firms *appears* to be borne out. In owner-controlled firms the β_1 coefficient of .131 is not significantly different from zero and is almost four times smaller than the coefficient obtained in the management-controlled sample. However, management-controlled firms had valuation ratios which were on average between 6.2 and 9.6 points above their industry's average, while the valuation ratios of owner-controlled firms were 10.4 and 6.2 points below average. The results for company-controlled firms are similar to those for management-controlled firms.

In Table 6.10 firms are cross-classified by size *and* control type.

Table 6.9: Corrective Discipline of the Market for Corporate Control

Equation number	Category	n	$\overline{VAL}_{t-1}$	$\overline{VAL}_t$	β_0	β_1	t-ratio $Ho:\beta=0$	t-ratio $Ho:\beta=1$	r^2	$\bar{r}^2$	MCC
By firm size:											
6.9.1	Small	63	1.034	1.114	.704	.397	(3.496)[a]	(5.322)[a]	.167	.153	?
6.9.2	Medium	81*	.935	.905	.543	.387	(3.104)[a]	(4.911)[a]	.109	.097	?
6.9.3	Large	49	1.065	.980	.614	.344	(2.615)[b]	(4.991)[a]	.127	.108	?
By control type:											
6.9.4	OC	68	.896	.938	.820	.131	(1.068)	(7.059)[a]	.017	.002	+
6.9.5	MC	75	1.062	1.096	.581	.485	(4.455)[a]	(4.729)[a]	.214	.203	?
6.9.6	CC	50*	1.050	.910	.408	.478	(3.525)[a]	(3.846)[a]	.206	.189	?

Notes: a denotes significance at the .01 level using a one-tail test; + indicates that the market for corporate control (MCC) operated perfectly; indicates that the market for corporate control operated imperfectly; * United Telecasters Ltd was exluded from the sample since its adjusted valuation ratio had a value of 128.

Table 6.10: Corrective Discipline of the Market for Corporate Control, by Firm Size and Control Type

Equation number	Control type	n	$\overline{VAL}_{t-1}$	$\overline{VAL}_t$	β_0	β_1	t-ratio Ho:β=0	t-ratio Ho:β=1	r^2	$\bar{r}^2$	MCC
Small firms:											
6.10.1	OC	31	.882	1.001	1.025	−.027	(.158)	(5.957)[a]	.001	<0	+
6.10.2	MC	18	1.226	1.360	.759	.492	(2.529)[b]	(2.611)[a]	.286	.241	?
6.10.3	CC	14	1.131	1.046	.488	.494	(1.657)[c]	(1.719)[c]	.186	.118	?
Medium-sized firms:											
6.10.4	OC	27	.832	.842	.667	.210	(.838)	(3.156)[a]	.027	<0	+
6.10.5	MC	28	.960	1.028	.542	.507	(2.039)[b]	(1.984)[b]	.138	.105	?
6.10.6	CC	26*	1.015	.837	.369	.461	(2.589)[b]	(3.027)[a]	.218	.186	?
Large Firms:											
6.10.7	OC	10	1.112	1.001	.640	.324	(1.405)[c]	(2.930)[a]	.198	.098	?
6.10.8	MC	29	1.061	.999	.633	.345	(1.872)[b]	(3.559)[a]	.115	.082	?
6.10.9	CC	10	1.026	.907	.565	.333	(1.073)	(2.148)	.126	.017	+

Notes: a, b and c denote significance at the .01, .05 and .10 levels respectively using a one-tail test; + indicates that the market for corporate control (MCC) operated perfectly; ? indicates that the market for corporate control operated imperfectly; * United Telecasters Ltd was excluded from the sample since its adjusted valuation ratio had a value of 128.

The results reveal basic differences between owner-controlled firms on the one hand and management- and company-controlled firms on the other. In the first group the β_1 coefficient increases with size and our statistical tests, applied literally, indicate that except in the case of large firms the market applied a perfect restraint. However, in management- and company-controlled firms the opposite is found, since the coefficient decreases as firm size increases.

Our tests show that, with the exception of large company-controlled firms, the corrective restraint was an imperfect disciplinarian on non-owner-controlled firms irrespective of firm size. Yet in the large firms group there is little separating the values of coefficients achieved in the three control-type sub-samples. Also, with the exception of the large firms category the average valuation ratios of owner-controlled firms (in relation to their industry averages) were considerably lower than those of management-controlled firms and, to a lesser degree, lower than those of company-controlled firms.

The results appear somewhat confusing. The major problem is that the test proposed by Holl is founded on logic which was employed by Stigler (1963) and Whittington (1971), who were searching for evidence of persistent *profitability* performance. It was argued that the unimpeded operation of market forces should eliminate high profits in some uses, for example through new entry — and low profits in other uses, for example by the exit or takeover of unprofitable firms. Thus, with perfect factor mobility there should be a tendency for above or below average profitability of individual industries and firms to be eliminated over time. In the context of Holl's model it is crucial to recognise that the value of the β_1 depends not only upon how firms with below-average valuation ratios are behaving, but also upon the behaviour of firms with above average valuation ratios.

It has been observed (for example by Singh, 1971) that a high valuation ratio does not necessarily provide protection from takeover. Also, Kuehn (1975) has observed that for different firms there exists a unique valuation ratio at which the probability of takeover is unacceptably high. Our theoretical approach proposes that one factor which determines the value of this critical valuation ratio is the firm's character of control. With a given valuation ratio we expect a dispersed ownership company to be more vulnerable than an owner-controlled company and that this difference in relative vulnerability should decline as firm size increases. It is not surprising that in Table 6.10 we find the average valuation ratio of small management-controlled firms to be almost 40 points higher than similar-sized owner-controlled firms, while in the medium-size category the difference is only 16 points. Thus, in the small and medium-sized firms categories management-controlled firms had valuation ratios which were more highly persistent than in owner-controlled firms, but they were also persistently higher. In our view this indicates that the market for corporate control was imposing greater discipline on management-controlled firms; in order to survive they needed to achieve above average valuation ratios and to maintain them at above average levels. By contrast, owner-controlled firms which had above average valuation ratios in 1966-7 to 1968-9 did not appear to have the same pressure on them to maintain their above average valuation.

Takeover: The Ultimate Discipline

These propositions can be explored further by taking a different view of Holl's model and examining the structure of actual takeover bids

Figure 6.1: Corrective Discipline of the Market for Corporate Control

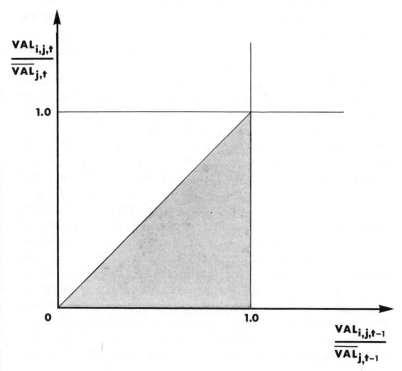

experienced in a subsequent period, 1975-6 to 1978-9. We can say with some assurance that firms which survive with below-average valuation ratios over an extended period without raising their valuation ratio towards the industry average and without experiencing a change in control must, in some way, have been able to avoid market discipline. These are firms which fall within the shaded area in Figure 6.1

The *Australian Financial Review* was examined for reports of takeover bids for companies in the sample over the period from 1975-6 to 1978-9. A total of 55 bids representing 28.3 per cent of the continuing firms sample were identified. As in the UK a high success rate was evident and most of the exceptions were bids for small and medium-sized owner-controlled firms. Table 6.11 displays the prior performances (in terms of post-tax rate of return on equity assets averaged over the period 1966-7 to 1974-5) of firms which experienced bids, together with those of firms which we have defined as evading the market for corporate control (MCC). The main focus will be on comparing the effectiveness of market discipline on management-controlled as opposed to owner-controlled firms.

Our first hypothesis is that given the size of the firm the market's discipline will be more effective in restraining management-controlled firms. Without reference to size we find that a higher proportion of owner-controlled firms (38 per cent) than management-controlled firms (28 per cent) could be said to have evaded the market's discipline. Yet the difference in proportions is particularly marked in the small firms category, is lower among medium-sized firms and is reversed in the large firms group.

The proportion of actual takeovers subsequent to 1974-5 is slightly higher among owner-controlled firms (29.4 per cent as against 26.7 per cent). But we also find that the performance of companies experiencing a bid, relative to those which did not, differed on the basis of control type. Owner-controlled firms which were subject to takeover earned higher profits than the average for all owner-controlled firms in a given size category, while management-controlled firms experiencing a bid generally had below average profitability. This can be explained by the fact that several of the owner-controlled firms which were taken over did so as a result of 'entrepreneurial' factors, while in management-controlled firms a raider more often took control of a firm with lagging performance. Despite these entrepreneurial effects within owner-controlled firms, the management-controlled firms which were taken over had earned

Table 6.11: Corporate Performance and the Market for Corporate Control, by Firm Size and Control Type

Size category	Control type	n_1	Companies subject to a takeover bid			Companies *not* evading the MCC which were subject to a takeover bid			Companies evading the MCC which were subject to a takeover bid			Companies evading the MCC which survived without a takeover bid			Companies evading the MCC			Average
			n_2	$\frac{n_2}{n_1}$ %	REA	n_3	$\frac{n_3}{n_1-n_6}$ %	REA	n_4	$\frac{n_4}{n_6}$ %	REA	n_5	$\frac{n_5}{n_6}$ %	REA	n_6	$\frac{n_6}{n_1}$ %	REA	REA
Small firms																		
	OC	31	9	29.0	11.7	6	30.0	13.9	3	27.3	7.4	8	72.7	7.7	11	35.5	7.6	10.4
	MC	18	7	38.9	12.4	5	31.2	13.5	2	100.0	9.9	0	0.0	—	2	11.1	9.9	12.9
	CC	14	6	42.9	16.6	5	41.7	17.9	1	50.0	10.4	1	50.0	5.3	2	14.3	7.8	12.9
Sub-total		63	22	34.9	13.3	16	33.3	15.0	6	40.0	8.7	9	60.0	7.4	15	23.8	7.9	11.7
Medium-sized firms																		
	OC	27	10	37.0	7.9	5	35.7	8.0	5	38.5	7.7	8	61.5	6.8	13	48.1	7.1	6.9
	MC	28	8	28.6	8.3	4	21.1	9.0	4	44.4	7.5	5	55.6	8.4	9	32.1	8.0	9.5
	CC	27	8	29.6	9.0	3	20.0	8.5	5	41.7	8.0	7	58.3	7.3	12	46.2	7.6	9.8
Sub-total		82	26	31.7	8.1	12	25.0	8.5	14	41.2	7.8	20	58.8	7.5	34	42.0	7.5	8.8
Large firms																		
	OC	10	1	10.0	7.6	1	12.5	7.6	0	0.0	—	2	100.0	8.4	2	20.0	8.4	9.5
	MC	29	5	17.2	8.5	3	15.8	9.9	2	20.0	6.3	8	80.0	7.9	10	38.5	7.6	8.6
	CC	10	1	10.0	14.3	0	0.0	—	1	33.3	14.3	2	66.7	8.2	3	30.0	10.2	8.9
Sub-total		49	7	14.3	9.2	4	11.8	9.3	3	20.0	9.0	12	80.0	8.0	15	32.6	8.2	8.8
All companies		194	55	28.3	10.3	32	24.6	11.9	23	35.9	8.2	41	64.1	7.6	64	33.0	7.8	9.7

Note: the following identities hold: $n_3 + n_4 \equiv n_2$, $n_4 + n_5 \equiv n_6$.

somewhat higher rates of return. Given that takeovers can occur for a variety of reasons, it is perhaps more relevant to consider the proportion of companies evading the market for corporate control which were able to survive without being contested. In each size category a higher proportion of owner-controlled firms evading the market survived with control intact.

Our second hypothesis is that the effectiveness of the market restraint will diminish with size, but that this effect will be stronger in the case of management-controlled firms. In Table 6.11 we find that the proportion of management-controlled firms able to evade the market increased with size, whereas in the owner-controlled category the highest proportion was in medium-sized firms. This pattern is replicated in the column showing firms which were subject to takeover. It is also of interest to note that only six of the 68 owner-controlled firms had what could be considered a strong institutional component in their structure of shareholdings. But five of these firms encountered a takeover offer and only one (McEwens Ltd) was able to survive with the original directors still in control.

Our hypothesis regarding company-controlled firms is that the external market for corporate control and firm size will be less relevant. In Table 6.11 it is apparent that the record for company control is unique in a number of respects. The proportion of firms which evaded market discipline was lowest in the small firms category. However, in relative terms, firms in this category experienced the greatest takeover activity. Another distinguishing feature is that in each size category the rate of return earned by those firms subject to takeover was higher than that of firms in other control types which experienced bids.

Here changes in control must be viewed as investment decisions made by the controlling company. Of the 15 firms which experienced a bid, in nine cases the controlling company was extending its shareholding and in six of these control was already 'strong' (i.e. more than 42 per cent of shares were held). In the six remaining instances the controlling firm was divesting itself of ownership in the company. In both the small and medium-sized firms categories, firms in which the controlling company was expanding its ownership were on average at least 2.4 percentage points more profitable than those in which the takeover represented a divestiture. Thus, companies preferred to integrate reasonably profitable firms and discard the relatively unprofitable ones. The fact that absorptions and spin-offs of small firms are much easier to effect probably explains why they were involved in such a high proportion of takeovers. However, there remained several company-controlled firms which had earned below-average profits and had evaded market discipline while not meeting with the same fate. Perhaps internal control measures were in the process of trying to improve performance, but since the period involved is quite long we cannot rule out the possibility that they were simply ineffective.

Summary

Our initial investigations showed that in Australia the profitability performance of listed companies is generally negatively associated with firm size, although among the top 100 firms the relation tends to level off. The lower profitability of very large firms is accompanied by lower variability of earnings. This picture conforms with the results frequently reported in UK and continental European studies. Thus, it appears that the advantages often ascribed to size, such as economies of scale or market power, are not being directed towards raising profitability. It has been suggested that the discretion which managers of large firms enjoy is instead being directed to the pursuit of non-profit-maximising objectives.

Small and medium-sized firms which operated in highly concentrated industries and were free of competitive restraints increased their rate of return over those in less concentrated industries. But the rates of return earned by large firms did not display any relationship to industry concentration. The implication of these findings is that, while some small firms may have been free of competitive pressure in their product market, unlike large firms they were not free of other market restraints on their behaviour. Our model proposes that the capital market restraint and the market for corporate control will impose greater discipline on small firms. That is, if they are to survive, they must perform satisfactorily in the face of these pressures.

Another striking feature of the results was that the shape and position of the size-profitability relationships depended on control type. It is our contention that this reflects the extent to which the effectiveness of market restraints is dependent on firm size. Of particular interest is the finding that the negative association between size and profitability was more pronounced in management-controlled than in owner-controlled firms. The following sections demonstrated that this was primarily the outcome of two factors.

First, in comparison to management-controlled firms, owner-controlled firms avoided the capital market restraint. Second, in management-controlled firms the effectiveness of the takeover restraint was more highly dependent on firm size.

In general, firms were found to display considerable interest in outside sources of funds. However, it has been the management- and company-controlled firms which have shown a strong preference for external funds when compared with private ownership companies. As in the UK it is the largest firms which have made proportionately greater use of external sources. Whether this capital market scrutiny was effective in constraining managers is another matter. Our tests revealed that the market's discipline was primarily directed at the elimination of below-average profitability performance. This corroborates the findings of Whittington in the UK. However, this discipline was most effective in raising the profitability of small and non-mature firms. Capital market discipline was not important in raising the profitability of company-controlled firms with below-average profitability. It may be that in these firms internal controls were important.

Our results have suggested that as in the US and the UK the market for corporate control in Australia has been a somewhat imperfect disciplinarian. We have confirmed that in general the extent of ineffectiveness increases with firm size but that this was most pronounced among management-controlled firms. In owner-controlled firms the incumbent ownership group could more often retain control despite prolonged periods of depressed earnings. Since this ability depended crucially on the composition of shareholdings it was more independent of firm size. In company-controlled firms the external market for corporate control was of little consequence, except in so far as it provided a guide to decisions made by the parent concern. If subsidiaries were not performing up to the standards set for them they were disposed of in the market, while good performers were internalised.

The relationships which have emerged in this chapter may be summarised with the aid of Figure 6.2. In the framework of our model the product market constraint sets the upper limit to profitability performance. One exception to this is when corporations reach a very large (and therefore conspicuous) size, where societal and governmental pressures are brought to bear. In general terms this upper bound is market specific, although it may vary within a market depending on the composition of mobility barriers (see Caves and

Figure 6.2: Performance Boundaries Set by the Market for Corporate Control

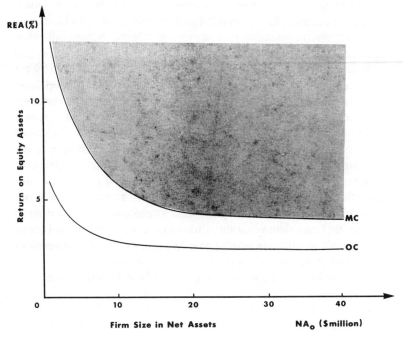

Porter, 1977) or strategic groups (Porter, 1979). Thus potential performance may vary within a product market.

The market for corporate control, on the other hand, sets the lower limit to acceptable performance. This constraint is economy wide and common to all firms. However, we have argued that it is affected by the control condition and by firm size. In Figure 6.2 the constraint is interpreted as the rate of return at each size level which must be achieved if takeover is to be averted. The two curves show the constraints for management-controlled (MC) and owner-controlled (OC) firms. The shaded area above MC shows that we would expect to find observations in that area for management-controlled firms.

In contrast, observations for owner-controlled firms will lie above OC. The general shapes of these curves indicate that size is a defence against takeover. However, the MC curve falls more steeply because small firms with dispersed ownership are more vulnerable to takeover than are small owner-controlled firms where incumbent directors are in possession of a strategic defensive shareholding. Thus, in the smaller size ranges the *difference* in discretion enjoyed by top management in management- and owner-controlled companies is large, but becomes progressively smaller as firm size increases. This is because it becomes almost as difficult to mount a successful raid on a large dispersed ownership company as on a large owner-controlled firm.

It is our contention that corporate performance within these bounds will depend on two more factors: the capital market constraint and managerial incentives. The capital market constraint, we have noted, is also economy wide, but the propensity to submit to it depends on control type, while its effectiveness depends on firm size and maturity. Managerial incentives, as represented by directorial shareholdings, are firm specific, although greater magnitudes tend to be associated with owner-controlled firms. In Chapter 4 we found that the responsiveness of profitability performance to directorial holdings tended to be roughly similar for management- and owner-controlled firms. The puzzling differences in intercepts estimated in equations run on owner- and management-controlled samples in Chapter 4 have been explained in the present chapter. In the next chapter we draw together all the strands of the model.

Notes

1. These hypotheses would appear to have particular relevance in a country such as Australia. Sheridan (1968) concluded that in 1961-2 about 47 per cent of Australia's most important industries were either monopolies or tight oligopolies. More recently Round (1976c) showed that Australian industries are more highly concentrated than in America. Also, see Karmel and Brunt (1966) and Brown and Hughes (1970).

2. For a review see Weiss (1974). Dissenting views have come from Stigler (1963), Brozen (1970, 1971a, 1971b, 1973) and Ornstein (1975).

3. Applying the test to the 'all companies' sample it was found that in the profitability equations we could reject the null hypothesis of homoscedasticity at the .01 level and, in the growth and risk equations, at the .05 level.

4. Even the return to holders on preference stock and debentures may be curtailed or delayed if overall profitability slumps considerably.

5. A 1 per cent cut-off point was employed to denote significant use of external finance since many companies with minority shareholders will appear to have grown by external means simply because they have retained a portion of profits attributable to these shareholders.

6. In Australia Sheridan (1974) found persistency in inter-firm profit rates, as have researchers elsewhere (e.g. Singh and Whittington, 1968; Whittington, 1971 in the UK and Mueller, 1977 in the US). The main problem, however, lies in the determination of which factor(s) *cause* the observed persistence to arise. For example, Porter (1979, p. 214) has stated that it was his intention to 'present a

theory of the determinants of companies' profits which rest[ed] on the *structure within industries* ... to provide ... an explanation ... for persistent intraindustry differences among firms' (emphasis in original).

7. The three non-mature domestically owned companies were excluded from the company-controlled category because of their exceptional behaviour. On average these firms were quite young. Two of the three maintained high rates of return throughout the study period and one went from making losses in the first sub-period to earn exceptionally high profits during sub-period 3. Since neither of these firms made new issues their profitability records made externally financed company-controlled firms appear relatively unprofitable.

8. As one writer put it, 'there are only 40 to 50 of the 1,420 listed corporations in Australia, which offer sufficient trading activity to attract the investment of overseas institutions' (Turnbull, 1976, p. 24).

9. See Hindley (1972) for a review of the literature in this area.

10. For example, consider the following statement of an experienced practitioner at a seminar on takeovers: 'it is essential to closely analyse the register of shareholders grouping large related holdings together ... The holding of institutions is also vital and broad links between the directors and the institutions should be studied' (Marks, 1977, p. 6).

11. One exception in this regard is a study by Davies and Kuehn (1977) which considered the influence of private ownership control and membership of declining industries as hindrances to the corporate control mechanism.

12. Inter-industry differences in valuation ratios in the UK are well documented in Singh and Whittington (1968) and Singh (1971).

7 OWNERS, MANAGERS AND MARKETS

Introduction

The tasks of the present chapter are threefold. The first task is to draw together the various elements of our model of the determinants of company performance. Thus, three sub-models, corresponding to the three control conditions identified in this study, are presented in the next section. There we introduce for the first time the effects of interrelationships between the performance variables which have often been overlooked by previous researchers. Second, we examine the determinants of performance *within* each control-type category. Our research has shown that internal and external influences on managerial performance vary according to the character of control. Yet previous researchers have ignored these interactions. Furthermore, it is our view that differences in performance *between* control types cannot be understood without reference to the determination of performance within them.

The third task is to consider the effect of control type on performance. This has been the principal focus of past studies in this area, but is approached somewhat differently here. Without first considering the determinants of performance within control types previous studies have been unable to furnish substantial reasons for why differences in performance arose or, for that matter, why no difference was found. Thus, if it was found that the profitability of owner-controlled firms was higher than in management-controlled firms, it was concluded that owner-managers had the incentive to maximise profits more closely. On the other hand, if there was no difference in profitability based on control type, it has been assumed that professional managers and owner-managers alike are maximising profits.

Our model stresses that performance will depend on the incentives available to managers and on the restraints on managerial discretion. Hence, with a given area of discretion which is determined by effectiveness of internal and external restraints on managerial behaviour, actual performance will depend on the incentives available to them. In Chapter 6 it was found that although large size is associated with relative freedom from product market restraints, it is also associated with freedom from stock market restraints — and this is what distinguishes large firms from small and medium-sized firms. Therefore, separate analyses are presented for large firms and for small to medium-sized firms. In the former category managers are largely insulated from external market restraints, while in the latter the area of discretion available to managers will depend on the effectiveness of both internal and external restraints. The chapter concludes with a summary and interpretation of the results.

The Model

Put over-simply, our model maintains that corporate performance (P) is determined by the net effects of managerial incentives and the internal and external restraints on managerial discretion. Thus,

Performance $\quad\Phi$ (managerial incentives, internal restraints, investment opportunities (maturity), market power, capital market restraints, the market for corporate control, ε) $\qquad$ (7.1)

where $\qquad\varepsilon$ is the stochastic error term

In turn, however, the nature of internal restraints will be a function of the firm's character of the control. Therefore, we have what are in effect three models, one for each character of control.

Model 1: Owner-controlled firms

$$P = \beta_0 + \beta_1 (\ln) \text{VDH} + \beta_2 \text{WOC} + \beta_3 \text{INST} + \beta_4 \text{NMAT} + \beta_5 \text{SIZE} + \varepsilon \qquad (7.2)$$

Model 2: Management-controlled firms

$$P = \beta_0 + \beta_1 (\ln) \text{VDH} + \beta_2 \text{INST} + \beta_3 \text{NMAT} + \beta_4 \text{SIZE} + \varepsilon \qquad (7.3)$$

Model 3: Company-controlled firms

$$P = \beta_0 + \beta_1 (\ln) \text{VDH} + \beta_2 \text{CHD} + \beta_3 \text{FOR} + \beta_4 \text{NMAT} + \beta_5 \text{SIZE} + \varepsilon \qquad (7.4)$$

where,

P	is firm performance, defined alternatively as RNA, pre-tax rate of return on net assets REA, post-tax rate of return on equity assets GHA, growth rate of net assets SDRNA, operating risk RET, retention ratio
(ln) VDH	is (the natural logarithm of) the value of directors' shareholdings
WOC	is a dummy variable which indicates weak owner control, taking a value of 1 when directors as a cohesive group accounted for between 10 and 42 per cent of issued shares, and zero otherwise.
INST	is a dummy variable indicating a strong institutional shareholding, taking a value of 1 when institutional holdings among the largest 20 cohesive groups accounted for more than 50 per cent of the groups' holdings and institutional holdings accounted for more than 15 per cent of shares of issue and zero otherwise.
CHD	is a dummy variable reflecting strong company control, taking a value of 1 if the firm had a company shareholding in excess of 42 per cent and zero otherwise.
FOR	is a dummy variable indicating foreign control, taking a value of 1 when the firm had a substantial foreign shareholding (i.e. $\geqslant 15$ per cent) and zero otherwise.
NMAT	is a dummy variable representing investment opportunities available to the firm, taking a value of 1 when the firm was non-mature and zero otherwise.
SIZE	defined as the reciprocal of opening net assets this variable is a measure of firm size and as such it

proxies for freedom from product market as well as stock market restraints.

These equations can be expanded to take account of interrelationships among the dependent variables. It is quite probable that the introduction of profitability, risk and growth as additional explanatory variables will introduce an element of multicollinearity into the estimation of the models. This is particularly so in the case of model 1 because of the relatively high simple correlations between SIZE and profitability (RNA, $r = .569$; REA, $r = .518$) and between SIZE and GNA ($r = .774$). However, it is of considerable interest to see whether the signs and significance of the explanatory variables in equations 7.2, 7.3 and 7.4 persist when these interrelationships are included, or are highly dependent on model specification.

As a final point some mention should be made of comparisons of performance between control types. Within the framework of our model, once the differences in managerial incentives (VDH), investment opportunities (NMAT) and market power (SIZE) are accounted for, any remaining differences in performance between control types must be due to differing internal restraints on managers. In earlier chapters it was argued that there will exist interaction effects between internal and external (stock market) restraints and between firm size and the effectiveness of stock market restraints.

To incorporate all these interaction effects in one equation explaining the determination of each performance variable would require a large number of interaction terms. It is not known exactly what form these interactions should take. Such a model would also be subject to a high degree of multicollinearity among the independent variables. In order to circumvent these problems our approach is to estimate separate equations for each control type and further to split the sample into two size categories with a cut-off point of $20 million in net assets in 1966. Dividing the sample by control type and size category has an associated advantage in that the statistical problems of heteroscedastic residuals are largely eliminated. This is because two of the *causes* of variations in performance — namely, the degree of discretion enjoyed by managers in firms of varying size and alternative characters of control — have been isolated. In 17 of the 20 equations for which the Goldfeld-Quandt test could be applied the null hypothesis of homoscedasticity could not be rejected at the .05 level of significance. Thus, in general no transformation of the data was necessary and OLS estimates are given.

Hypotheses

Interrelationships among Dependent Variables

The dependent variables reflecting corporate performance are: pre-tax rate of return on net assets (RNA); post-tax rate of return on equity assets (REA); growth rate of net assets (GNA); operating risk (SDRNA); and the retention ratio (RET). However, it is of some interest to consider the possible interrelationships between these variables. Previous studies have tended to ignore relationships between performance variables, even though these may be important. For instance, several studies employing more than one performance variable in comparing owner- and management-controlled firms have found that, when the former were more profitable, they also grew faster and were more risky (see Chapter 2). We shall consider the possible relationships between the dependent variables in turn.

Profitability. Theory suggests that growth can have either a positive or a negative effect on profitability. A growing firm can provide a stimulating atmosphere for management and, to the extent that growth requires additional finance to be obtained in the capital market, we should expect a positive relationship between growth and profitability. On the other hand, if a firm grows too rapidly, its managerial resources may become strained and as a result profitability will turn down. However, in a cross-sectional study it is unlikely that a parabolic relationship will be observed, since firms in the sample will have different investment opportunities. Hence, we would expect to find a positive growth-profitability relationship.

It is almost axiomatic in the economics and financial literature that, *ceteris paribus*, higher risks are compensated by higher returns. That is, we should expect that if higher risks are taken by managers, these will need to be rewarded with a higher rate of return. Therefore, our hypothesis is that the assumption of greater risk will have a positive influence on profitability.

Growth. A firm's profitability will have a profound influence on its *ability* to grow. High profits will mean that new investment can be financed out of retained earnings and a good record of current profitability will heighten the firm's chances of attracting external finance. Hence, a positive profitability–growth relationship is hypothesised. This raises the problem of simultaneity in the determination of profitability and growth. However, a single equation format is retained.[1]

Risk. There is also likely to be an element of simultaneity in the determination of risk and profitability. Thus, the level of risk assumed by a firm is expected to be influenced by the level of profitability sought by management. If managers wish to attain a high rate of profit they will need to endure the possibility of greater variations in profits. Again, simultaneous estimation will not be attempted.[2]

Retentions. A firm's profitability is expected to be a leading determinant of its retention ratio. The demonstration of high rates of return will provide management with a rationale for retaining a large proportion of profits within the company. Tax differentials on dividends and capital gains encourage this practice since, if earnings are reinvested profitably, rather than distributed as dividends and taxed in the hands of shareholders, they can be recouped at a later date as capital gains. On the other hand, if profitability is low, management may be concerned about the possibility of a takeover bid and will be anxious not to drop the dividend payout. In order to maintain shareholder loyalty, then, these low profitability firms can be expected to exhibit low retention ratios. For these reasons it is hypothesised that profitability will be positively related to the retention ratio.

The Independent Variables

Managerial Incentives. A major element of the incentive structure open to managers is the value of shareholdings in their possession. Up to a point, more shareholdings by directors are expected to promote a unity of interest with other shareholders. However, interests may conflict when directors' shareholdings become very large (i.e. the directors will then be in a higher personal income tax bracket than the average investor), or where these shareholdings are seen by directors as being essential to their continued control over the company. Nevertheless, it is argued that directors' shareholdings (VDH) will be positively related to profitability, growth and the retention ratio and negatively related to business risk.

The Character of Control and Internal Restraints. Since the director-led cohesive ownership group (DCG) in *owner-controlled firms* (OC firms) is by definition the dominant shareholder (with at least 10

per cent of the shares), votes are concentrated in its hands. The higher
is the proportion of shares held by the director group, the less
opportunity there is for a dissident faction outside the group to
organise an effective opposition to it.

Because directors in weak owner-controlled firms (WOC) have
more to fear from shareholders we would expect their profitability to
be higher, and their risk exposure to be lower, than in firms where
directors have absolute control. Also, the survival strategies of
directors in these WOC firms are likely to differ from those of
directors with absolute control. The latter will be intent on retaining
their commanding position in the shareholding structure and this will
require a high retention ratio and minimal reliance on external
finance. Thus, a positive relationship is hypothesised between WOC
and growth, while a negative relationship is hypothesised between
WOC and retentions.

In *management-controlled firms* (MC firms) the most effective
internal restraint on managerial discretion is that which can be
applied by alert and well-informed investors — the financial institutions. The investment departments of the larger institutions closely
monitor the performance of companies in which they have interests.
Managers of firms with strong institutional shareholdings will need to
maintain good relations with institutions, because they may require
their support in capital raisings and in order to avert a takeover bid.

Strong institutional shareholding applies predominantly to
management-controlled companies, but it is also found in a few
companies under weak owner control. In order to survive, such firms
will need to maintain their efficiency levels and thus a positive
relationship is expected between INST and profitability. Since
institutions are long-term investors they will prefer a higher growth
rate and growth will entail more external finance and higher retentions. In Australia these effects are likely to be reinforced by the
limited investment opportunities open to institutions. The fact that
institutions must compete with foreign capital inflows, their inability
to invest internationally and the high foreign ownership levels in
Australian industries all combine to suggest that institutions would
prefer to see direct reinvestment of corporate profits. As institutions
are generally risk averse and are removed from day-to-day decision-
making in companies which make up their portfolio, we should
expect INST to be negatively related to operating risk.

We know there are a variety of motives for inter-company shareholdings which result in *company-controlled firms* (CC). As a result

it is difficult to formulate hypotheses regarding their behaviour. However, the discretion available to managers in these firms is likely to be lower where the controlling company has a strong shareholding (CHD) and greater where the controlling firm is a foreign concern (FOR), because it is more difficult to control the activities of an international subsidiary. Since firms where managerial discretion is greatest will presumably be able to engage in more X-inefficient practices, profitability and growth should be higher where company control is strong and lower where foreign control is present. Since retentions represent greater discretion, we should expect these to be higher in foreign-controlled firms and lower in strong company-controlled firms. However, another reason for high retentions in foreign subsidiaries may be the wish to forestall payment of with-holding tax on dividends. It is more difficult to formulate a hypothesis regarding risk. On the one hand, the absence of an internal restraint can relieve pressure on management to smooth fluctuations in earnings. On the other hand, the more involved the controlling firm becomes in the day-to-day operations of its 'subsidiary', the less alarmed it will be when earnings do fluctuate.

The Product Market Restraint. The concept of market power has so many dimensions that it has been notoriously difficult to quantify. As a 'catch all' proxy for market power firm size is a good candidate. The size of a firm will be related to entry barriers, as for example those associated with capital costs, advertising and research and development expenditures. Firm size is also likely to be positively, if by no means perfectly, correlated with market share. Finally, following the 'shared assets' view of market power, firm size is likely to be positively related to the four-firm concentration ratio.[3] In view of these arguments size should be positively associated with profitability. But since size emancipates managers from the restraint of the product market it also allows them to pursue non-profit-maximising objectives. This consideration is especially significant if firm size is also coupled with relative freedom from other market restraints on managerial discretion. Therefore, we will make no *a priori* judgements as to the expected relationships between firm size and profitability, growth and retentions. However, there are strong reasons for expecting operating risk to be related negatively to firm size. First, because large firms tend to be more highly diversified than small ones. Second, because lower risk may be an element of the managers' utility functions. That is, managers may wish to trade the possibility of higher returns for more stable returns and the discretion which market power allows may be used to smooth fluctuations in earnings. Another factor which adds to this expectation is that the typical manager's portfolio is generally less diversified than that of the typical investor.

Stock Market Restraints. Greater reliance on the capital market will enable firms to grow more rapidly. However, if the *capital market* is efficient it will allocate funds to those firms which can make the best use of these resources. Thus, if firms wish to grow through external financing they will be constrained by the capital market to earn a satisfactory rate of return on new investment.

Our findings indicate that large size is not indicative of independence from the capital market. On the contrary, since large firms are more heavily traded and can make new issues more cheaply, their reliance on the capital market has been substantial. However, the capital market does not appear to be highly selective in allocating funds to large firms. In contrast, small to medium-sized and non-mature firms which approach the market earn significantly higher future rates of return than otherwise similar internally financed companies. Thus, the managers of large firms enjoy a degree of discretion as a result of the capital market being less discriminating in allocating finance to them. Therefore, size proxies for freedom from capital market restraint and on this count we should expect profitability to be negatively associated with firm size. Also, it should be noted that in many cases owner-controlled firms (particularly where directors have absolute control) avoid the capital market restraint altogether, choosing instead to finance entirely from internal sources. Thus, on the basis of capital market scrutiny we should expect management-controlled firms to be more profitable than owner-controlled firms of a given size.

Given the financial performance of a firm, the effectiveness of the *market for corporate control* will depend on two factors: firm size and the structure of shareholdings. Where the ownership structure is widely dispersed size will be the most important consideration. However, institutional domination of the share register could make a market raid easier to effect. In owner-controlled firms where directors have absolute control, there is no reason to fear an uninvited bid for the control of the company. But directors of weak owner-controlled firms will have more to fear from a raider, especially when their shareholdings are matched or surpassed by institutional holdings. Yet the directors of owner-controlled firms, even when this control is said to be 'weak', will enjoy considerably greater freedom from the takeover restraint than will the directors of a similar sized management-controlled firm. In company-controlled firms the market indicators are important in so far as they provide a guide to the controlling company on the effectiveness of their internal restraint on management. Hence, our hypothesis is that large firms will have less reason to fear a takeover bid and therefore less pressure to maximise profits but, for a given size, management-controlled firms will be more vulnerable than owner-controlled firms.

Firm Maturity. The stage of maturity will reflect the investment opportunities available to the firm. As such, non-maturity (NMAT) will have repercussions on both the incentives and restraints faced by managers. When investment opportunities exceed internally generated funds we would expect managers to engage in greater external financing (see Chapter 6) and therefore to attract the attention of the financial community. The managers of non-mature firms may wish to grow rapidly, but they will prefer profitable growth, as this will affect the firm's future growth prospects. If investment opportunities are high we would also expect managers to accept greater risk in their operations. Thus, our hypotheses are that non-maturity will be positively related to profitability, growth, risk and retentions.

The predicted signs are summarised in Table 7.1.

Results for Small and Medium-Sized Firms

Owner-Controlled Firms

The results of the model explaining firm performance within the owner-controlled category are displayed in Table 7.2. The equations which exclude interrelationships between the dependent variables are of primary interest. Here application of the test devised by Farrar and Glauber (1967) revealed that multicollinearity is only a problem between NMAT and SIZE.

As expected, directorial shareholdings are positively and significantly related to both profitability and growth. The coefficient on VDH in the risk equation (7.2.7) is negative, but the effect is very minor. Whether directors held large or small shareholdings in their company made little difference to the riskiness of the firm's oper-

Table 7.1: Predicted Signs on Independent Variables

Dependent variable	ln VDH	VDH	WOC	INST	CHD	FOR	NMAT	SIZE	RNA	GNA	SDRNA	SDREA
RNA	+		+	+	−	+	?		+	+	+	
REA	+		+	+	−	+	?		+		+	
GNA	+		+	+	−	+	?	+				
SDRNA		−	−	−	?	?	+	+	+			
RET		+	−	+	−	+	+	?	+			

ations. In fact, none of the variables included in the analysis had much effect at all and taken together they do not provide a significant explanation of risk (as is indicated by the low F-value). The positive coefficient on INST is unexpected, since we have argued that institutional shareholders are risk averse. However, given that these owner-controlled firms with a strong institutional shareholding performed no worse in terms of profitability and growth, it is perhaps the risk factor which prompted institutions to sell their holdings in these firms to takeover bidders in 1975-9.

It is somewhat surprising to find a negative coefficient on VDH in the retentions equations (7.2.9 and 7.2.10). Positive simple correlations between profitability and the value of directors' holdings and between profitability and retentions inflate the negative value of the VDH coefficient in equation 7.2.10. However, despite statistical significance at the .05 level the effect of VDH is still of relatively minor consequence. In owner-controlled firms the value of directors' holdings does not seem to affect retentions. What is most important as a determinant of retentions is the strength of control exerted by directors as a cohesive group. The coefficient of −.106 on WOC in equation 7.2.8 indicates that directors who had 'absolute' control pursued a restrictive payout policy.

It appears that directors with weak control may have been under more pressure from other shareholders to return a greater fraction of earnings in the form of dividends. This would seem to be a rational strategy for survival given that the shareholding structure in these firms would make a takeover bid more feasible. On the other hand, the survival strategy of directors who had absolute control is very clear. They prefer to retain their proportional interest in the company. As a result external finance was rarely sought and retentions remained at high levels. It might be expected that these differences in

Table 7.2: Complete Model, Small and Medium Owner-Controlled Firms

Equation number	n	Dependent variable	Constant	ln VDH	VDH	WOC	INST	NMAT	SIZE (1/NAo)	RNA	GNA	SDRNA	SDREA	R^2	$\bar{R}^2$	F-ratio
7.2.1	58	RNA	.024	.017 (2.339)[b]		.005 (.249)	.005 (2.197)[b]	−.015 (.597)	.118 (4.329)[d]					.445	.392	8.348[a]
7.2.2	58	RNA	.049	.011 (1.323)[c]		−.518E-3 (.032)	.059 (2.327)[b]	−.020 (.765)	.083 (2.100)[e]		.281 (1.349)[c]	−.216 (.716)		.468	.393	6.279[a]
7.2.3	58	REA	.014	.009 (2.079)[b]		.008 (.732)	.009 (.598)	−.003 (.187)	.056 (3.501)[d]					.338	.275	5.321[a]
7.2.4	58	REA	.048	.004 (.984)		.008 (.820)	.013 (.995)	−.009 (.657)	.043 (2.148)[e]		.132 (1.224)		−.526 (4.164)[a]	.510	.441	7.436[a]
7.2.5	58	GNA	−.063	.020 (4.170)[a]		.019 (1.530)[c]	−.003 (.176)	.012 (.695)	.134 (7.550)[d]					.714	.687	25.998[a]
7.2.6	58	GNA	−.066	.018 (3.597)[a]		.018 (1.494)[c]	−.009 (.539)	.014 (.802)	.124 (5.856)[d]	.117 (1.274)				.723	.691	22.194[a]
7.2.7	58	SDRNA	.032		−.183E-5 (.259)	.587E-3 (.071)	.016 (1.421)[c]	−.005 (.427)	.017 (1.342)[c]					.092	.004	1.049
7.2.8	58	SDRNA	.035		−.117E-5 (.161)	.881E-3 (.100)	.018 (1.506)[c]	−.005 (.454)	.017 (1.426)[c]	(.540)				.097	<0	.911
7.2.9	54	RET	.488		−.419E-4 (1.031)	−.106 (2.072)[b]	.077 (1.116)	.019 (.290)	.124 (1.748)[f]					.176	.090	2.047[c]
7.2.10	54	RET	.257		−.660E-4 (2.195)[b]	−.110 (2.949)[a]	−.073 (1.309)[c]	.041 (.846)	−.074 (1.220)	.188 (6.488)[a]				.565	.510	10.182[a]

Notes: figures in brackets are t-ratios; a, b and c denote significance at the .01, .05 and .10 levels respectively using a one-tail test; d, e and f denote significance at the .01, .05 and .10 levels respectively using a two-tail test.

financing policies should somehow be reflected in the profitability and growth performances of owner-controlled firms.

The simple correlation coefficients between non-maturity (NMAT) and profitability (RNA, REA) and growth (GNA) are positive and highly significant. But once other influences on performance are included, particularly that of firm size, the firm maturity coefficient becomes insignificant and in several equations it is of the wrong sign. Thus, the non-mature owner-controlled firms, all of which had opening net assets of less than $5 million, did not perform very differently from other similar sized owner-controlled firms. However, it is probable that multicollinearity has biased the coefficients on NMAT.

Firm size itself consistently has a negative effect on the performance variables. It is interesting to note that, while firm size has a negative influence on operating risk, the coefficient is relatively small and is barely significant at the .10 level. One reason for this weak relationship may be that diversification (which is normally cited as the rationale for expecting a negative association between firm size and risk) is resisted by owner-managers as the size of the firm increases.

Another interesting feature of the results is that when the effect of profitability on retentions is included (in equation 7.2.10) the firm size coefficient changes sign and is now non-significant. Thus, when variations in profitability are accounted for there is little association between firm size and the retention ratio.

When included as independent variables, profitability (RNA) and growth (GNA) have the anticipated positive signs. Yet the profitability-growth relationship is insignificant in equation 7.2.6. It may be that this has arisen because of collinearity between firm size (SIZE), profitability (RNA) and growth (GNA). However, the inclusion of RNA in the growth equation does not materially alter the values or significance of the other explanatory variables. Instead, it may reflect the fact that the profitability-growth relationship depends partly on the relationship between profitability and external finance. More profitable firms will enjoy wider access to external finance than will unprofitable ones. If, as appears to be the case in owner-controlled firms, external financing decisions are dependent on such considerations as the retention of control by the director-dominated group, this is likely to distort the profitability-growth relationship.

Even more surprising is the lack of a significant relationship between operating risk (SDRNA) and the return on net assets in equation 7.2.8 and the highly significant negative relationship between shareholder-related risk (SDREA) and the rate of return on equity assets in equation 7.2.4. It is difficult to reconcile such a 'perverse' (that is, negative) risk-return relationship with conventional theories. However, similar results using firm level data have been achieved in the US by Shepherd (1975) and Winn (1977). Shepherd's explanation was that either the 'risk premium' had not been measured properly (i.e. it was related to structural variables), or simply that risk 'does not in fact command the premium which has conventionally been assumed' (p. 204). Winn's hypothesis was that managers have alternative objectives to higher profits. That is, when confronted with a risky situation managers might strive for greater diversification and integration of the firm's operations.

Management-Controlled Firms

Table 7.3 shows the results for the complete model analysing the performance of management-controlled firms. Once again the value of directors' shareholdings has a positive and significant effect on profitability and growth and a weak but insignificant negative effect on operating risk. This may indicate that, unlike owner-managers, the managers of management-controlled firms undertake more diversification.

In management-controlled firms the value of directors' shareholdings had a strong and significant impact on the retention ratio. The coefficient of .000294 on VDH in equation 7.3.9 indicates that an increase of $100,000 in the value of directors' shareholdings was associated with an increase of almost three points in the retention ratio. However, when the influence of profitability (RNA) on retentions is included in equation 7.3.10 the value of the coefficient on VDH is halved and is now significant only at the .10 level. The coefficient on RNA is three and a half times larger than in the owner-controlled firms sample. Its value indicates that a 10 percentage points increase in the rate of return on net assets was associated with a 6.73 points increase in the retention ratio. This provides further evidence for the view that in management-controlled firms investment opportunities (as reflected by the rate of return) were a more significant determinant of payout policy than in owner-controlled firms.

The coefficients on the dominant institutional shareholdings dummy (INST) all have the predicted signs. In equation 7.3.1 we find that institutionally dominated companies earned a 2.9 percentage

Table 7.3: Complete Model, Small and Medium Management-controlled Firms, n = 46

Equation number	Dependent variable	Constant	ln VDH	VDH	INST	NMAT	SIZE (1/NAo)	RNA	GNA	SDRNA	SDREA	R^2	$\bar{R}^2$	F-ratio
7.3.1	RNA	.031	.024 (3.140)[a]		.029 (1.701)[b]	.010 (.486)	.198 (5.695)[d]					.532	.487	11.661[a]
7.3.2	RNA	.009	.021 (2.752)[a]		.029 (1.756)[b]	−321E-4 (.022)	.161 (4.331)[d]		.180 (1.526)[c]	.614 (1.518)[c]		.587	.524	9.245[a]
7.3.3.	REA	.003	.016 (3.940)[a]		.014 (1.664)[c]	.012 (1.105)	.091 (4.963)[d]					.532	.487	11.674[a]
7.3.4	REA	−.017	.014 (3.723)[a]		.021 (2.442)[a]	.004 (.445)	.068 (3.955)[d]		.116 (2.002)[b]		.664 (2.706)[a]	.665	.613	12.894[a]
7.3.5	GNA	.011	.017 (1.709)[b]		.019 (.893)	.008 (.305)	.113 (2.543)[e]					.207	.130	2.675[b]
7.3.6	GNA	.001	.009 (.832)		.010 (.453)	.005 (.184)	.048 (.830)	.327 (1.672)[c]				.259	.166	2.793[b]
7.3.7	SDRNA	.032		−.812E-6 (.032)	−.007 (1.033)	.014 (1.842)[b]	.027 (2.045)[b]					.182	.102	2.282[c]
7.3.8	SDRNA	.021		−.207E-4 (.809)	−.009 (1.449)[c]	.012 (1.680)[c]	.007 (.418)	.098 (1.701)[b]				.237	.142	2.489[b]
7.3.9	RET	.321		.294E-3 (2.630)[a]	.095 (3.112)[a]	.013 (.369)	.104 (1.672)					.364	.302	5.863[a]
7.3.10	RET	.246		.158E-3 (1.336)[c]	.076 (2.572)[a]	.004 (.105)	−.029 (.362)	.673 (2.518)[a]				.451	.382	6.568[a]

Notes: figures in brackets are t-ratios; a, b and c denote significance at the .01, .05 and .10 levels respectively using a one-tail test; d and e denote significance at the .01 and .05 levels respectively using a two-tail test.

points higher rate of return on net assets. The value of the coefficient remains unchanged and is still significant at the .05 level when growth and risk are included in equation 7.3.2. The rate of return on equity assets was also higher in institutionally dominated companies and the coefficient on (INST) is almost significant at the .05 level. However, when the effects of growth and risk are incorporated in equation 7.3.4 significance is found at the .01 level.

Given that companies with a strong institutional component in their shareholding structure, through their ties with suppliers of capital, are likely to have greater means for expansion, it is surprising that their growth rate was not significantly higher. This finding is even more surprising since institutional dominance was associated with both a higher rate of return and a higher retention ratio. In equation 7.3.9 it can be seen that the retention ratio of institutionally dominated companies was 9.5 points higher and a large differential in the retention ratio persists when the effect of profitability is accounted for in equation 7.3.10. This indicates that even those management-controlled firms which were not dominated by institutions raised substantial amounts of external finance. Hence, while greater dispersion in their shareholdings may have afforded them some protection from takeover (in addition to their higher dividend payout), these firms were not free of capital market restraint. Indeed, our data show that in the 13 non-institutionally dominated management-controlled firms 53.5 per cent of growth was externally financed, while the corresponding figure for institutionally dominated companies was 43.6 per cent.

Although in the operating risk equation (7.3.7) the institutional dummy takes a negative sign, it is not significant. However, when RNA is included in equation 7.3.8, significance borders on the .05 level. This raises the question of the direction of causation: were institutionally dominated companies less risky because of the institutional influence, or were they institutionally dominated because they were less risky? A similar argument could be extended to each of the performance variables under consideration.

It is our contention that causation runs primarily from institutional dominance to performance. That is to say, where institutions hold a dominant position in the structure of shareholdings they can impose an internal restraint on managerial performance. There have been instances where this restraint has been rather direct. In these cases institutional investors have given management notice that their performance is lagging.[4] Thus, the significance of institutional dominance is not so much that these institutions will intervene directly in the operating decisions of firms, but that their strategic position may sharpen the capabilities of the market for corporate control. In addition, a strong institutional shareholding could be used to promote further external financing by the company and this will impose a greater capital market restraint.

An alternative hypothesis is that the causal mechanism works in the opposite direction. That is, successful companies attract the attention of institutional investors, which take up larger shareholdings through purchases and when new issues are made. However, in two-thirds of the owner-controlled firms more than 15 per cent of shares on issue was held by the largest four institutional investors. Thus, a large number of owner-controlled firms might have been labelled institutionally dominated if the remaining shareholdings had not been concentrated in private hands — particularly in the hands of the directors' groups. In contrast, the ownership of the majority of management-controlled firms was classified as being dominated by institutions. This was in spite of the fact that the absolute percentage held by them may have been of a similar magnitude to that in owner-controlled firms. The crucial difference was that in management-controlled firms other shareholdings were dispersed.

Turning our attention back to Table 7.3 we find that non-maturity had little apparent effect on firm performance, although the signs on the coefficients relating to NMAT are generally consistent with expectations. The only statistically significant effect is that the earnings of non-mature firms fluctuated more than in otherwise similar mature firms. This may have been because the products of non-mature firms were subject to greater fluctuations in demand. However, it might also reflect the fact that managers of non-mature firms were more willing to take risks in the expectation of higher profitability.

Firm size generally had a negative influence on performance. However, the inclusion of growth and risk do have some effect on the value of the SIZE coefficients in the profitability equations, making the negative relationships less pronounced. But with the relatively strong effect of profitability on growth (that is, relative to that observed in owner-controlled firms), the negative relationship between firm size and growth is much weaker in equation 7.3.6. Also, as was the case in the owner-controlled sample, the negative relationship between firm size and retentions (in equation 7.3.9) disappears when profitability is included (in equation 7.3.10). But, unlike owner-controlled firms, the inclusion of profitability (RNA) as a determinant of risk (in equation 7.3.8) does eliminate the effect of size on risk. Finally, it will be noted that in management-controlled firms the risk-profitability relationships are strong and positive. From theory this is what we would expect, although it is the opposite to what was found in the owner-controlled sample.

Company-Controlled Firms

Company-controlled firms constitute something of a special case. The origins of company control can be diverse, so that it is difficult to generalise about the performance of this group. With this reservation in mind the performance within small and medium-sized company-controlled firms is examined in Table 7.4. Although the value of directors' holdings generally has the expected sign, its effect is quite small in comparison with those found in the owner and management-controlled samples. This may be due to performance restraints imposed by the parent company. Thus, even where directors' holdings were small the imposition of a minimum performance restraint would tend to flatten the observed relationship.

Strong company control (CHD) was associated with somewhat higher profitability, but the coefficients are not significant. In equation 7.4.5 we find that growth was 3.8 percentage points higher in strong company-controlled firms and the coefficient on CHD is almost significant at the .05 level. However, it is possible that these firms had come under strong company control *because* they had better prospects. The only other significant effect of strong company control was that operating risks were much higher in these firms. Fluctuating earnings might be viewed differently when the controlling firm is in possession of a strong controlling interest.

Foreign control was associated with lower rates of return once the effects of maturity were taken into consideration. In equation 7.4.3 the coefficient on FOR indicates that the rate of return on equity assets in foreign-controlled companies was 4.8 percentage points lower than that of otherwise similar domestic company-controlled firms. However, foreign-controlled companies were considerably less risky and, when risk is included in the profitability equations, the differentials are reduced substantially. From this it would appear that foreign parents place a premium on stability in reported earnings. It has often been noted that foreign-controlled companies tend to retain a higher fraction of earnings than domestic companies (e.g.

Table 7.4: Complete model, Small and Medium Company-Controlled Firms

Equation number	n	Dependent variable	Constant	ln VDH	VDH	CHD	FOR	NMAT	SIZE $(1/NAo)$	RNA	GNA	SDRNA	SDREA	R^2	$\bar{R}^2$	F-ratio
7.4.1	41	RNA	.164	-.002 (.230)		.024 (1.028)	-.026 (.955)	.067 (2.399)[b]	.048 (1.906)[f]					.287	.185	2.817[b]
7.4.2	41	RNA	.088	-.205E-3 (.032)		-.509E-3 (.022)	-.003 (.118)	.005 (2.065)[b]	.026 (1.067)		.328 (2.109)[b]	.799 (1.808)[b]		.440	.322	3.711[a]
7.4.3	41	REA	.075	.004 (.546)		.018 (.828)	-.048 (1.935)[b]	.088 (3.529)[a]	.003 (.148)					.309	.210	3.129[b]
7.4.4	41	REA	.039	.003 (.454)		.017 (.838)	-.021 (.869)	.053 (2.118)[b]	.845E-3 (.045)		.193 (1.399)[c]		.212 (3.206)[a]	.481	.371	4.371[a]
7.4.5	41	GNA	.080	.007 (.805)		.038 (1.605)[c]	.637E-3 (.032)	-.005 (.164)	.050 (1.978)[f]					.160	.040	1.334
7.4.6	41	GNA	.019	.008 (.944)		.029 (1.280)	-.029 (.395)	-.029 (1.038)	.032 (1.284)	.372 (2.329)[b]				.276	.148	2.157[c]
7.4.7	41	SDRNA	.045		-.451E-4 (1.445)[c]	.019 (2.247)[e]	-.026 (2.772)[d]	.014 (1.382)[c]	.007 (.798)					.271	.166	2.597[b]
7.4.8	41	SDRNA	.027		-.358E-4 (1.167)	.016 (1.925)[f]	-.023 (2.471)[e]	.007 (.677)	.002 (.184)	.109 (1.847)[b]				.337	.220	2.882[b]
7.4.9	39	RET	.485		-.297E-4 (.187)	.007 (.164)	-.017 (.356)	.129 (2.486)[a]	-.005 (.114)					.202	.081	1.668
7.4.10	39	RET	.371		.295E-4 (.195)	-.008 (.187)	.005 (.114)	.087 (1.650)[c]	-.037 (.825)	.663 (2.260)[b]				.312	.183	2.414[c]

Notes: figures in brackets are t-ratios; a, b and c denote significance at the .01, .05 and .10 levels respectively using a one-tail test; d, e and f denote significance at the .01, .05 and .10 levels respectively using a two-tail test.

Brash, 1966). One factor pressing in this direction is that a 15 per cent withholding tax is paid on dividends remitted overseas. Yet we find that there was no difference in the retention policies of domestic and foreign company-controlled firms. In both cases parent corporations appeared to prefer a low dividend payout policy.

In contrast to the situations in owner and management-controlled firms, non-maturity had significant effects on the performance of company-controlled firms. Non-mature firms were significantly more profitable and remained more profitable even after their higher risk was taken into account. In equation 7.4.9 we find that non-mature firms retained 12.9 per cent more of their earnings, but when the effect of profitability is introduced in equation 7.4.10 the difference reduces to 8.7 per cent and is significant only at the .10 level. As in management-controlled firms the profitability of company-controlled firms was an important determinant of payout policy. Given that non-mature firms earned considerably higher profits and retained a larger fraction, it is surprising to find that they did not grow at a faster rate than mature firms. This may indicate that mature company-controlled firms were growing too fast and that profitability levels were being depressed as a result of this excessive growth.

Firm size had a comparatively minor influence on the performance of company-controlled firms. Perhaps this was due to their being relatively insulated from external influences on performance. However, profitability had approximately the same effect on growth as in management-controlled firms. Also, the growth-profitability and risk-return relationships were positive and significant. In this sense the performance of company-controlled firms was more akin to that of management, rather than owner-controlled firms.

Comparisons Between Control Types

The main drawback to results of studies employing the 'traditional' methodology is that they do not take full account of the various interaction effects between control type and the independent variables, which we have found to be significant. Rather than include all these interactions as additional independent variables, an alternative approach is to calculate estimates of the performance which could be expected from a 'typical' company in each control category from the coefficients estimated in the last three sections. Nevertheless, estimates using the traditional approach are presented in Appendix Table A.7.1 for comparative purposes.

The mean characteristics of companies within each control

category are provided in Appendix Table 7.2. The 'typical' OC company was mature and weak owner-controlled, its directors held shares valued at $471,826 and its net assets were $5.883 million. The 'typical' MC company was also mature, but was dominated by institutional shareholders, its directors held shares valued at only $135,784, and its net assets were $7.471 million. However, the frequency distributions for opening net assets and value of directors' holdings were strongly positively skewed, so that the mean values cannot be considered as representative. To correct for this bias, median values were calculated for these variables and these have been employed in the analysis. It is much less meaningful to speak of a 'typical' CC firm. Indeed, it would be a misnomer to describe the typical CC firm as being mature and having a strong domestic company shareholding, since less than a quarter of the sample would fit such a description (in contrast to 48 per cent for OC firms and 58 per cent for MC firms). Hence the calculated performance statistics shown in Table 7.5 relate only to owner- and management-controlled firms. As the median opening net assets of small to medium-sized firms was approximately $5 million, the figures have been calculated from that base.

In view of our previous findings the first two columns in Table 7.5 show the relative performances of the most constrained management- and owner-controlled firms. That is, those firms in which

Table 7.5: Comparative Performance of 'Typical' Small to Medium Owner- and Management-Controlled Firms

Performance indicator	MC (1)	OC (2)	OC* (3)	MC-OC (4)	MC-OC* (5)
RNA	20.9	14.9	13.0	6.0	7.9
REA	10.8	8.4	7.4	2.4	3.4
GNA	13.0	9.6	7.4	3.4	5.6
SDRNA	3.0	3.5	3.6	—0.5	—0.6
RET	46.4	38.7	40.3	7.7	6.1

Notes: an asterisk indicates that the performance figures for the typical owner-controlled firm have been calculated on the assumption that its directors held the same value of shareholdings as the median value for directors in management-controlled firms; figures are shown in percentage points.

directors had the least discretionary powers in relation to other firms with a similar character of control. In column (4) *differences* in the performances of MC and OC companies are shown. The figures in column (3) are 'hypothetical' in the sense that they are calculated on the assumption that the directors of owner-controlled firms had the same value of shareholdings in the firm as the directors of the typical management-controlled firm. This has the effect of eliminating discrepancies in the performances of OC and MC firms which can be attributed to differing incentive structures. Thus, the figures shown in column (5) provide an indication of performance differentials when 'all other factors are constant' (apart from control type). They therefore reflect the actual difference in the discretion possessed by directors of these firms.

At first sight it appears extraordinary that firms in which the directors held shares with a median value three times greater than those of directors of management-controlled firms should be significantly less profitable than the latter.[5] The intuitive answer to this apparent anomaly can be seen from a comparison of the figures in columns (4) and (5) of Table 7.5. In owner-controlled firms the *incentive effect*, which for each variable is the difference between the two values (column (5) − column (4)), was outweighed by the difference in managerial discretion (column (5)).

Several reasons may be advanced to explain why directors of the weak owner-controlled firm in our example had more discretion than the directors of the institutionally dominated management-controlled firm. First, internal restraints on the directors of the owner-controlled firm were rather weak. Although institutions may have held a significant proportion of shares in this firm, these holdings were relatively ineffectual when compared with the voting strength of directors as a cohesive group. By contrast, institutional dominance of management-controlled firms was associated with significantly higher profitability and retained earnings, somewhat higher growth and slightly less risk. In other words, where institutions were capable of exerting a strong internal restraint on managers, the performance of these firms accorded quite closely with our hypotheses regarding the objectives of these investors. Thus, if we were to compare the performance of a 'typical' owner-controlled firm in which directors had absolute control (and where internal restraints would be virtually non-existent) the profitability and growth differentials in column (5) would widen.

Second, external restraints on managerial discretion were more effective in the typical management-controlled firms. Management-controlled firms financed a larger proportion of their growth externally. The capital market appeared to place a severe restraint on the performance of relatively small companies, but in many owner-controlled firms this restraint was not allowed to operate. Finally, since these were relatively small companies the restraint of the market for corporate control was more effective in checking managerial discretion in management-controlled firms. Unlike the directors of owner-controlled firms, in the event of a takeover bid the directors of management-controlled firms could not rely on the strength of a large shareholding in the company. Instead the shareholding structure was relatively dispersed, except that a strategic block of shares was held by a few institutional investors. If the firm was not performing well, one or two of these institutions might consider selling their holdings to a market raider. Once such a foothold is obtained by a raider, the remaining institutional shareholders generally follow suit, as they are frightened of becoming 'locked in' minority shareholders.

These factors explain *why*, despite their lower shareholdings, the directors of management-controlled firms had the incentive to maintain high rates of return. There are also several possible explanations as to *how* they were able to earn higher rates of return. First, it is possible that management-controlled firms were more efficient. For example, one means of attaining more efficient operations is to institute reforms in organisational structure and it may be that these changes were being resisted by some owner-managers. Second, the fact that directors of owner-controlled firms tended to shun external finance may indicate that these firms were not taking advantage of all investment opportunities which presented themselves. Third, in Chapter 6 we found some evidence to suggest that management-controlled firms took greater advantage of positions of market power. That is, the four-firm concentration ratio had a greater positive effect on the profitability of management-controlled firms.

The faster growth of the typical management-controlled firm can be explained by the fact that it was more profitable, retained a higher proportion of earnings and engaged in more external financing. Some part of the higher retention ratio observed in the typical management-controlled firm may be attributable to the fact that it was more profitable and profitability was a leading determinant of payout policy. Another important influence was that institutional dominance was associated with significantly higher retentions. We have argued that since they are long-term investors institutions will prefer capital growth. Even so, management-controlled firms did not retain a higher fraction of their (larger) profits than absolute owner-controlled firms. Finally, despite their higher rates of return, management-controlled firms have been shown to be slightly less risky. It has been suggested that this was the result of their being more widely diversified.

Results for Large Corporations

Owner-Controlled Firms

From a statistical point of view it is unfortunate that the number of owner-controlled firms among the top 100 was so small. In fact, only ten of our sample of 68 continuing owner-controlled firms fell into this category. However, these ten large owner-controlled firms had relatively uniform characteristics. Nine of their number were weak owner-controlled, which indicates that while it is rare for large companies to be owner-controlled it is very rare to find the dominant ownership group owning more than 42 per cent of shares. Furthermore, all of these firms were classified as mature and in no case could institutions be said to have held a dominant shareholding.

In the profitability and growth equations (7.6.1, 7.6.3 and 7.6.5) in Table 7.6 we find that the coefficients on ln VDH are very similar to those obtained with the small to medium-sized owner-controlled sample. Once again the value of directors' shareholdings had a weak and insignificant impact on operating risk. However, the coefficient on VDH in the retentions equation (7.6.8) is significant at the .05 level and its value suggests that on average an increase of $1 million in the value of directors' holdings was associated with a 4.56 points increase in the retention ratio.

We have seen that only in one company were directors as a cohesive group in control of a large proportion of the ordinary shares in their company. Hence the coefficients on WOC must be viewed with caution. It could be argued, along similar lines to Radice (1971) and Steer and Cable (1978), that firms such as this must have been extraordinarily efficient to grow large without diluting the interest of the dominant ownership group. That is, to have grown mainly through internally generated funds, or through the issue of long-term debt rather than equity. Or, it could be argued that such firms have enjoyed long-standing positions of market power.

Table 7.6.: Complete Model, Large Owner-Controlled Firms, n = 10

Equation number	Dependent variable	Constant	ln VDH	VDH	WOC	NAo	RNA	GNA	SDRNA	SDREA	R^2	$\bar{R}^2$	F-ratio
7.6.1	RNA	.044	.018 (2.305)[b]		-.023 (.826)	.269E-3 (.937)					.586	.378	2.826
7.6.2	RNA	-.038	.023 (2.597)[b]		.021 (.729)	.340E-3 (1.642)		.355 (1.210)	2.292 (2.599)[b]		.860	.684	4.895[c]
7.6.3	REA	.074	.007 (1.809)[c]		-.036 (2.811)[b]	.127E-3 (.953)					.720	.580	5.143[b]
7.6.4	REA	.016	.012 (3.780)[a]		-.009 (.900)	.222E-3 (1.969)		-.304 (2.658)[b]		1.349 (4.159)[a]	.858	.745	7.564[b]
7.6.5	GNA	-.110	.023 (2.997)[b]		.062 (2.271)[b]	-.289E-4 (.100)					.660	.491	3.888[c]
7.6.6	GNA	-.097	.029 (2.566)[b]		.055 (1.835)[c]	.509E-4 (.158)	-.297 (.699)				.691	.443	2.789
7.6.7	SDRNA	.028		.749E-6 (.513)	-.010 (1.102)	-.267E-4 (.279)					.227	-.156	.586
7.6.8	SDRNA	-.010		.171E-5 (1.176)	-.003 (.382)	-.120E-3 (1.515)	.245 (2.486)[b]				.654	.378	2.364
7.6.9	RET	.271		.456E-4 (2.175)[b]	.164 (1.290)	.145E-3 (.105)					.490	.235	1.920
7.6.10	RET	.346		.505E-4 (1.621)[c]	.150 (.984)	.331E-3 (.195)	-.487 (.230)				.495	.091	1.226

Notes: figures in brackets are t-ratios; a, b, and c denote significance at the .01, .05 and .10 levels respectively using a one-tail test.

While in small and medium-sized owner-controlled firms profitability had a strongly negative association with firm size, here we find weak and statistically insignificant positive associations. The growth rate and operating risk were weakly negatively related to firm size. Finally, there is an insignificant and weak positive coefficient on firm size (NAo) in the retentions equation (7.6.9). Overall, then, once the effects of directors' holdings are taken into consideration, firm size had a negligible impact on the performance of large owner-controlled companies. The directors of these companies had considerable discretionary powers. In no instance were institutions or other shareholders outside the directors' group capable of imposing an internal restraint on them. Protection from the possibility of takeover was provided not only by the concentrated shareholding of the directors' cohesive group, but also by the size of these firms. However, the median shareholdings of directors in large owner-controlled firms was quite substantial at $1.7 million and this provided the incentive to maintain high profitability and growth levels.

The negative growth-profitability, profitability-growth and profitability-retentions relationships must be treated with reserve, because of collinearity between the value of directors' holdings, profitability and growth. On the other hand, the positive and significant risk-return relationships are more reliable, since our risk measures showed relatively strong and positive simple correlations with profitability and were only weakly correlated with the value of directors' holdings. This contrasts with the behaviour of small and medium-sized owner-controlled companies, where risk and rates of return were negatively related.

Management-Controlled Firms

The majority of large companies had a dispersed ownership structure. In Table 7.7 we find that the value of shares held by directors had positive effects on profitability performance and in the rate of return on equity assets equation the coefficient on ln VDH is almost significant at the .05 level. But the values of these coefficients are lower than in comparable equations estimated for small to medium-sized owner-cntrolled firms and for large owner-controlled firms. In equation 7.7.5 the value of directors' holdings had no apparent effect on the growth rates of large management-controlled firms. Furthermore, directors' holdings had negligible effects on risk and on the level of retentions.

These results are very different from those found in the small to

Table 7.7: Complete Model, Large Management-Controlled Firms, n = 29

Equation number	Dependent variable	Constant	ln VDH	VDH	INST	NMAT	NAo	RNA	GNA	SDRNA	SDREA	R^2	$\hat{R}^2$	F-ratio
7.7.1	RNA	.136	.008 (1.305)		−.018 (1.118)	.012 (.495)	−.183E-3 (.942)					.116	< 0	.788
7.7.2	RNA	.087	.008 (1.518)[c]		−.037 (2.295)[b]	.002 (.077)	−.270E-4 (.141)			−.020 (.032)		.344	.164	1.919
7.7.3	REA	.067	.005 (1.689)[b]		−.008 (1.002)	.024 (1.957)[b]	−.211E-4 (.219)					.197	.063	1.473
7.7.4	REA	.086	.005 (1.844)[b]		−.015 (1.687)[c]	.025 (1.689)[c]	.189E-4 (.182)		.187 (1.482)[c]		−.172 (.530)	.321	.136	1.735
7.7.5	GNA	.088	−.645E-3 (.122)		.033 (2.293)[b]	.018 (.845)	−.278E-3 (1.657)					.301	.185	2.585[c]
7.7.6	GNA	.027	−.004 (.860)		.041 (3.167)[a]	.013 (.672)	−.195E-3 (1.298)	.449 (2.823)[a]				.481	.368	4.262[a]
7.7.7	SDRNA	.031		−.421E-5 (.538)	−.003 (.604)	.008 (.880)	−.896E-4 (1.316)[c]					.126	< 0	.863
7.7.8	SDRNA	.036		−.362E-5 (.447)	−.004 (.659)	.008 (.897)	−.952E-4 (1.348)	−.030 (.407)				.132	< 0	.700
7.7.9	RET	.305		.960E-5 (.134)	.082 (1.576)[c]	.033 (.412)	.341E-3 (.077)					.096	< 0	.637
7.7.10	RET	.466		−.214E-4 (.329)	.106 (2.232)[b]	−.050 (.694)	.469E-4 (.600)	1.553 (2.671)[a]				.310	.160	2.066

Notes: figures in brackets are t-ratios; a, b and c denote significance at the .01, .05 and .10 levels respectively using a one-tail test.

medium-sized management-controlled firms sample. Two possible explanations come to mind. First, the directors of large management-controlled firms may have less power to influence the company's performance than directors of small management-controlled firms. That is, the boards of these large companies may have either been dominated by executive directors with little direct equity interest in the firm, or simply acted as a 'rubber stamp' for decisions made by senior management. Second, it is possible that the overall wealth of these directors was more highly diversified than that of directors in smaller management-controlled firms; it was certainly more diversified than that of directors in large owner-controlled firms. Thus, the pecuniary interests of directors in large management-controlled firms would not have been as dependent on the profitability, growth and payout policies pursued in these firms.

The coefficients found on the institutional dominance dummy (INST) are of considerable interest. Ignoring the effects of inter-relationships between the dependent variables we find that institutionally dominated companies were slightly *less* profitable, although the coefficients are not significant. However, institutional dominance *was* associated with a significantly faster rate of growth of net assets. This faster growth was achieved through an 8.2 points higher retention ratio and greater external financing. In fact large management-controlled firms with shareholding structures dominated by institutions financed 60 per cent of their growth from external sources, which compares with a figure of 37 per cent for other large management-controlled firms. There was no significant difference in the operating risks faced by the two groups of firms.

It could be argued that the negative coefficients on INST in the profitability equations may be discounted because of the significantly faster growth achieved by institutionally dominated firms. Since they were faster growing, higher depreciation charges probably under-stated the reported profitability of this group relative to other firms. Yet, when the positive and significant growth-profitability effects are included in equations 7.7.2 and 7.7.4, the coefficients on INST become more negative and statistical significance is found. Also, when profitability (RNA) is included as an explanatory variable in the growth and retentions equations (7.7.6 and 7.7.9) the positive coefficients on INST increase both in size and in statistical significance. Therefore, the results are supported when interrelationships among the dependent variables are taken into consideration. However, it must be recognised that in the profitability equations collinearity between INST and GNA ($r = .445$) may have caused some random distortion.

The capital market and the market for corporate control appear to place minor restraints on the performance of large companies. Substantial new equity and debt issued were not associated with significant improvements in future profitability. This provides a partial explanation for our finding that despite their greater recourse to external finance, large institutionally dominated companies did not show higher rates of return. Also, large management-controlled firms are less vulnerable to the possibility of takeover and we have argued that this is the primary instrument by which institutions may exercise influence over a firm's management. Thus, the evidence appears strong that the managers of large institutionally dominated companies were pursuing growth maximisation policies. Indeed, the managers of these firms might have reasoned that the most effective means of retaining security of tenure (i.e. averting takeover) would be to grow more rapidly — even if this was at the expense of raising the institutional component of their firm's shareholding structure. Further evidence in support of this contention is that large non-mature management-controlled firms were significantly more profitable in terms of the rate of return on equity assets, but did not grow significantly faster than mature firms.

Firm size had relatively weak negative and statistically insignificant effects on profitability and growth. Operating risk also showed a weak negative association with firm size, and the coefficient is significant at the .10 level using a one-tail test. However, there was no relationship between firm size and the retention ratio. As a final point it is interesting to note that the risk-return relationship was negative but insignificant in the large management-controlled firms sample. This is reminiscent of the behaviour found only in small to medium owner-controlled firms. The most satisfying hypotheses explaining such behaviour is that managers of large management-controlled companies were risk averse, preferring relatively low but stable earnings to higher but less certain ones.

Comparisons between Control Types

Table 7.8 displays performance results calculated for 'typical' large owner and management-controlled firms. Here, the 'typical' large owner-controlled firm was weak owner-controlled, had net assets valued at \$34.22 million and its directors held shares valued at \$1.72 million. On the other hand, the 'typical' large management-

Table 7.8: Comparative Performance of 'Typical' Large Owner-
and Management-Controlled Firms

Performance indicator	MC (1)	OC (2)	OC* (3)	MC-OC (4)	MC-OC* (5)
RNA	14.7	16.4	10.9	−1.7	3.8
REA	8.0	8.6	6.4	−0.6	1.6
GNA	10.9	12.2	5.1	−1.3	5.8
SDRNA	2.5	1.8	1.7	0.7	0.8
RET	38.9	51.9	44.4	−13.0	−5.5

Notes: an asterisk indicates that the performance figures for the typical owner-controlled firm have been calculated on the assumption that its directors held the same value of shareholdings as the median value for directors in management-controlled firms; figures are shown in percentage points.

controlled firm had a strong institutional shareholding, net assets valued at $37 million and its directors held shares valued at $79,050. Hence, the computations compared the performances of owner- and management-controlled firms with assets of $35 million.

The typical management-controlled firm was less profitable, grew more slowly, was more risky and retained a smaller fraction of earnings than the typical owner-controlled firm. It is evident that the outstanding difference was in payout policy. Column (5) shows the performance differences between owner- and management-controlled firms on the assumption that the directors of the owner-controlled firm held $79,050 worth of shares in their company. Now we find that the typical management-controlled firm would be *more* profitable and grow significantly *faster* than the owner-controlled firm. However, the management-controlled firm would still be more risky and retain a lower fraction of earnings.

The fact that given the same incentive (as proxied by the value of directors' holdings) the owner-controlled firm would be less profitable is interesting, for it implies that the directors of a large owner-controlled firm still have greater discretion *available* to them than their counterparts in a similar sized management-controlled firm. Both firms could be expected to enjoy considerable market power and the capital market restraint could not be relied upon. But while in both instances the absolute size of the firm might afford a measure of protection from takeover, the directors of an owner-controlled firm would have the additional advantage provided by the control of a significant minority interest. However, since the directors of the typical owner-controlled firm actually *did* have a substantial incentive to raise profitability, much of this discretionary power remained unrealised.

A corollary following from the above proposition is that the top managers of the typical large management-controlled firm, who had much less personal incentive to maximise profitability but similar freedom from restraints, *did* exercise more of the discretionary powers available to them. True, most large management-controlled firms had a shareholding structure which was dominated by institutional investors and this provided a potentially strong internal restraint on managers. However, while strong links with institutions enabled these firms to increase their rate of growth, profitability was not improved relative to other management-controlled firms. Indeed, when account is taken of the fact that growth generally had a positive effect on profitability, these institutionally dominated firms were significantly *less* profitable. Hence it would seem that, in large firms at least, strong institutional shareholdings facilitated the growth aspirations of managers. This was most probably because managers felt secure in the knowledge that institutions would not easily be persuaded to sell in the event of a takeover bid. At the same time their more rapid growth would provide added protection against takeover.

This does not necessarily mean that all large management-controlled firms were bad investments from the viewpoint of institutional investors. Many were themselves frequently engaged in the acquisition of smaller firms, and thereby receiving a great deal of publicity in the financial press. The large size of these firms, coupled with their significant institutional holdings, yielded high share marketability, which is valued by large investors seeking liquidity. Thus, many of these firms were highly rated by the stock market.

In column (5) of Table 7.8 we find that given the same value of directors' shareholdings the typical owner-controlled firm would grow at a rate of 5.8 percentage points lower than the 'typical' management-controlled firm. This reflects the fact that the growth rate of owner-controlled firms was more highly dependent upon profitability and retention of earnings. Thus 53 per cent of the growth of all large management-controlled firms was externally financed, while only 41 per cent of the growth of large owner-controlled firms was achieved through the capital market. Yet the value of directors' holdings made little impact on the difference in operating risks — large owner-controlled firms as a group were slightly less risky. For comparative purposes an analysis employing the traditional dummy variable approach is shown in Appendix Table A.7.3.

Summary and Interpretation

The approach adopted in this chapter has been first to examine the determinants of performance *within* control types and employ the knowledge gained to explain differences in performance *between* control types. Perhaps the most significant result to emerge has been the finding that it is not control type *per se* which is of crucial importance in determining company performance, but the nature of interactions between managerial incentives and the restraints on managerial discretion. It was reasoned that firm size will have an important bearing on these interactions since large size, of itself, confers freedom from market restraints. Thus, separate analyses were conducted on small to medium-sized firms and on large firms, where 'large' was roughly defined as membership of the largest 100 listed corporations in Australia. Attention was directed to comparing the performance of 'owner'- and 'management'-controlled firms for two reasons. First because this distinction has been central to the 'new' or 'alternative' theories of the firm. Second, the firms which were classified as 'company-controlled' had an extremely diversified composition. Without intimate knowledge of the circumstances leading to a large company shareholding, or of the actual control situations applying to each case, it is difficult to categorise such firms.

The main relationships may be most clearly visualised in Figure 7.1 which is a stylised representation of the determination of the rate of return on equity assets in owner-controlled (OC) and manage- ment-controlled (MC) firms. Quadrant 1 shows the relationships between firm size and the *limits* to managerial discretion in OC and MC firms which were discussed at the end of Chapter 6. These limits show the lower bounds of profitability which must be achieved by firms of each control type if takeover is to be avoided.

Quadrants II and III are simply 45° line transformations of the firm size (NA_o) axis. Quadrant IV shows the relationship between firm size and the value of directors' shareholdings. In dispersed ownership companies there is no discernible relationship (MC_4 is a straight line), although this naturally implies that the *proportion* of total equity which is owned by directors falls as firm size increases. In owner- controlled companies there is a U-shaped relationship between firm

Figure 7.1: Determinants of Corporate Profitability Performance

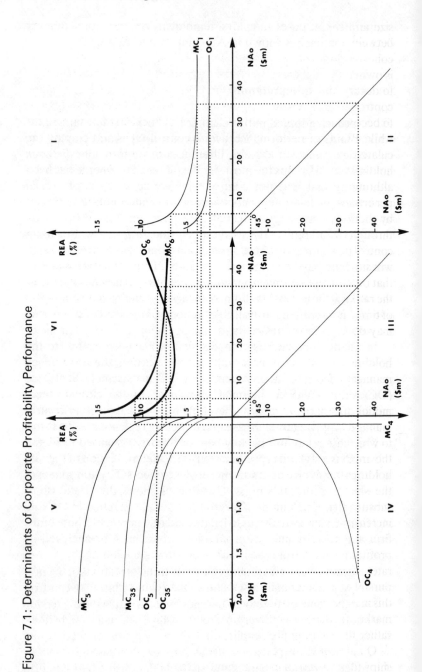

size and the value of directors' holdings. There is no relationship between firm size and the proportion of shares held by directors as a cohesive group. The proportion of the cohesive group's share which is owned by directors (PDH) falls rapidly at first and then continues to decline monotonically with increases in firm size. Larger owner-controlled firms tend to be older and so the family shareholdings tend to become more and more diffused among successive heirs. Second, while PDH progressively declines as firm size increases, it is calculated from a larger absolute base (in terms of the *value* of shareholdings held by directors as a cohesive group). This means that although in very large companies directors may account for only 15 per cent of the cohesive group's shareholding, the absolute value held by them is large. In practice very few owner-controlled firms pass through the 'trough' in this relationship. Directors fearing the loss of control place greater reliance on internal sources of finance and this will slow the growth rate relative to other firms. From this it follows that only exceptionally profitable OC firms will eventually penetrate the ranks of the largest 100 listed companies in a relatively short space of time (say, one generation), although some very old OC companies may do so over several generations.

In quadrant V the relationships between the value of directors' holdings and rate of return on equity assets are drawn for owner- and management-controlled firms with opening net assets of $5 million ($OC_5, MC_5$) and $35 million ($OC_{35}, MC_{35}$). In the context of our model this incentive effect is assumed to be additive to the level of managerial discretion shown in quadrant I. In other words, the extent to which the discretion available to directors is *exercised* depends on the incentives available to them. The value of directorial shareholdings is only one of the competing incentives available. In essence the shape of this relationship reflects a falling marginal rate of substitution of profitability for other objectives as the rate of profit increases. Alternative objectives may include raising the size of the firm and thereby increasing salary and prestige (although raising profitability is in some degree complementary to raising the growth rate), extracting tax-free perquisites from gross revenues and the pursuit of a quiet life (for example, if the firm has a high market share this may be maintained through a conservative limit pricing policy, or market power may be employed in reducing earnings fluctuations rather than raising profitability).

Quadrant VI displays the 'observed' size-profitability relationships for owner and management-controlled firms.[6] These relationships show the net outcome of the incentives and restraints acting on top management in these firms. It is now apparent why a typical $5 million OC firm should be markedly less profitable than a similar sized MC firm, while the $35 million OC firm should be slightly more profitable than a similar sized MC firm. In both cases the incentive to raise profitability (as indicated by the value of directorial share-holdings) is higher in owner-controlled firms. But the discretionary power available to directors is also always greater in owner-controlled firms and because this power is in large measure dependent on the shareholdings controlled by the cohesive owner-ship group it is not as dependent on firm size. Thus, if the managers of small to medium-sized MC firms were to sacrifice profitability for other objectives they would quickly fall prey to a takeover raider, and these firms would disappear as independent companies. In contrast, the directors of OC firms can pursue alternative objectives to a greater extent and continue to survive without being taken over. In the $30 million size range the managerial discretion and incentive effects tend to cancel one another and, as firm size increases beyond this point, the former comes to dominate the latter effect in the case of management-controlled firms. Since the large firms in our sample had median opening net assets of approximately $35 million the observed difference in profitability between MC and OC firms was relatively small (1.7 per cent in the case of return on equity assets). Figure 7.1 implies that the larger the firm the greater this difference would become, but it cannot be confirmed empirically without additional OC observations in the larger size ranges.

The size-growth relationships for owner- and management-controlled firms have similar shapes to the size-profitability relation-ships. However, the differences between control types are propor-tionally larger. Compared with OC firms the typical small to medium-sized MC firm — in addition to being significantly more profitable and retaining a higher proportion of earnings —achieves a much higher proportion of its growth through external finance. In the large firms category owner-controlled firms are slightly more profitable and, while they finance a somewhat smaller proportion of their growth externally, they retain a much higher fraction of their earnings.

The relationship between firm size and operating risks is negative and seems to be due to greater diversification in larger firms. Overall there are no significant differences in the operating risks borne by owner- and management-controlled firms. But the relationship is more steeply negative for MC firms in the lower size ranges and this may indicate that these firms begin diversification programmes earlier.

It appears that the discretion available to managers in most company-controlled firms is effectively circumscribed by the controlling firm. That is, the rate of profit earned by similar sized company-controlled firms is not significantly less than that of small to medium-sized management-controlled firms, nor is it significantly less than that earned by large owner-controlled firms. Yet the growth and retentions policies of company-controlled firms are interesting. For example, when a company-controlled firm is small or non-mature, high ploughback and growth policies are pursued, but in large company-controlled firms greater dividend payments are preferred.

In sum, our evidence suggests that internal organisation and external restraints are important determinants of company performance. Yet distinctions *between* control types are only important in so far as they are associated with a specific set of incentives and restraints facing managers. Our research indicates that over a wide range of firm sizes these factors tend to cancel one another. Thus, large management-controlled firms are about as profitable as large owner-controlled firms because, even though managers in the former may have less to gain personally by raising profitability, they have relatively stronger internal and market restraints acting on them. However, there is ample evidence to suggest that large size is not only associated with increased discretionary power, but that this power is used by managers to pursue objectives apart from profits.

Notes

1. As Hurdle (1974, p. 485) has argued, to unravel the relationships exogenous variables are required to identify each equation in the system. Like Hurdle, we have the difficulty that there exist few exogenous variables which are related to one or other of the endogenous variables, but not to both of them. Steer and Cable (1978, p. 19) have held that 'consistent estimates are obtained from a single equation model as long as there is a lag in the feedback from profit and growth'. Furthermore, they argued that OLS and TSLS estimates have in any case often turned out to describe 'essentially the same picture'. Steer and Cable cited Strickland and Weiss (1976), who employed a three-equation model of the determinants of advertising, concentration and price-cost margins.

2. Recent Australian estimates of these relationships by Round and Ryan (1980) have found little difference between OLS and TSLS estimates.

3. In Australia Phillips (1978, p. 166) found that the simple correlation coefficient between the four-firm concentration ratio and the turnover of the

largest four firms in 1968-9 was .345.

4. A particular case in our sample is that of Bradmill Industries Ltd, which we classified as being institutionally dominated. The four largest institutional investors in this company held 15.2 per cent of issued shares and the AMP was the largest single shareholder with 5.8 per cent. After informing Bradmill's management a year or two in advance of its intention to dispose of the holding, in 1977 the AMP granted an option to the Lew-Fayman-Goldberg group, which used it to launch a raid on the company. See the *Australian Financial Review*, 26 April 1978, p. 48.

5. This in fact appears to raise considerable doubts about the contention that directors buy into those firms which they feel are likely to be more profitable. Or, if they do, it suggests that inside knowledge is an imperfect indicator.

6. It will be noticed that the OC_6 curve displays a quadratic relationship. The upward sloping segment is merely conjectural. Tests of the relationship between firm size and profitability conducted in Chapter 6 cannot be relied upon because the bulk of observations lay in the small size ranges and would have swamped any positive effect. However, the coefficients on NA_o appearing in the profitability equations for the large owner-controlled firms sample were positive and approached statistical significance when the effects of growth and risk were included. Nevertheless, many more observations in the large firms category would be required before arriving at a firm conclusion on the nature of the true relationship.

8 SUMMARY AND CONCLUSIONS

Our analysis has proceeded on the assumption that corporate decision makers — top management — are at the centre of the process by which corporate performance is determined. The empirical evidence has yielded considerable support for a model of corporate performance which focuses on the nature of incentives, internal and external restraints on managerial discretion — in short, on the relationships between owners, managers and their various market environments.

When confronted with similar findings regarding the profitability performances of large US corporations Larner (1970, p. 29) concluded that 'proponents of theories of managerial discretion have expended much time and effort in describing a phenomenon of relatively minor importance'. Studies which also included a consideration of firm growth policies arrived at somewhat different conclusions. For example, in the UK Radice (1971, pp. 561-2) felt that 'the managerial theories ... are basically theories of the large modern firm, not theories of the managerial firm, and ... they need not be based on the separation of ownership from control'. In a later US study, Sorenson (1974, p. 148) was also of the opinion that 'if the modern corporation has abandoned profit maximization as its primary goal, the source of this abandonment may be in the sheer size of the firm or possession of market power, but not in a change in corporate control'.

All three researchers made valid observations in the context of results generated by a particular methodology, while failing to see the underlying mechanisms. Our methodology of first establishing the reasons for differences in corporate performance within control-type categories has enabled us to gain a deeper understanding of the fundamental reasons behind differences (or the lack of differences) in performance between these categories. Furthermore, past studies have generally confined their investigations to the very largest corporations in an economy, which has also contributed to a blinkered view of the underlying processes. Our sample included a large range of firm sizes. What emerges from the present study is this. As suggested by critics of the managerial theories there do exist non-market and market restraints on firm behaviour and performance, but at the same time the managerial theorists appear to be correct in proposing that these mechanisms are subject to failure. Categorisation into control type is useful in indicating the nature of incentives and restraints which are likely to predominate. However, the relationships are likely to be complex. There is no simple formula tying control type and performance. Thus, it is the operation of the mechanisms themselves, rather than control type *per se*, which are of vital concern to issues of economic theory and policy.

Implications for the Structure-Conduct-Performance Paradigm

Our results suggest that the expediency of following in the Bain (1968, p. 329) tradition of testing 'indirectly for net associations of structure and performance, leaving the detailed character of the implied linkage of conduct substantially unascertained' is called into question. Expanding the traditional structure-conduct-performance triad to include elements such as the internal organisation of firms and stock market restraints has the effect of directing attention back to decisions taken at the firm level (firm conduct). Thus, while market structure may be an important determinant of the potential performance of the firm, the extent to which this potential is realised will be dependent on the incentives of managers and the internal and external stock market restraints which must be satisfied in order to ensure their survival. For example, in Chapter 6 we found that, where stock market restraints were most effective, in management-controlled and smaller firms, the positive relationship between market concentration and profitability was stronger than among groups of firms in which these restraints were less effective (i.e. large and owner-controlled firms).

The 'shared assets' view of market power suggests that the concentration-profitability relationships for large and small firms should be roughly parallel. The alternative view proposed by Demsetz (1973) holds that high concentration results from the superior efficiency displayed by some firms. In other words, efficient and profitable firms eventually come to dominate the markets in which they operate. On this view we should expect that large firms will be more profitable than small firms and that the difference will become more marked with increases in seller concentration. Our results suggest that a second alternative hypothesis, which might be termed the shared assets managerial discretion hypothesis, should also be considered. This hypothesis proposes that managerial discretion is related not only to market power, as indicated by the degree of seller concentration, but to firm size as well. Discretion in the product market allows firms to raise profits (in the long run) above competitive levels. On the other hand, the weaker stock market and shareholder constraints associated with large size allow managers more freedom to pursue non-profit-maximising goals. Smaller firms, particularly those with a dispersed ownership structure, will need to perform close to the potential set by the product market in order to survive, so the concentration-profitability relationship should be more steeply positive for these firms. Our results support this view, but must be viewed with caution owing to the highly aggregate nature of the data.

This provides a plausible explanation for several Australian and UK findings of very weak or negative market concentration-profitability relationships. In both countries studies have generally revealed a negative relationship between firm size and profitability. However, since industry profitability is the weighted average of firm rates of return, and in highly concentrated industries large firms will account for a greater proportion of assets, it is not difficult to see how negative, or weak positive associations could emerge in industry level studies. There is even evidence to support the suggestions of these researchers that their findings conflict with those found in the US because of differences in managerial motivation. In Chapter 4 we showed that in the US managerial incentives appear to be more closely geared to profit maximisation than in Australia.

Implications for the Theory of the Firm

For some time speculation has existed about the relevance of the neoclassical theory of the firm in light of the fact that ownership and control of business enterprise have become increasingly separated. Defenders of the neoclassical position have not denied that the functions of ownership and management have been separated in many cases, but argue that the restraints acting on corporate managers are of such a nature that major revision of the theory is unwarranted. It has been alleged that a Darwinian 'survival of the fittest' will ensure that only profit-maximising firms will continue in the long run.[1] A pervasive theme of the present study is that the ability to survive constitutes a fundamental determinant of corporate performance, since it sets the limits to managerial discretion. But while neoclassical theory proposes that profitability *alone* will determine the chances of survival, we have found that due to certain market imperfections control type and firm size play important roles in this process.

In the UK Singh (1971) suggested that the market for corporate control was acting in a perverse manner since, though managers of small-medium firms could reduce their chances of being taken over by raising profitability, the best strategy for managers of large firms was rapid growth. Our results show that large firms were well placed to survive for extended periods of time. While few large firms earned exceptionally high rates of profit, they rarely showed very low rates of profit. Since large firms were favoured by the stock market they could make new equity issues and raise long-term debt on favourable terms and achieve a steady rate of growth of net assets while maintaining a relatively low retentions policy. They could finance a large proportion of their growth through external sources and in Chapter 6 it was found that greater exposure to the capital market restraint did not result in a significant improvement in their future profitability performance.

However, it is also apparent that the *concentration* of ownership also provides a means for survival. In the UK this fact was noted by Kuehn (1975) and Singh (1971). They found that firms in the smallest-size classes had the greatest chance of survival and suggested that tight family ownership was the cause. In Chapter 6 it was discovered that a number of closely held private-ownership-controlled firms in the small and medium-size categories had survived the study period while displaying valuation ratios which were consistently below their industry average. These tended to be older established firms in which the original family shareholdings had become dispersed among a number of heirs. Yet the directors appeared to maintain control through family voting trusts, the pyramidal structure of family investment companies and family loyalty to the firm. The fact that such firms could survive with control intact attests that the market for corporate control was not effective in eliminating inefficient management. In addition, these owner-controlled firms often retained a high proportion of their profits and avoided external finance, so that capital market pressures could not operate as a spur to managerial efficiency. Finally, in Chapter 7 we found evidence to suggest that in small to medium-sized owner-controlled firms such considerations as retention of control by the dominant family were taking precedence over rational investment policy.

Very little is known about the implied relationships of company control and their effects on performance. In some cases inter-company shareholdings may act as a buffer against an unfriendly takeover bidder and thereby lessen the efficiency of the market for corporate control. However, there were indications that in most cases (relating to domestically controlled companies at least) these share-holdings were evidence of the market in operation. Many of them were built up either through on-market purchases, or as a result of a partial takeover bid, following a poor performance by existing management. This, in turn, made it difficult to separate the per-formance effects of company control from factors which caused these firms to come under company domination in the first instance. Inter-company shareholdings were quite fluid. Those companies which were showing good prospects for recovery or further improvement in performance were later subjected to a full bid, while 'subsidiaries' exhibiting continually poor performance were often sold to another company. Yet divestment of shares in very large company-controlled firms was rare, even if performance were lagging.

The methodology employed by the present study makes it difficult to deliver firm judgements about whether some companies were maximising growth at the expense of profitability. It can be argued that in comparison with the directors of management- and company-controlled firms, the directors of owner-controlled firms had a greater *incentive* to maximise profitability — because they held much larger shareholdings in their firm. In fact, our results showed that directorial shareholdings had a positive effect on the profitability levels achieved once the effects of the firm size and control type were accounted for, but once the holding exceeded $300,000 the effect was rather minor. Directorial shareholdings also had a significant and positive effect on the growth rate of firms.

In our small to medium firms management-controlled firms grew significantly faster than owner-controlled firms, but the former were also significantly more profitable. This was in spite of the fact that the directors of owner-controlled firms held shares valued three times higher than those held by directors of management-controlled firms. These important differentials in performance were explained by the fact that the internal and external restraints on small to medium-sized management-controlled firms were far greater than those applying to similar owner-controlled companies. Thus, small and medium-sized management-controlled firms were more vulnerable to takeover and only those which maintained high profitability and growth rates (and therefore, high valuation ratios) survived. However, another reason for the superior performance displayed by small to medium-sized management-controlled firms was that they had more frequent recourse to the capital market, while owner-controlled firms relied more heavily on retained earnings. That is, management-controlled firms were subjected to greater capital market pressures to raise their profitability to the average for industry as a whole.

In the large firms sample, owner-controlled firms earned slightly higher rates of return and also grew at a slightly faster rate than management-controlled firms, but neither of these differences was found to be statistically significant. This result appears to conform quite closely to the findings reported by several overseas researchers who generally restricted their sample to very large firms. A plausible explanation is that the restraints on managers of management-controlled firms declined more rapidly with increases in firm size.

In the small to medium firm size category management-controlled firms with dominant institutional shareholdings had significantly higher profitability and growth rates than other management-controlled firms. The institutionally dominated firms also retained a significantly higher proportion of their earnings. But among large firms only the growth rate and retention ratio were higher in management-controlled firms with a strong institutional component. Thus, in large management-controlled firms the presence of institutions appeared to facilitate managerial growth aspirations and this relatively fast growth had the added effect of making these firms even less vulnerable to takeover. Indeed, it seems that during the period of study large management-controlled firms could count on institutions to remain loyal in the unlikely event of an outside bid for control. In so far as the more rapid growth of large institutionally dominated management-controlled firms was not associated with higher profitability, they could be considered to be maximising growth. However, large owner-controlled firms were also growing significantly faster than large non-institutionally dominated management-controlled firms, while not earning significantly higher profits. By the same criteria, then, owner-controlled firms could be considered as growth maximisers.[2] Being extremely wealthy the directors of large owner-controlled firms could be expected to prefer capital gains over current dividend income. In light of this fact it is not surprising that the retention ratio of large owner-controlled firms was significantly higher (indeed, some 16 points higher) than that of similar sized management-controlled firms.

Throughout this study it has been striking to note the important role played by the survival mechanism and this fact holds important implications for studies which compare the performances of owner and management-controlled firms, since it determines the nature and composition of the sample under consideration. Thus, among small firms we found relatively few dispersed ownership companies, but a proportionately large number of family-dominated concerns. Small owner-managed firms operated with varying levels of efficiency, their owner-managers faced different incentives and enjoyed varying degrees of control over their firms. On average, however, the restraints facing owner-managers were far less severe than those confronted by the professional managers of similar sized dispersed ownership companies. The latter group of firms was composed of survivors. Since their small size and dispersed ownership structure made them vulnerable to takeover, only the above-average performers were observable.

In contrast, the large firms sample, which coincided approximately with membership of the top 100 group of listed companies, had a relatively small proportion of firms which could be described as 'owner-controlled' — that is, controlled by a small cohesive group of shareholders associated with the board of directors. Hence the norm was dispersed ownership and again survival was important given the differing patterns of financing observed between owner- and management-controlled firms. Except for early periods in their development (non-maturity) owner-controlled firms tended to finance the bulk of their expansion from internal sources, while management-controlled firms were more inclined to seek funds in the capital market. In addition, management-controlled firms appeared to engage more frequently in takeover activity. Under these circumstances it is likely that the owner-controlled firms which achieved, or retained, positions in the top 100 group of listed companies had special attributes.

Implications for Owners and Managers

Our examination of the structure of shareholdings within Australian listed companies has revealed that in two-thirds of the cases, strategic blocks of shares were held by other companies or by private individuals with direct representation on the board of directors. In the remaining third there were no significant private or company shareholdings (i.e. less than 10 per cent in the hands of a cohesive group of private individuals, or less than 15 per cent in the case of a company shareholder). These firms were designated as management-controlled. However, in two-thirds of these firms, financial institutions were dominant shareholders. The degree of concentration in ownership is higher than in either the US or the UK, although those countries are moving in the same direction. Because of the concentration in ownership small shareholders are effectively disenfranchised.

We have demonstrated that dominant shareholders have different interests, which will not coincide with the interests of smaller shareholders. We have also seen that in Australia managers lack incentives to align their interests with those of shareholders. Bonuses tied to profitability performance are minimal, the value of directors' shareholdings in most companies which are not 'owner-controlled' are relatively small and executive stock option schemes are quite rare. Australian shareholders have traditionally frowned on incentive plans for managers. Sometimes this suspicion has been justified; for example, generous stock option plans have at times been proposed for top executives who already have a substantial equity interest in the firm. Our results have suggested that in such cases additional incentives would be unlikely to elicit improved performance.[3] These problems are not confined to Australia. In the US there have been cases of shareholder discord arising from managerial remuneration policy. Baker (1977) has argued that difficulties involved in the construction of equitable reward systems, together with the proliferation of such schemes in the US, robs them of their effectiveness. In Australia, however, there remains ample room for experimentation with, and extension of, the managerial incentive structure.

Our study suggests that the potential shareholder constraints on management — and this means shareholders who are not also part of management — need to be activated. For instance, we found that in private-ownership-controlled companies which lacked these constraints the incentive provided by substantial directorial shareholdings was not enough to promote maximum performance. In fact it was the very existence of this large ownership stake which created a divergence from the interests of other shareholders. After an extensive review of the international literature, a recent Australian study by Davies (1982) has suggested that mandatory cumulative voting[4] be introduced along with the European system of two-tier boards. However, he still thought the financial institutions are the brightest prospect for improved monitoring of performance.

In the UK, Mr. P.E. Moody (1979), the group chief investment manager of the Prudential Corporation, has also suggested that institutions could champion the cause of small shareholders. But there are problems. Financial institutions have a variety of objectives and are not as highly concentrated in the UK as they are in Australia. Paradoxically, the more contacts are made between institutions and industrial corporations, the wider the disparity between them and smaller shareholders becomes, and the more their flexibility is restricted by fear of insider trading. Also, the exercise of institutional power could invite a social and political backlash.

In the past in Australia, as in the US and UK, institutions have generally acted passively. As a top executive of the Australian Mutual Provident Society, Australia's largest investor, put it, 'One could be certain that they would readily support the incumbent board and management ... Sale of a holding was almost unknown, and takeover offers were accepted only after a strong acceptance recommendation from the existing board' (Craig, 1979, pp. 2-3). In recent years institutions have become far more receptive to takeovers and as a consequence companies with significant institutional shareholdings, even many large companies, have become vulnerable to takeover. The heightened share-market activity has had a demonstration effect.[5] Large institutions (as well as the managers of industrial companies) have come to recognise the power embodied in their shareholdings. This may indicate that in the future the investment managers of major institutions will be more likely to 'talk to' management if they are unhappy with a company's performance and that managers will take heed.

If the remarks of Sir Robert Crichton-Brown (1980) as president of the Australian Institute of Directors are any indication, such moves are likely to meet stiff resistance. Sir Robert has condemned 'the evident desire of some major institutions to take an active management role in some of their corporate investments ... [since it] can only serve to further concentrate economic power in this country and to place constraints on capital market efficiency'. In his view, 'the original passive institutional investment philosophies are far more consistent with a free enterprise system than what we are seeing today' (Crichton-Brown, 1980, p. 15). However, the argument betrays the vested interests of incumbent directors. It is argued that small shareholders are often 'left out in the cold' during takeover raids and that they will have even less chance to participate as institutions increasingly trade with each other directly. However, Sir Robert sees nothing wrong with large corporate or private shareholders being able to sell control to another party off-market without making a similar offer to minority shareholders. He also suggests such innovations as restricting voting rights and allowing directors the right to refuse transfers.

Organisation costs and the free-rider problem ensure that small shareholders will never realise their voting potential without some institutional adaptation brought about by government legislation. The Shareholders' Associations and Corporate Democracy Inc. are the efforts of capable and enthusiastic individuals working for principles of fairness rather than vested interest. Apart from gaining some publicity, they are unlikely to make a crucial difference to the outcomes. But the legislative alternative, which would drastically alter the power relationship in society, would be met with considerable opposition.

Conclusions for Public Policy

In terms of our model the role of government policy towards industry and commerce is seen as regulating the various market mechanisms to enhance the efficiency of their operation. But governments have goals apart from efficiency. Furthermore, government intervention imposes social costs which will need to be weighed against benefits. Finally, there is the delicate problem associated with the possibility of conflicting policy prescriptions, both within and between alternative arms of the government sector.

Ideally, as a market mechanism the market for corporate control is concerned with eliminating inefficient or incompetent management, or facilitating the realisation of economies of scale. But experience shows it to be imperfect. Efficiency will not be served by empire building or monopolisation, and equity will not be attained in lightning takeover raids employing nominees, warehousing[6] and back-room deals. In the US the Securities and Exchange Commission which was established in the wake of abuses leading to the Great Crash of 1929 carries the responsibility for regulation of corporate securities dealings. In the UK self-regulation is practised through the stock exchange and the City of London Takeover Panel. In Australia in 1980 self-regulation by the stock exchanges was effectively replaced by the National Companies and Securities Commission (NCSC).

The NCSC administers the Companies (Acquisition of Shares) Act 1980, which has the twin objective of obtaining equal opportunity for all shareholders in an offeree company, and providing sufficient time, disclosure of information and alternative opinion for all shareholders to be able to arrive at an objective conclusion about accepting or rejecting an offer. Under the new provisions an acquirer may in any manner, and over any period of time, accumulate a holding of up to 20 per cent of the voting shares in another company. Once a 20 per cent interest has been established the acquirer can only proceed by (a) purchasing shares in any way as long as the increment to his holding does not exceed 3 per cent of voting shares in any six monthly period, (b) lodging a formal takeover offer, which may be conditional upon a minimum percentage of acceptances, or (c) making an on-market bid, i.e. standing in the market for one month after making an announcement to accept unconditionally all shares offered at a declared price.

Inherent in the new approach to regulating takeovers is a tradeoff between equity and efficiency. The provision of time for all shareholders to become acquainted with the terms of an offer, and the greater disclosure of information about its adequacy, may place small shareholders in a better position to benefit. But the provision of time and the very complexity of the legislation may allow an inefficient management to put into effect blocking tactics which could inhibit the market's operation (see Santow, 1979; Ormandy, 1980). One observer has concluded that 'the effect of the new Take-Over Code will be to inhibit takeovers and to assist in entrenching incumbent directors and controllers of companies' (Vrisakis, 1980, p. 14). The present study suggests that such a result would indeed serve to perpetuate inefficient management of resources.

Another possibly unfortunate aspect of the new legislation is that it militates against partial takeovers. An offeror making an on-market announcement may run the risk of being locked into a no-control situation. Also, under a formal takeover offer an offeror who for strategic reasons purchases more than 20 per cent of the shares outside of this scheme will lose the advantage conferred by a minimum acceptance condition. In its submission to the Senate Select Committee on Securities and Exchange, merchant banker Hill Samuel outlined possible abuses of inter-company shareholdings which could be detrimental to minority shareholders and proposed that these be eliminated as far as possible (see Rae, *et al.*, 1974, p. 14.133). However, in Chapter 6 of the present study it was found that partial takeovers, resulting in company control, could play an important role in the market for corporate control. That is, while an acquiring company might be hesitant in purchasing complete control from the outset, a period of *effective* control might demonstrate whether a complete and permanent merging of operations is justified. In our view such a process should be accompanied by provisions for the equitable treatment of minority shareholders. Thus, the new legislation stipulates that where there exists a significant relationship (defined as ownership of 30 per cent or more of voting shares) between offeror and offeree, the board of the offeree must obtain independent advice on the adequacy of a bid. However, it is doubtful whether a report commissioned by the incumbent board will very often diverge from the position adopted by the directors. One solution to this problem might be for the NCSC to exercise its discretion in cases where an independent assessment is deemed appropriate and nominate an investigator of its own. This proposal, however, raises yet another question: that of formulating equitable funding procedures.

Another problem relates to the threshold level of 20 per cent ownership. The findings of this study suggest that in many companies effective control can be achieved with 20 per cent ownership which can be firmly established through creeping acquisition (at the rate of 3 per cent every six months). Management circles (Crichton-Brown, 1980) have urged a lowering of the threshold to 10 per cent. The problem with this suggestion, however, is that it will entrench incumbent directors even more and may inhibit the investment policies of financial institutions.

This question draws attention to the problems posed for legislators by the expanding power of financial institutions. In the US Soldofsky and Boe (1975) and Welles (1974) have suggested that limits might need to be imposed on the amount that any financial institution be permitted to own in any one company and on the total assets controlled by a single institution. Soldofsky (1971) questioned the 'legitimacy' of institutional power, proposing that the income-receiving and investment aspects of their operations be separated from the voting function. The latter function, it was suggested, could be vested in a Stockholders' Voting Council composed of the holders of paper issued by the institutions, i.e., superannuation and insurance policy holders, investment company shareholders, etc. Such suggestions, however, call into question the legitimacy of any agent-principal relationship, without which no society can function.

The holders of institutional paper have objectives which are as varied as those of shareholders in industrial corporations. The executives of institutions must balance the interests and objectives of their shareholders or policy holders, just as the executives of industrial concerns must presumably balance the objectives of their shareholders (not to mention employees, creditors and society at large). The present study has concluded that if the various market and non-market restraints on management are effective, more optimal performances are likely to result. We have not considered the situation within financial institutions in detail. The largest equity-owning financial institutions in Australia are mutual associations in which policy holders exercise practically no influence on the behaviour or composition of top management. If these institutions had a control mechanism such as is provided in the joint-stock company, their operating efficiency might be improved and the institutions themselves might be motivated to take a greater interest in the efficiency of industrial companies. In the US, O'Hara (1981) has demonstrated empirically the superior efficiency of stock-based savings and loan associations over the mutual form. The latter continue to survive as an organisational form, she argues, because of government regulation restricting entry and exit. All this suggests that some attention should be focused on the accountability of executives in financial institutions and how the legislative framework affects the market and non-market mechanisms.

A public policy issue deserving some attention is the possibility of a tradeoff between X-efficiency and allocative efficiency. Australian Trade Practices Legislation was traditionally based on the UK *rule of reason* model. Though the merger provisions of the 1974 Trade Practices Act moved closer to the *per se* approach of the US, a public benefit test recognising the importance of economies of scale was provided. New legislation passed in 1977 restricted the ban on mergers to cases where a bidder would as a result of the acquisition 'be in a position to control or dominate a market, or substantially strengthen his power to control or dominate a market'. Although the new provisions will hamper the achievement or extension of dominance by merger or takeover of further markets, and thereby perhaps promote allocative efficiency, at the same time many existing monopolists and oligopolists are made less vulnerable to takeover, which impairs the effectiveness of the market for corporate control.

Such a state of affairs does not augur well in light of the findings of this study; if managers of firms are free of internal and product market restraints and the threat of takeover is also removed, complacency and inefficiency are likely to result. At the same time many more mergers and takeovers are now free to take place if dominance is not present, so that over a significant range of industry the market for corporate control can now work more effectively.

Other contentious policy issues relate to double taxation of corporate income and differential rates of tax on dividends and capital gains. Presently Australia operates under the 'classical' system whereby companies are taxed and shareholders are then taxed separately on their dividend income. Capital gains on sale of property are not taxed unless realised within twelve months of purchase. Both these issues came under the scrutiny of the Taxation Review Committee (Asprey, *et al.*, 1975).

The Committee thought that non-taxation of capital gains would encourage investments in areas returning little current income and would encourage the ploughback of current income. Similarly, double taxation of corporate earnings was criticised for creating a bias towards greater retention of earnings. However, the Committee was careful to qualify this point by saying that 'whether the distortion is a ground for criticism depends on the view that is taken of company self-financing through retention of profits, compared with financing by resort to the market' (p. 227). In this respect Chapter 6 of the present study indicates that there should be some cause for concern. There it was shown that externally financed firms with similar (below average) past profitability records to firms mainly financed internally earned significantly higher rates of profit in the future. This effect was stronger within small and medium-sized firms and in newly established (non-mature) companies than in large well-established concerns. However, implications for the efficiency of reinvestment of retained earnings are made clear when we consider evidence recently provided by Praetz (1979). Employing a sample of 50 large Australian corporations, Praetz concluded that 'the most important part of [his] cross-section regressions is that retained earnings was unimportant as a determinant of second period earnings growth' (p. 158). This is reminiscent of the UK findings reported by Little and Rayner (1966).

The owner control/management control distinction is an important one in this context. There are two reasons why the directors of owner-controlled firms would wish to retain a large fraction of earnings within the firm. First, the dominant shareholders will be wealthier than the average shareholder and a high retention policy will result in under-taxation. Second, if the controlling group of shareholders wishes to maintain a tight grip over the company new equity will be restricted, so that finance for expansion will need to come from new debt issues (which will be limited by gearing considerations) and retentions. In Chapter 7 it was found that in the small to medium-size category the retention ratio did not differ markedly as between owner- and management-controlled firms. However, the retentions policy followed by management-controlled firms was far more sensitive to variations in profitability: management-controlled firms with more profitable operations and new investment opportunities tended to retain a greater share of their earnings stream. Since the retention ratio of small to medium owner-controlled firms did not show a great deal of variation with the value of directors' holdings and these firms would (because of their size) be more vulnerable to takeover if the shareholding of the dominant ownership group were reduced, it seems that fear of loss of control provides a more important explanation of their retention policy. On the other hand, in the large firms sample it was found that owner-controlled firms had significantly higher retention ratios than similar sized management-controlled firms. However, retentions were again found to be relatively insensitive to the value of directors' holdings. Again it seems that control was a vital concern even though in several of these firms the shareholdings of the director group could have been diluted without jeopardising directors' control. The influence of double taxation cannot be dismissed, however, since in small to medium-sized management-controlled firms the retention ratio was positively and significantly related to the value of directors' holdings.

The Taxation Review Committee recommended that an imputation system of taxation replace the 'classical' approach. Under an imputation system shareholders would be allowed a credit against income tax on dividends to counter some or all of the tax already paid by the company, but this plan was not implemented. High-income earners would still favour retentions because of a higher marginal tax rate, but less than under double taxation. Of course, if high retentions are motivated by questions of survival and control is firmly held, it is doubtful whether imputation would result in much more liberal payouts. However, some form of imputation has been introduced in France (1963), the UK (1973) and West Germany (1977). As a preliminary measure a lump sum concessional allowance on the first

$500 of dividend income received by shareholders has been introduced in the US. Pressures for reform are mounting in Australia and the first step towards removal of double taxation was made in the 1982 Budget. Now personal income tax on the first $1,000 of dividend income from resident companies is reduced by $300.

In relation to the taxation of capital gains, there remain several conceptual problems which require careful analysis and public debate. For example, the taxation of unrealised gains would be inequitable as would the practice (under a progressive tax system) of taxing several years of accrued gains as one year's income. Further problems arise under inflationary conditions because much of the capital gain is likely to represent a purely nominal addition to wealth. Though the equity question is clearly a difficult one, the deleterious efficiency effects could be mitigated by allowing listed companies to purchase their own shares.[7] This practice is widespread in the US and some European countries and has recently been proposed for adoption in Australia by the Australian Financial System Inquiry (see Campbell, *et al.*, 1981) and in the UK by the British Department of Trade. The Department's argument is that this relaxation would permit companies with surplus cash flow to return that cash to shareholders and thereby promote a speedy reallocation of resources to areas with higher marginal investment opportunities. A proof of this proposition has been provided by Mueller (1972, pp. 206-8), but he qualified his support by suggesting that prospective purchases be announced well in advance, so as to minimise the possibility of abuse arising from insider trading by corporate officers. We should go further to propose that such a condition be legislated, so that share repurchase could not be used to thwart takeover attempts.[8]

Suggestions for Future Research

A number of avenues for future research have been suggested. Perhaps the most fundamental point is to call into question the methodology by which the performance consequences of the separation of ownership and control are assessed. Rather than plunge directly into a comparison of the relative performances of 'management-' and 'owner-'controlled firms, we have demonstrated that the results will be far more illuminating if the forces shaping performance *within* control types are understood first. Given superior data and better specified models, future research along these lines would be capable of yielding deeper insights into the determinants of corporate performance.

Research could be directed, in the first instance, at more detailed investigations into the behaviour and performance of the three characters of control identified here. This research could be integrated with a study of the strategic policies (for example, mergers and diversification) and internal organisational structures adopted by firms in response to internal and external pressures on management.[9]

In the UK, Channon (1973) noted that family-controlled firms tended to resist organisational change, were slow to diversify and tended to retain a unitary form of control. Many business histories (see Hannah, 1976) provide examples of conservative family control retarding business policy. We have found that in Australia family-controlled companies still feature prominently. It would be interesting to enquire whether this fact has had some influence on the rate of change of *industrial* structure taking place in these countries, since both have in recent decades experienced low rates of structural change within the OECD group. It has been conjectured that this slow adaptation to changing economic circumstances has contributed to their relatively slow rates of growth. For public policy it would be of considerable importance to examine the influences of alternative ownership-control patterns on the rate of structural adaptation. Such knowledge would greatly assist in the design of appropriate policy responses to changing conditions. For instance, it seems reasonable to suggest that structural changes will be more difficult to effect, and more easily resisted, if a firm remains single product and can avoid the discipline of the market for corporate control.

Company-controlled firms, we have found, often represent the market for corporate control in action. These firms are frequently part of a holding company structure, although in some cases company control may be preliminary to divisionalisation. It is clear that relatively little research effort has been devoted to the study of holding company structures (see Daems, 1978). In Chapter 6 it was noted that the control situation in company-controlled firms is fluid over time, suggesting an on-going process of adjustment. Since disaggregated and standardised accounts are available for listed company-controlled firms, a time-series analysis tracing the relative performances of firms before and after the establishment of a dominating company shareholding could be instructive. For example, if a partial takeover bid were launched on a firm with inefficient management, the approach could aid in quantifying the extent of the inefficiency. Alternatively, it could help in resolving the question of whether the market for corporate control provides a greater social benefit as an *ex ante* threat to incumbent managers, than as an *ex post* spur to managerial efficiency (see Meeks, 1977).

Given the importance of financial institutions demonstrated in the present study, it is clear that further careful research into their investment behaviour is called for, particularly in the UK and Australia, where the growth and concentration of institutional shareholdings are well advanced, but also in the US. For example, it would be of interest to trace inter-company and inter-industry flows of institutional funds in response to their performance. Comparative studies of Anglo-American corporations and continental European firms might be fruitful.

In the present study firm maturity was rather crudely measured. However, some interesting results were achieved, particularly with regard to company-controlled firms. A definitive study would require a longitudinal approach employing data on marginal rates of return on investment and the marginal cost of capital for individual firms.[10] Such a study, tracing the development of young enterprising firms and the problems encountered in raising finance and maintaining a rapid rate of growth, could yield information which would be instructive for policy-makers concerned with the efficiency of market mechanisms which regulate the flow of resources into high-yielding areas.

Finally, the tentative support for the shared assets-managerial discretion hypothesis which was found in Chapter 6 suggests that further research is required in that direction. Differences in the concentration-profits and firm size-profits relationships have been observed between US, UK, Australian and continental European firms. Our analysis suggests that an international study might resolve these questions by examining such factors as managerial incentives, and the alternative market and institutional frameworks.

Notes

1. See, for example, Alchian (1950). More recently a theory of the survival of organisational forms has been proposed by several writers (Jensen, 1983; Fama and Jensen, 1983). This theory states that the most profitable or efficient organisational *form* will tend to dominate, through survival, various activities. However, it does not speak specifically of the survival characteristics of individual organisations.

2. Note, however, that faster growing companies may *report* profits which are understated relative to slower growing firms because of higher provision for depreciation.

3. The Australian Shareholders' Association makes regular protests against executive stock option plans on the grounds that they dilute the existing shareholders' interest, invite insider trading and may assist incumbent boards during a takeover.

4. The system of cumulative voting originated in the US during the 1870s. It allows a minority of shareholders to elect representatives to the board depending on their proportionate shareholding. In the US, banks and utilities are subject to mandatory cumulative voting in some states.

5. This is indicated by several articles appearing in the financial press. For example, see 'AMP Caught in the John Takeover Tug-o-war', *Australian Financial Review (AFR)*, 20 November 1975, p. 36; 'Institutions Discover the Value of their Vote', *AFR*, 22 March 1976, p. 32; 'AMP's Mighty Equities Muscle', *AFR*, 26 April 1978, p. 48; 'Investment Manager's Dilemma', *AFR*, 15 June 1978, p. 40; 'AMP Investment Style Showing More and More Arrogance', *Age*, 24 November 1979, p. 31.

6. The term 'warehousing' describes an agreement whereby a market raider employs agents (other companies or individuals) to purchase shares in a target company and re-sell them to the raider under specified conditions later.

7. Coombes and Tress (1977, 1979) have advocated that Australian companies be allowed to repurchase shares.

8. The use of share repurchase as a tactic to foil takeover bids in the US is documented by Hayes and Taussig (1967).

9. The US and European studies which have appeared in the last decade are reviewed in Caves (1980). In Australia a first step in this direction has been made by Chenhall (1979); however, this study lacked the firm theoretical structure which is envisaged.

10. Hiller (1978) has produced some evidence along these lines.

APPENDIX

Table A.1.1: Alphabetical Listing of Companies (for notes, see end of table)

Company name	(a) Primary industry	(b) Control type	(c) Firm maturity	(d) Non-continuing
Abel Lemon Holdings Ltd	46	MiO		
Acmil Ltd	31	MC	*	
Acrow Australia Ltd	33	OC	*	*
Actrol Ltd	33	MC		
William Adams and Co. Ltd	33	MC	*	
Adelaide Brighton Cement Ltd	28	MiO		
Adelaide and Wallaroo Fertilizers Ltd	27	MC		*
Adelaide Steamship Co. Ltd	53	MC		
Advertiser Newspapers Ltd	26	DC		
Aldus Ltd	33	MiO		
Allens Confectionery Ltd	21	MC		
Allied Mills Ltd	21	MC		
Amalgamated Holdings Ltd	91	MiO		
Amalgamated Wireless (Australasia) Ltd	33	MC		
Ampol Petroleum Ltd	27	MC		
Angus and Coote (Holdings) Ltd	48	MiO		
Ansett Transport Industries Ltd	54	DC		
ARC Industries Ltd	31	DC		
Associated Pulp and Paper Mills Ltd	26	JDO		
Austral Bakeries (Holdings) Ltd	21	DC		
Australian Consolidated Industries Ltd	28	MC		
Australian Fertilizers Ltd	27	OC		
Australian Gypsum Industries Ltd	28	MC		
Australian Motor Industries Ltd	32	JDO		
Australian Paper Manufacturers Ltd	26	MC		
Automatic Totalisators Ltd	33	MC		
Ballarat Brewing Co. Ltd	92	MC	*	
Barrett Burston (Australia) Ltd	21	MC		
Bennett and Fisher Ltd	46	MC		
Bennett and Wood Ltd	32	MC		
Berlei Hestia Ltd	24	DC		*
Bestobell Australia Ltd	31	OC		*
Bliss Welded Products Ltd	33	OC		*
Blue Circle Southern Cement Ltd	28	JDO		
Blue Metal Industries Ltd	28	MC		
Bonds Coats Patons Ltd	24	OC	*	*
Boral Ltd	28	MC	*	
Borg Warner (Australia) Ltd	32	OC	*	
Bradford Insulation Holdings (S.A.) Ltd	28	DC		

239

Company name	(a) Primary industry	(b) Control type	(c) Firm maturity	(d) Non-continuing
Bradken Consolidated Ltd	29	DC		
Bradmill Industries Ltd	23	MC		
Brambles Industries Ltd	51	MC		
Brick and Pipe Industries Ltd	28	MC		
Brickworks Ltd	28	DC		
Bruck (Australia) Ltd	23	MC	*	
Buckley and Nunn Ltd	48	MC	*	
Bushells Investments Ltd	21	MjO		
Byrne and Davidson Industries Ltd	31	MiO	*	*
A.G. Campbell Holdings Ltd	46	MiO		
Capitol Motors Ltd	48	MjO	*	*
Carlton and United Breweries Ltd	21	MC		
W.R. Carpenter Holdings Ltd	46	MiO		
C.C. Bottlers Ltd	21	MiO	*	
Century Storage Battery Co. Ltd	32	MC		
A.J. Chown Holdings Ltd	46	DC		
Clark Rubber Stores Ltd	48	MiO	*	
Cleckheaton Ltd	23	MC	*	
Clifton Brick Holdings Ltd	28	MiO		
Clyde Industries Ltd	31	MC		
G.J. Coles and Co. Ltd	48	MC		
Collie (Australia) Ltd	27	MiO		
Comeng Holdings Ltd	32	DC		
Commonwealth Industrial Gases Ltd	27	OC		
Concrete Industries (Monier) Ltd	28	OC		
Consolidated Foods Ltd	21	MC		
Consolidated Press Holdings Ltd	26	MjO		*
Containers Ltd	31	MC		
Sydney Cooke Ltd	31	MC		
Courtaulds Hilton Ltd	24	OC		*
G.E. Crane Holdings Ltd	31	MiO		
Crestknit Ltd	24	MC	*	
Cuming, Smith and Company Ltd	27	MiO		
Dalton Brothers Holdings Ltd	26	DC		
Davis Consolidated Industries Ltd	21	MiO		
Dennys, Lacelles Ltd	46	MC		
Dickson Primer (Consolidated) Ltd	31	MiO		
Doulton Australia Ltd	28	OC	*	*
Edwards Dunlop and Co. Ltd	26	MC		
Elder Smith Goldsborough Mort Ltd	46	MC		
Electrical Equipment of Australia Ltd	33	MiO		
Email Ltd	33	MC		
EMI (Australia) Ltd	33	OC	*	
Ensign Holdings Ltd	24	MC		
John Fairfax Ltd	26	MjO		
Farley and Lewers Ltd	28	DC		

Company name	(a) Primary industry	(b) Control type	(c) Firm maturity	(d) Non- continuing
F.H. Faulding and Co. Ltd	27	MiO		
T.A. Field Holdings Ltd	21	MjO		
Fielders Ltd	21	MiO		
J. Fielding and Co. Ltd	26	MiO		
Fleetways (Holdings) Ltd	51	OC		
Flexdrive Industries Ltd	32	MiO	*	
Frozen Food Industries of Australia Ltd	21	DC	*	
J. Gadsden Australia Ltd	31	MiO		
Georges Australia Ltd	48	MC		*
Gerrard Co. of Australasia Ltd	33	MC		
Gibson Chemical Industries Ltd	27	MC		
Gillespie Brothers Holdings Ltd	21	MiO		
Glass Containers Ltd	28	OC	*	*
Glen Iris Brick Consolidated Ltd	28	DC		*
Gollin Holdings Ltd	46	MiO		
Gordon and Gotch (Australasia) Ltd	26	MC		
Gowing Brothers Ltd	48	MiO		
Grace Brothers Holdings Ltd	48	MiO		
Group Engineering Ltd	31	MiO	*	
GUD Holdings Ltd	32	MC	*	
James Hardie Asbestos Ltd	28	MiO		
Hardie Trading Ltd	27	DC		
Keith Harris and Co. Ltd	21	MC		
Henderson's Industries Ltd	31	MiO		
The Herald and Weekly Times Ltd	26	MC		
Hills Industries Ltd	31	MiO	*	
John Holland Holdings Ltd	41	MiO	*	
Humes Ltd	28	MC		
Hunter Douglas Ltd	31	OC	*	
Huttons Ltd	21	MC		
Hygienic Lily Ltd	26	OC	*	*
Industrial Engineering Ltd	33	MiO		
International Combustion Australia Ltd	33	OC		
Jasco Holdings Ltd	26	OC	*	
Jaques Ltd	33	MC		
M.B. John Ltd	31	DC		
Henry Jones (IXL) Ltd	21	MC		
Johns and Waygood Perry Engineering Ltd	33	MC		*
Kelvinator Australia Ltd	33	MC		
Kemtron Ltd	33	MC		*
The Kiwi International Co. Ltd	27	MjO		*
Lane Ltd	27	OC	*	
Lanray Industries Ltd	46	MiO	*	
Alfred Lawrence Holdings Ltd	27	MC		

Company name	(a) Primary industry	(b) Control type	(c) Firm maturity	(d) Non- continuing
Life Savers (Australasia) Ltd	21	MC		
Lightburn and Co. Ltd	33	MjO		
LNC Industries Ltd	48	MC		
Gilbert Lodge Holdings Ltd	33	MiO		
Lowes Ltd	48	MiO		
K.G. Luke Group Industries Ltd	31	MiO		
Macquarie Broadcasting Holdings Ltd	91	DC	*	
Malco Industries Ltd	33	MiO		
Malleys Ltd	33	OC	*	
Marrickville Holdings Ltd	21	MC		
Martin Bright Steels Ltd	29	MiO		
John Martin and Co. Ltd	48	MiO		
Mauri Brothers and Thomson Ltd	21	DC		
Mayne Nickless Ltd	51	MC		
Meggitt Ltd	21	DC		
Michaelis Bayley Ltd	34	MiO		
James Miller Holdings Ltd	23	MiO		
Charles Moore Australia Ltd	48	MiO		
Malcolm Moore Industries Ltd	32	MC		
Phillip Morris Australia Ltd	22	OC	*	
Myer Emporium Ltd	48	MiO		
Mytton's Ltd	31	MiO		
McEwans Ltd	48	MiO		
John McIlwraith Industries Ltd	31	MiO		
McIlwraith McEacharn Ltd	53	OC		
Ralph McKay Ltd	33	OC	*	
McPherson's Ltd	33	MiO		
National Consolidated Ltd	32	MC		
Newbold General Refractories Ltd	28	DC		
News Ltd	26	MiO		
Nicholas International Ltd	27	MiO		*
Oliver J. Nilsen Australia Ltd	33	MjO		
NKS (Holdings) Ltd	31	MC		
Norman Ross Discounts Ltd	48	MjO	*	*
Nylex Corporation Ltd	34	OC		
Olympic Consolidated Industries Ltd	32	MC		
OPSM Industries Ltd	34	MC		
Overseas Corporation (Australia) Ltd	31	MC	*	
Ozapaper Ltd	26	OC		
Penfold Wines Australia Ltd	21	MjO		
W.C. Penfold Holdings Ltd	26	MiO		
Petersville (Australia) Ltd	21	MC		
Philips Industries Holdings Ltd	33	OC		*
Pioneer Concrete Services Ltd	28	MC	*	
Pizzey Ltd	33	MiO		

Company name	(a) Primary industry	(b) Control type	(c) Firm maturity	(d) Non-continuing
Protean Holdings Ltd	21	MjO	*	*
Protector Safety Industries Ltd	93	DC		*
Pye Industries Ltd	33	OC	*	
Reckitt and Colman Holdings Ltd	21	OC	*	*
Reed Consolidated Industries Ltd	26	OC		
Repco Ltd	32	MC		
Rocla Industries Ltd	28	MC		
Rothmans of Pallmall (Australia) Ltd	22	OC	*	
Sebel Ltd	25	MiO	*	
B. Seppelt and Sons Ltd	21	MiO		*
Siddons Industries Ltd	33	MiO		
Simpson Pope Holdings Ltd	33	MjO		
Sims Consolidated Ltd	29	MC		
H.C. Sleigh Ltd	27	OC		
Washington H. Soul Pattinson and Co. Ltd	48	DC		
S.A. Brewing Co. Ltd	21	MC		
Steamships Trading Co. Ltd	46	MC		
Steggles Holdings Ltd	21	MiO		
Stramit Ltd	31	OC	*	
Sun Electric Consolidated Ltd	33	MiO		
Swift and Co. Ltd	27	OC		
David Syme and Co. Ltd	26	DC		
Taubmans Industries Ltd	27	OC		
Television Corporation Ltd	91	DC	*	*
Textile Holdings Ltd	23	MiO		
Thomas Nationwide Transport Ltd	51	MC	*	
Tooheys Ltd	21	MC		
Transport Development Australia Ltd	51	OC	*	*
Travelodge Australia Ltd	92	OC	*	
Tubemakers of Australia Ltd	29	JDO		*
Tyree Industries Ltd	33	OC	*	*
Union Carbide Australia and New Zealand Ltd	27	OC		*
United Telecasters Sydney Ltd	91	DC	*	
Vickers Australia Ltd	32	OC		*
Victorian Broadcasting Network Ltd	91	MiO		
Vulcan Industries Ltd	33	MC	*	
F.J. Walker Ltd	21	DC		
Waltons Ltd	44	MC		
Warburton O'Donnell Ltd	33	MC		
Wattyl Ltd	27	MC		
Waugh and Josephson Holdings Ltd	46	MiO		
Martin Wells Holdings Ltd	34	MiO	*	
Joe White Maltings Ltd	21	MiO		

Company name	(a) Primary industry	(b) Control type	(c) Firm maturity	(d) Non-continuing
Winchcombe Carson Ltd	46	MC		
Wilke and Co. Ltd	26	DC		
Winns Ltd	48	MiO		
Woodhall Ltd	31	OC	*	*
Woolworths Ltd	48	MC		
Wormald International Ltd	33	MC		
Yates Seeds Ltd	46	MiO		
York Motors (Holdings) Ltd	48	MC		
J.B. Young Holdings Ltd	48	DC		

Notes

(a)   Industrial classification

ASIC code

21-22	Food, beverages and tobacco
21	Food and beverages
22	Tobacco
23	Textiles
24	Clothing and footwear
25	Wood, wood products and furniture
26	Paper and paper products, printing and publishing
27	Chemical, petroleum and coal products
28	Glass, clay and other non-metallic mineral products
29	Basic metal products
31	Fabricated metal products
32	Transport equipment
33	Other industrial machinery and equipment and household appliances
34	Leather, rubber and plastic products and manufacturing n.e.c.
41	General construction
46	Wholesale trade
48	Retail trade
51, 53, 54	Transport and storage
51	Road transport
53	Water transport
54	Air transport
91, 92, 93	Entertainment, recreation, restaurants, hotels and personal services
91	Entertainment and recreational services
92	Restaurants, hotels and clubs
93	Personal services

(b)   Control-type classification

Code	
MjO	Majority ownership control
MiO	Minority ownership control
MC	Management control

DC	Domestic company control
OC	Overseas company control
JDO	Joint domestic/overseas company control

(c) *Maturity*

Firms designated as non-mature are marked with an asterisk.

(d) *Continuing companies*

Firms which did not continue (or for which data were not available) over the whole period are marked with an asterisk.

Table A.1.2: Raw Data Variables Employed

Variable number (V)			Description
		Balance sheet	
Current assets			
VI	Cash and liquids	—	Cash and bank balances
		—	Short-term deposits
V2	Trade debtors	—	Trade debtors
		—	Other debtors
V3	Stocks	—	Stocks on hand and in transit
V4	Other current assets	—	Expenses paid in advance
Long-term assets			
V5	Net plant and property	—	Properties and storage facilities
		—	Plant and equipment
V6	Intangible assets	—	Debenture issue expenses
V7	Investments	—	Shares in other corporations
V8	Deferred assets	—	Future income tax benefit
		—	Secured loans to directors
Current liabilities			
V9	Bank overdraft	—	Bank overdraft: secured
		—	Bank overdraft: unsecured
V10	Trade Creditors	—	Trade creditors and accrued charges
		—	Trade bills payable — secured
V11	Provision for income tax		
V12	Debt due one year	—	Provisions for long service leave, holidays and sundry
V13	Other current liabilities	—	Provision for dividend
Long-term liabilities			
V14	Long-term debt	—	Mortgage loans — secured

		—	Bank term loans — secured
		—	Registered debenture stock
V15	Other deferred liability	—	Provision for retirement allowances
		—	Provision for maintenance

Capital and Reserves

V16	Minority interest		
V17	Preferred capital		
V18	Ordinary equity	—	Issued ordinary stock units
		—	Asset revaluation reserve
		—	Capital profits reserve
		—	Exchange fluctuation reserve
		—	Retained profits
		—	Premium on share issues
		—	Premium on consolidation

Summary

V19	Current assets
V20	Long-term assets
V21	Current liabilities
V22	Long-term liabilities
V23	Capital and reserves

Capital and reserves (V23) + current liabilities (V21) + long-term liabilities (V22) = current assets (V19) + long-term assets (V20)

Income account

V24	First operating income
V25	Depreciation
V26	Second operating income (V24 – V25)
V27	Investment income
V28	Other normal income
V29	Earned before interest and tax (V26 + V27 + V28)
V30	Interest paid
V31	Pre-tax group profit (V29 – V30)
V32	Current tax provisions
V33	Group net profit (V31 – V32)
V34	Minority dividends
V35	Preference dividends
V36	Earned for ordinary (V33 – V34 – V35)
V37	Ordinary dividends
V38	Retained from normal operations (V36 – V37)
V39	Non-normal surplus loss
V40	Total retained (V38 ± V39)

Additional variables

Funds obtained from new share issues

V41	Rights issue
V42	Public placement
V43	Private placement
V44	Issue made in connection with acquisitions
V45	Allotment
V46	Employee shares

V47	Exercise of executive options
V48	New equity issues (V41 to V47)

Share price data

V49	Average post balance data price
V50	Average of high and low prices
V51	Median monthly volume of trading
V52	Median monthly value of trading
V53	Shares on issue (fully paid)
V54	Equivalent fully paid shares
V55	Number of executive share options outstanding

Other variables

V56	Revaluation of assets
V57	Australian standard industrial classification code
V58	Four-firm concentration ratio (for two-digit manufacturing industries)

Ownership and control data

V59	Number of shares on issue
V60	Directors' holdings
V61	Directors as a cohesive group
V62	Holdings of largest 20 cohesive groups
V63	Number of directors
V64	Significant Australian company holding
V65	Significant UK company holding
V66	Significant US company holding
V67	Significant other overseas company holding
V68	Chairman's holding
V69	Managing director's holding
V70	Deputy chairman's holding
V71	Chairman and managing director's holding
V72	Deputy chairman and managing director's holding
V73	General manager/chief executive's holding
V74	Company secretary's holding
V75	Deputy managing director's holding
V76	Other significant private holding
V77	Private holdings in largest 20 cohesive groups
V78	Institutional holdings in largest 20 cohesive groups
V79	Company holdings in largest 20 cohesive groups
V80	Nominee holdings in largest 20 cohesive groups
V81	US company holdings in largest 20 cohesive groups
V82	UK company holdings in largest 20 cohesive groups
V83	Other overseas company holdings in largest 20 cohesive groups

Data on firm maturity

V84	Initiation date of company
V85	Date of extraordinary events

Table A.1.3: Definition of Variables

Notation

m	=	last year of a period
p	=	first year of the period
o	=	year p *minus* one year
n	=	number of years in the period
	=	m — o
y	=	corporate tax rate

The values of m, p, o and n are as follows:

'Whole period' :	m = 9, p = 1, o = 0, n = 9
'Sub-period 1' :	m = 3, p = 1, o = 0, n = 3
'Sub-period 2' :	m = 6, p = 4, o = 3, n = 3
'Sub-period 3' :	m = 9, p = 7, o = 6, n = 3

where '0' refers to 1965-6 and '9' to 1974-5.

Net assets (NA):

$$[V20 + V19 - (V21 + V15)]$$

Net assets — opening $(\text{net assets})_o$

Net assets — closing $(\text{net assets})_m$

Aggregate net assets:

$$\frac{(\text{Net assets})_m + (\text{net assets})_o}{2} + \sum_{p}^{m-1} (\text{net assets})$$

This procedure gives half weight to both opening and closing values of net assets in order that an average may be derived which is comparable with flows such as profits. It is based on the arbitrary assumption that the change in net assets between two accounting dates is linear.

Growth rate of net assets (GNA): *

$$n\sqrt{\frac{(\text{Net assets})_m}{(\text{net assets})_o}} - 1$$

Pre-tax rate of return on net assets (RNA):

$$\frac{\sum_{p}^{m} (V24 + V27 + V28 + V39 - V25)}{(\text{Aggregate net assets})}$$

Equity assets:

$$[V23 - (V16 + V17)]$$

Aggregate equity assets:

$$\frac{(\text{Equity assets})_m + (\text{equity assets})_o}{2} + \sum_{p}^{m-1} (\text{equity assets})$$

Post-tax rate of return on equity assets (REA):

$$\frac{\sum_{p}^{m} (V37 + V40)}{(\text{Aggregate equity assets})}$$

External growth rate (EXG):

$$\sqrt[n]{\frac{\sum_{p}^{m} V48 + (V17_m - V17_o) + (V16 + V14)_m + (V18)_o}{(\text{net assets})_o}} - 1$$

Valuation Ratio (VAL):

$$\frac{\sum_{p}^{m} (V53 \times V49)}{\sum_{p}^{m} V18}$$

Retention ratio (RET):

$$\frac{\sum_{p}^{m} (V38)}{\sum_{p}^{m} (V38 + V37)}$$

Gearing (GEAR):

$$\frac{\sum_{p}^{m} [V30\,(1-y) + V35]}{\sum_{p}^{m} [V30\,(1-y) + V37 + V35 + V40]}$$

Operating risk (SDRNA):

$$\sqrt{\frac{\sum_{p}^{m} (RNA_t - R\hat{N}A_t)^2}{n}}$$

where: RNA_t is the pre-tax rate of return on net assets in any year t between p and m.

$R\hat{N}A_t$ is the value for RNA_t predicted from a linear time series regression of the form $RNA_t = a + bt$.

---

* In their study, Singh and Whittington (1968, p. 236) estimated the numerator, closing size, by adding sources and uses figures to opening values and summing this with actual closing figures for minority interests and long-term liabilities. This was done because of the inclusion of companies which had changed their accounting date. Thus, the problem does not arise in our analysis.

Table A.2.1: Summary of Earlier Research on the Separation of Ownership and Control

Author(s)	Period	Sample	Definition of control type	Methodology, approach	Performance variables	Verdict
a) UNITED STATES						
Monson, Chiu and Cooley (1968)	1952-63	500 largest industrials	OC: One party has > 10% and is on BOD, or has > 20% MC: no block > 5%	Analysis of variance and analysis of co-variance	NI/NW	OC > MC*
Kamerschen (1968)	1959-64	200 largest non-financial	OC: > 10% owned by a party MC: < 10% owned by a party	Multiple regression	REA	OC > MC
Hindley (1970)	1930-50	variety of samples	OC: largest 20 hold > 40% MC: largest 20 hold < 20%	Multiple regression and other tests	ln R	ln R negatively related to % hold by largest 20
Larner (1970)	1956-62	187 of largest 500 non-financial	OC: one party has > 10% MC: no party has > 10%	Multiple regression	1) REA 2) risk: variance of REA	1) OC > MC* (not economically sig.) 2) MC > OC
Boudreaux (1973)	1952-63	72 of 500 largest industrials	OC: one party has > 10%, is on BOD or otherwise known to control, or has > 20%	Analysis of variance and analysis of co-variance	1) Rp = NI/NW 2) risk: Dp = standard deviation of Rp	1) OC > MC* 2) OC > MC*

			MC: no block > 5% and no recent evidence of control				
Palmer (1973a) (1973b)	1961-9	500 largest corporations	SOC: one party has > 30% WOC: one party has between 10 & 30% MC: no party has > 10%	Analysis of variance corrected for heteroscedasticity Mann-Whitney U-test	1) NI/NW 2) CV of NI/NW (ie $\sigma/\bar{x}$)	1) OC > MC* when high monopoly power 2) MC > OC sig. only in 4th 125
Ware (1975)	1960-70	74 large, well-established firms in food and beverage industry	OC: one party has > 15% and is on BOD, or has > 25% MC: no evidence of OC, and no block > 5%	Analysis of variance	1) NI/NW 2) $AP_L = NS/E$ 3) LTD/TA 4) RET	1) MC > OC* 2) MC < OC* 3) MC > OC 4) OC > MC*
McEachern (1975) (1978)	1963-72 1964-73	48 large industrials in 3 industries nearly all in top 500	EC: dominant interest has > 4% and is not part of management OM: chief executive owns > 4% MC: no interest has > 4%	Multiple regression	1) Market rate of return 2) Payout ratio 3) risk: β coefficient 4) growth of sales	1) OM > EC*, EC > MC* 2) OM < EC 3) OM > EC*, MC > EC* 4) OM > MC*

Table A.2.1 continued

Author(s)	Period	Sample	Definition of control type	Methodology, approach	Performance variables	Verdict
Holl (1977)	1962-72	343 of top 500	as for Palmer	Matched samples by size and mkt structure, identified MC firms evading market for corporate control (MCC)	Average market rate of return (i.e. dividend and stock price appreciation)	all OC > MC* evading MCC
Sorrenson (1979)	1948-66	30 OC and 30 MC firms in 11 industries	OC: one party has > 20% MC: no block > 5%	Analysis of variance	1) NI/NW	1) OC > MC generally MC > OC* in 1 industry
					2) Market rate of return	2) OC > MC generally MC > OC* in 1 industry
					3) Payout ratio	3) MC > OC generally MC > OC* in 2 industries
					4) Growth of NW	4) OC > MC generally MC > OC* in 2 industries
					5) Growth of sales	5) OC > MC generally OC > MC* in 1 industry

	Sample	Classification	Method	Dependent variables	Results
Bothwell (1980) 1960-7	150 large industrials in top 500	as for Palmer	Multiple regression, with interaction effects for high, substantial and low BTE	1) risk adjusted (CAPM) economic profit margin on sales 2) REA	1) SOC, WOC > MC* when BTE and market share high or substantial 2) SOC, WOC > MC
b) UNITED KINGDOM Radice (1971) 1957-67	86 'large' firms (NA > £5m in 1963) in three 2-digit industries	OC: a cohesive group has > 15% MC: no group has > 5%	Multiple regression	1) RNA 2) GNA	1) OC > MC* 2) OC > MC*
Holl (1975) 1948-60	183 quoted companies	OC: 1) if > 50% by one person or 2) if 20-50% by largest shareholder or, 3) > 20% by largest 20 holders and a) main holders are persons, or b) BOD has > 10% or c) 2 Board members are in top 20 share holders	Discriminant analysis, and generalised (Mahalanobis) distance analysis, with matched samples	1) RNA 2) GNA 3) Variance of RNA	1) OC > MC 2) indecisive 3) OC > MC large overlap between groups

Table A.2.1 continued

						Results	
Steer and Cable (1978)	1967-71	82 out of top 250	OC: if > 15% by a cohesive group or, > 3% by managers	Multiple regression including variables reflecting organisational structure	1) Π/EA 2) Π/EA+LTD) 3) Π 4) Growth of capital	1) OC > MC* 2) OC > MC* 3) OC > MC* 4) OC > MC*	
c) WEST GERMANY Thonet and Poensgen (1979)	1961-70	52 to 92 quoted companies	OC: cohesive group has > 25% MC: no group has > 25% excludes: > 25% owned by government, other Company or institutions	Multiple regression (GLS + OLS) on pooled yearly data	1) REA 2) Market rate of return 3) VAL 4) GTA 5) Variance of REA	1) MC > OC* 2) MC > OC 3) MC > OC* 4) MC < OC (sig. in high CR) 5) high CR: OC > MC low CR: OC < MC	
d) FRANCE Jacquemin and de Ghellinck (1980)	1970-74	103 of 200 largest	Case by case approach to find who exercises control. Divided into familial (FA) and non-familial (NFA)	Multiple regression using multi plicative dummy variables across pooled data (FA and NFA)	NCF/EA	Firm size had a greater positive influence on FA companies	

| e) AUSTRALIA Round (1976) | 1956-64 | 289 large companies | OC: > 10% held by persons among top 20

MC: persons hold < 5%

CC: > 15% held by another company | Multiple regression. Examined effect of overseas control | NI/TA | 1) Full sample OC > MC
2) 50 of top 100 OC > MC*
3) Overseas control* |

Notes:

* statistical significance was claimed by author(s)

OC: owner control
SOC: strong owner control
CC: company control
OM: owner-managed
REA: return on equity assets
NI: net income
R: book value of company/market value of company
GNA: growth rate of net assets
II: profit after interest and depreciation
LTD: long-term debt
TA: total assets
GTA: growth rate of total assets
VAL: valuation ratio = market value of company/book value
NS: net sales
AP$_L$: average product of labour

MC: management control
WOC: weak owner control
EC: externally controlled
RNA: return on net assets
NW: net worth
EA: equity assets
T: turnover
NCF: net cash flow
E: employees
RET: retention ratio

Table A.4.1: Chow Test of Equality of Coefficients Between Control-Type Samples

Dependent variable	Firm Samples Compared		
	OC vs. MC	OC vs. CC	MC vs. CC
RNA	11.159[a]	5.054[a]	6.685[a]
	(4,135)	(4,111)	(4,118)
REA	9.945[a]	3.803[a]	3.601[a]
	(4,135)	(4,111)	(4,118)
GNA	5.526[a]	7.256[a]	1.208
	(4,135)	(4,111)	(4,118)
SDRNA	1.194	1.038	2.290[c]
	(4,135)	(4,111)	(4,118)
RET	1.959	1.721	3.981[a]
	(4,131)	(4,105)	(4,116)

Notes: figures in brackets denote (V_1, V_2) degrees of freedom; a and c denote significance at the .01 and .10 levels respectively using a one-tail 'F' test.

Table A.5.1: Effects of Family Domination on the Performance of Management-Controlled Firms, n = 75

Equation number	Dependent variable	Constant	FAM	ln VDH	VDH	NMAT	SIZE (1/NAo)	R^2	$\bar{R}^2$	F-ratio
5.1.1	RNA	.171	.050 (3.140)[a]					.120	.107	
5.1.2	RNA	.147	.023 (1.706)[b]			.019 (1.158)	.187 (5.981)[d]	.434	.408	18.028[a]
5.1.3	RNA	.078	.006 (.424)	.016 (2.827)[a]		.015 (.921)	.212 (6.816)[d]	.491	.461	16.852[a]
5.1.4.	REA	.093	.024 (2.915)[a]					.104	.092	
5.1.5	REA	.082	.013 (1.773)[b]			.021 (2.343)[b]	.076 (4.470)[d]	.359	.332	13.258[a]
5.1.6	REA	.035	.002 (.207)	.011 (3.617)[a]		.018 (2.155)[b]	.092 (5.669)[d]	.460	.429	14.907[a]
5.1.7	GNA	.111	.014 (.899)					.011	< 0	
5.1.8	GNA	.095	−.003 (.170)			.021 (1.134)	.118 (3.352)[d]	.170	.135	4.833[a]
5.1.9	GNA	.042	−.016 (.935)	.012 (1.840)[b]		.018 (.960)	.137 (3.792)[d]	.208	.163	4.593[a]
5.1.10	SDRNA	.029	.007 (1.508)[c]					.030	.017	

Table A.5.1 continued

Equation number	Dependent variable	Constant	FAM	In VDH	VDH	NMAT	SIZE (1/NAo)	R^2	$\bar{R}^2$	F-ratio
5.1.11	SDRNA	.024	.003 (.589)			.012 (2.163)[b]	.031 (2.995)[a]	.202	.169	6.004[a]
5.1.12	SDRNA	.025	.004 (.749)		−.756E-5 (.875)	.012 (2.133)[b]	.030 (2.746)[a]	.211	.166	4.680[a]
5.1.13	RET	.402	.063 (2.046)[b]					.054	.041	
5.1.14	RET	.381	.042 (1.315)[c]			.025 (.636)	.146 (2.009)[e]	.114	.076	3.038
5.1.15	RET	.373	.037 (1.116)		517E-4 (.864)	.026 (.660)	.159 (2.140)[e]	.123	.073	2.457

Notes: figures in brackets are t-ratios; a, b and c denote significance at the .01, .05 and .10 levels respectively using a one-tail test; d and e denote significance at the .01 and .05 levels respectively using a two-tail test.

Table A.6.1: Size and Performance — Domestic and Company-Controlled Firms

Dependent variable	Domestic-company-controlled					Overseas-company-controlled					Chow test
	n	Constant	SIZE (1/NAo)	r^2	$\bar{r}^2$	n	Constant	SIZE (1/NAo)	r^2	$\bar{r}^2$	
RNA	27	.159	.125 (1.710)[c]	.105	.069	24	.178	.057 (2.106)[b]	.168	.130	.356 (2,47)
REA	27	.093	.100 (1.067)	.044	.005	24	.093	.017 (1.122)	.054	.011	.772 (2,47)
GNA	27	.110	.109 (1.557)	.088	.052	24	.115	.051 (1.963)[c]	.149	.110	.287 (2,47)
SDRNA	27	.036	.064 (1.921)[e]	.129	.094	24	.037	.004 (.541)	.013	< 0	2.968 (2,47)[c]
RET	26	.482	.008 (.089)	.000	< 0	23	.494	.054 (1.046)	.050	.004	.342 (2,45)

Notes: figures in brackets are t-ratios; b and c denote significance at the .05 and .10 levels respectively using a two-tail test; e denotes significance at the .05 level using a one-tail test; Chow test: figures in brackets denote (V_1, V_2) degrees of freedom; c indicates significance at the .10 level using a one-tail 'F' test.

Table A.6.2: Structure of New Equity Issues, Whole Period, by Control Type/Maturity

Type of issue	(1) Rights issues		(2) Issues in acquisitions		(3) Private placements and allotments		(4) Public placements		(5) Total new issues		(6) No. in sample	(7) (5)/(6)%
Control Type/ Maturity classification	%	n	%	n	%	n	%	n	%	n	n	
Non-mature:												
2. Minority ownership	74.0	10	51.7	7	33.3	6	6.7	1	162.3	10	10	100.0
3. Management	45.1	10	29.4	7	28.1	4	1.7	2	104.2	10	11	90.9
4. Domestic company	47.2	2							47.2	2	3	66.7
5. Overseas company	11.5	5	33.5	7	20.4	5	6.5	3	71.9	10	12	83.3
Mature:												
7. Majority ownership	4.8	1	11.7	1	.02	1			16.5	2	7	28.6
8. Minority ownership	10.1	22	5.6	25	1.9	17	1.6	9	19.2	37	51	72.6
9. Management	17.5	42	16.4	39	2.2	19	.9	7	37.0	57	64	89.1
10. Domestic company	16.3	11	17.4	10	24.2	7	2.2	2	60.1	16	21	76.2
11. Overseas company	17.2	8	40.8	7	11.6	6	.4	1	69.9	10	12	83.3
12. Joint domestic/ overseas company	4.5	1	10.9	1	11.4	2			26.8	3	3	100.0

Summary:

13. Non-mature	42.1	27	34.5	21	24.6	15	4.5	6	105.7	32	36	88.9
14. Mature	14.1	85	14.6	83	5.8	52	1.2	19	35.7	125	158	79.1
All companies	19.3	112	18.3	104	9.3	67	1.8	25	48.7	157	194	80.9

Statistically significant differences: Rights issues: $2 > 5^c$, $3 > 5^c$, $8 < 9^b$, $13 > 14^a$.
Issues in acquisitions: $13 > 14^b$.
Private placements and allotments: $7 < 8^a$, $7 < 9^a$, $7 < 11^a$, $8 < 9^b$, $8 < 11^b$, $9 < 11^b$, $13 > 14^b$.
Public placements: $13 > 14^c$.
Total new issues: $8 < 9^b$, $8 < 10^b$, $8 < 11^c$, $13 > 14^a$.

Notes: a, b and c denote significance at the .01, .05 and .10 levels respectively; tests between control types use a two-tail 't' test, while the comparison between non-mature and mature groups is made using a one-tail test.

Table A.6.3: Structure of New Equity Issues, Whole Period, by Firm Size

Type of issue	(1) Rights issues		(2) Issues in acquisitions		(3) Private placements and allotments		(4) Public placements		(5) Total new issues		(6) No. in sample	(7) (5)/(6)%
	%	n	%	n	%	n	%	n	%	n	n	
Size category ($m. net assets in 1966)												
1. 0 < 5	32.5	39	28.3	37	13.9	26	3.3	10	78.0	51	63	81.0
2. 5 < 10	13.0	22	16.4	23	12.9	15	.8	4	43.1	36	47	76.6
3. 10 < 20	13.0	23	18.5	16	6.8	14	2.5	7	40.8	30	35	85.7
4. 20 < 40	15.7	16	7.6	13	2.2	8	.9	4	26.4	24	28	85.7
5. 40 < 80	9.6	6	10.1	8	1.6	3			21.3	8	10	80.0
6. ≥ 80	9.0	6	2.5	7	.3	1			11.8	8	11	72.7
All companies	19.3	112	18.3	104	9.3	67	1.8	25	48.7	157	194	80.9

Statistically significant differences:

Rights issues: $1 > 2^a$, $1 > 3^a$, $1 > 4^c$, $1 > 5^a$, $1 > 6^a$.

Issues in acquisitions: $1 > 4^a$, $1 > 5^b$, $1 > 6^a$, $2 > 6^b$, $3 > 6^b$, $4 > 6^c$.

Private placements and allotments: $1 > 4^a$, $1 > 5^a$, $1 > 6^a$, $3 > 5^c$, $3 > 6^b$, $4 > 6^c$.

Public placements: $1 > 2^c$, $1 > 5^b$, $1 > 6^b$, $3 > 5^c$, $3 > 6^c$.

Total new issues: $1 > 2^c$, $1 > 3^b$, $1 > 4^a$, $1 > 5^a$, $1 > 6^a$, $2 > 6^b$, $3 > 5^c$, $3 > 6^a$, $4 > 6^c$.

Note: a, b and c denote significance at the .01, .05 and .10 levels respectively using a two-tail test.

Table A.7.1: Effects of Control Type on Performance, Small and Medium-Sized Firms

Equation number	n	Dependent variable	Constant	MC	CC	NMAT	SIZE (1/NAo)	RNA	GNA	SDRNA	SDREA	R^2	$\hat{R}^2$	F-ratio
8.5.1	145	RNA	.132	.049 (3.764)[d]	.027 (1.962)[f]	.028 (1.920)[b]	.088 (5.392)[d]					.287	.266	14.057[a]
8.5.2	145	RNA	.091	.041 (3.311)[d]	.014 (1.074)	.019 (1.416)[c]	.053 (3.126)[c]		.351 (4.170)[a]	.402 (1.927)[b]		.391	.364	14.744[a]
8.5.3	145	REA	.073	.023 (2.446)[e]	.016 (1.633)	.034 (3.355)[a]	.028 (2.445)[e]					.189	.166	8.165[a]
8.5.4	145	REA	.050	.020 (2.330)[e]	.005 (.596)	.022 (2.326)[b]	.013 (1.150)		.206 (3.584)[a]		.211 (5.138)[a]	.358	.330	12.824[a]
8.5.5	145	GNA	.079	.025 (2.001)[e]	.028 (2.229)[e]	.017 (1.261)	.089 (5.790)[d]					.267	.246	12.723[a]
8.5.6	145	GNA	.036	.008 (.691)	.020 (1.618)	.008 (.618)	.060 (3.777)[d]	.330 (4.409)[a]				.357	.333	15.406[a]
8.5.7	145	SDRNA	.034	$-.801E{-}3$ (.161)	.007 (1.328)	.006 (1.126)	.009 (1.510)[c]					.059	.032	2.182[c]
8.5.8	145	SDRNA	.024	$-.449E{-}2$ (.868)	.005 (.946)	.004 (.753)	.003 (.421)	.075 (2.352)[b]				.095	.062	2.908[b]
8.5.9	139	RET	.413	.020 (.726)	.073 (2.525)[e]	.064 (2.184)[b]	.049 (1.473)					.127	.100	4.853[a]
8.5.10	139	RET	.261	$-.027$ (1.126)	.048 (1.936)[f]	.037 (1.457)[c]	$-.043$ (1.378)	1.086 (7.197)[a]				.371	.348	15.714[a]

Notes: figures in brackets are t-ratios; a, b and c denote significance at the .01, .05 and .10 levels respectively using a one-tail test; d, e and f denote significance at the .01, .05 and .10 levels respectively using a two-tail test.

Table A.7.2: Mean Characteristics of Small and Medium-Sized Companies, by Control Type

Variable	Owner-controlled		Management-controlled		Company-controlled	
	Mean	Standard dev.	Mean	Standard dev.	Mean	Standard dev.
RNA	.1648	.0762	.2065	.0704	.1934	.0797
REA	.0879	.0406	.1083	.0372	.1087	.0729
GNA	.1104	.0709	.1274	.0692	.1391	.0737
SDRNA	.0376	.0275	.0360	.0199	.0453	.0281
SDREA	.0355	.0331	.0273	.0163	.0654	.1604
RET	.4412	.1609	.4551	.1088	.5224	.1340
ln VDH	5.6587	1.0883	4.4655	1.0261	3.7519	1.4263
VDH	471.8257	522.8836	135.7837	125.6367	94.322	135.9806
WOC	.7414	.4417				
INST	.1207	.3286	.7174	.4552		
CHD					.5122	.5061
FOR					.4634	.5049
NMAT	.1724	.3810	.1739	.3832	.3415	.4801
SIZE	.3164	.3613	.2283	.2228	.2818	.4765
NAo	5.8830	4.1350	7.4710	4.5780	7.9550	5.4130
	Median		Median			
VDH	289.2700		93.8400			
NAo	4.6750		7.0600			

Table A.7.3: Effects of Control Type on the Performance of Large Firms, n = 49

Equation number	Dependent variable	Constant	MC	CC	NMAT	NAo	RNA	GNA	SDRNA	SDREA	R^2	$\bar{R}^2$	F-ratio
8.9.1	RNA	.172	−.016 (1.151)	−.006 (.361)	.025 (1.266)	−.134E-3 (.833)					.082	< 0	.980
8.9.2	RNA	.120	−.012 (.825)	−.714E-3 (.045)	.014 (.720)	−.850E-5 (.055)		.353 (2.319)[b]	.346 (.784)		.188	.072	1.619
8.9.3	REA	.094	−.011 (1.412)	−.008 (.872)	.019 (1.711)[b]	.349E-4 (.389)					.090	.007	1.082
8.9.4	REA	.069	−.009 (1.180)	−.009 (.900)	.011 (.967)	.771E-4 (.851)		.142 (1.634)[c]		.350 (1.815)[b]	.182	.065	1.555
8.9.5	GNA	.125	−.018 (1.313)	−.026 (1.585)	.026 (1.319)[c]	−.275E-3 (1.750)[f]					.143	.065	1.829
8.9.6	GNA	.072	−.013 (.972)	−.024 (1.531)	.018 (.936)	−.233E-3 (1.536)	.312 (2.216)[b]				.230	.141	2.576[b]
8.9.7	SDRNA	.023	.005 (.994)	.011 (1.948)[f]	.006 (.837)	−.834E-4 (1.541)[c]					.150	.073	1.941
8.9.8	SDRNA	.020	.005 (1.022)	.011 (1.942)[f]	.005 (.756)	−.813E-4 (1.474)	.016 (.308)				.152	.053	1.540
8.9.9	RET	.525	−.165 (3.558)[d]	−.134 (2.407)[e]	.028 (.431)	−.229E-4 (.045)					.228	.158	3.252[b]
8.9.10	RET	.297	−.143 (3.296)[d]	−.126 (2.445)[e]	−.006 (.095)	.156E-3 (.319)	1.332 (2.942)[a]				.358	.283	4.786[a]

Notes: figures in brackets are t-ratios; a, b and c denote significance at the .01, .05 and .10 levels respectively using a one-tail test; d, e and f denote significance at the .01, .05 and .10 levels respectively using a two-tail test.

Table A.7.4: Mean Characteristics of Large Companies, by Control Type

Variable	Owner-controlled		Management-controlled		Company-controlled	
	Mean	Standard dev.	Mean	Standard dev.	Mean	Standard dev.
RNA	.1660	.0320	.1507	.0383	.1627	.0431
REA	.0951	.0181	.0862	.0204	.0885	.0269
GNA	.1134	.0352	.0947	.0381	.0903	.0409
SDRNA	.0195	.0078	.0239	.0137	.0315	.0144
SDREA	.0185	.0082	.0215	.0142	.0316	.0269
RET	.5244	.1378	.3624	.1230	.3932	.0947
ln VDH	7.2493	1.1100	4.5533	1.2630	4.0077	2.0698
VDH	2171.8810	1941.7424	214.3072	344.3146	245.8790	418.0993
WOC	.9000	.3162				
INST			.6897	.4708		
CHD					.6000	.5164
FOR					.5000	.5270
NMAT			.1034	.3099	.1000	.3162
NAo	42.773	29.424	54.2172	39.1505	39.9440	23.0815
	Median		Median			
VDH	1715.9000		79.0500			
NAo	34.2200		37.0200			

BIBLIOGRAPHY

Alchian, A.A. (1950), 'Uncertainty, Evolution and Economic Theory', *Journal of Political Economy*, LVIII (June), pp. 211-21.

Alchian, A.A. (1969), 'Corporate Management and Property Rights', in H.G. Manne (ed.), *Economic Policy and the Regulation of Corporate Securities*, Washington, American Enterprise Institute, pp. 337-60.

Asprey, K.W. *et al.* (1975), *Taxation Review Committee: Full Report*, Canberra, Australian Government Publishing Service.

Australian Bureau of Statistics (1974), *Industry Concentration Statistics: Details by Industry Class, 1968-69*, Canberra.

Australian Bureau of Statistics (1975), *Industry Concentration Statistics: Manufacturing Census, 1972-73*, Canberra.

Australian Bureau of Statistics (1976), *Foreign Ownership and Control in Manufacturing Industry, 1972-73*, Canberra.

Australian Institute of Management (1975), *National Executive Salary Survey 1975*, Sydney.

Bain, J.S. (1951), 'Relation of Profit Rate to Industry Concentration: American Manufacturing, 1936-40', *Quarterly Journal of Economics*, 65 (August), pp. 293-324.

Bain, J.S. (1956), *Barriers to New Competition*, Cambridge, Mass., Harvard University Press.

Bain, J.S. (1968), *Industrial Organization*, 2nd edn, New York, John Wiley and Sons.

Baker, J.C. (1938), *Executive Salaries and Bonus Plans*, New York, McGraw-Hill.

Baker, J.C. (1977), 'Are Corporate Executives Overpaid?', *Harvard Business Review*, 55 (July-August)), pp. 51-6.

Baker, S.H. (1969), 'Executive Incomes, Profits and Revenues: A Comment on Functional Specification', *Southern Economic Journal*, 25 (April), pp. 379-83.

Baldwin, W.L. (1964), 'The Motives of Managers, Environmental Restraints, and the Theory of Managerial Enterprise', *Quarterly Journal of Economics*, 78 (May), pp. 238-56.

Baran, P.A. and P.M. Sweezy (1966), *Monopoly Capital: An Essay on the American Economic and Social Order*, New York, Monthly Review Press.

Barna, T. (1962), *Investment and Growth Policies in British Industrial Firms*, Occasional Papers XX, National Institute of Economic and Social Research, Cambridge University Press.

Baumol, W.J. (1959), *Business Behaviour, Value and Growth*, New York, Macmillan.

Baumol, W.J. (1965), *The Stock Market and Economic Efficiency*, New York, Fordham University Press.

Baumol, W.J. (1967), *Business Behavior, Value and Growth*, New York, Harcourt.

Baumol, W.J. and P. Heim, B.G. Malkiel and R.E. Quandt (1970), 'Earnings Retention, New Capital and the Growth of Firms', *Review of Economics and*

Statistics, 52 (November), pp. 345-55.

Becker, G.S. (1962), 'Irrational Behavior and Economic Theory', *Journal of Political Economy,* 70 (February), pp. 1-13.

Benishay, H. (1961), 'Variability in Earnings — Price Ratios of Corporate Equities', *American Economic Review,* 51 (March), pp. 81-94.

Berle, A.A. and G.C. Means (1932), *The Modern Corporation and Private Property,* New York, Macmillan.

Bonbright, J.C. and G.C. Means (1932), *The Holding Company, Its Public Significance and Its Regulation,* New York, MacGraw-Hill.

Boudreaux, K.J. (1973), 'Managerialism and Risk-Return Performance', *Southern Economic Journal,* 39 (January), pp. 366-72.

Bothwell, J.L. (1980), 'Profitability, Risk and the Separation of Ownership from Control', *Journal of Industrial Economics,* 28 (March), pp. 303-12.

Brash, D.T. (1966), *American Investment in Australian Industry,* Canberra, Australian National University Press.

Briston, R.J. and R. Dobbins (1978), *The Growth and Impact of Institutional Investors,* Institute of Chartered Accountants in England and Wales, London.

Brittain, J.A. (1966), *Corporate Dividend Policy,* Washington, DC, Brookings Institution.

Brown, P. and H. Hughes (1970), 'The Structure of Australian Manufacturing Industry, 1914 to 1963-4', in C. Forster (ed.), *Australian Economic Development in the Twentieth Century,* George Allen and Unwin.

Brozen, Y. (1970), 'The Antitrust Task Force Deconcentration Recommendation', *Journal of Law and Economics,* 13 (October), pp. 279-92.

Brozen, Y. (1971a), 'Bain's Concentration and Rates of Return Revisited', *Journal of Law and Economics,* 14 (October), pp. 351-69.

Brozen, Y. (1971b), 'The Persistence of "High Rates of Return" in High-Stable Concentration Industries', *Journal of Law and Economics,* 14 (October), pp. 501-12.

Brozen, Y. (1973), 'Concentration and Profits: Does Concentration Matter?', in J.F. Weston and S.I. Ornstein (eds.), *The Impact of Large Firms on the US Economy,* Lexington, Mass., D.C. Heath, pp. 59-70

Burch, P.H. (1972), *The Managerial Revolution Reassessed,* Lexington, Lexington Books.

Bushnell, J.A. (1961), *Australian Company Mergers, 1946-59,* Melbourne, Melbourne University Press.

Campbell, J.K. *et al.* (1981), Australian Financial System Inquiry, *Final Report of the Committee of Inquiry,* AGPS, Canberra.

Caves, R.E. and B.S. Yamey (1971), 'Risk and Corporate Rates of Return: Comment', *Quarterly Journal of Economics,* LXXXV (August), pp. 513-17.

Caves, R.E. and M.E. Porter (1977), 'From Entry Barriers to Mobility Barriers: Conjectural Decisions and Contrived Deterrence to New Competition', *Quarterly Journal of Economics,* XCI (May), pp. 241-61.

Caves, R.E., J. Khalilzadeh-Shirazi and M.E. Porter (1975), 'Scale Economies in Statistical Analyses of Market Power', *Review of Economics and Statistics,* 57 (May), pp. 133-40.

Caves, R.E. (1980), 'Industrial Organization, Corporate Strategy and Structure', *Journal of Economic Literature,* XVIII (March), pp. 64-92.

Chandler, A.D. (1969), *Strategy and Structure,* Cambridge, Mass., Massachusetts

Institute of Technology Press.

Chandler, A.D. (1977), *The Visible Hand: The Managerial Revolution in American Business*, Cambridge, Mass., Harvard University Press.

Channon, D.F. (1973), *The Strategy and Structure of British Enterprise*, Boston, Harvard University Press.

Chenhall, R.H. (1979), 'Some Elements of Organizational Control in Australian Divisionalised Firms', *Australian Journal of Management*, 4 (April), supplement, pp. 1-36.

Chevalier, J. (1969), 'The Problem of Control in Large American Corporations', *Antitrust Bulletin*, 14 (Spring), pp. 153-80.

Chow, G.C. (1960), 'Tests of Equality between Sets of Coefficients in Two Linear Regressions', *Econometrica*, 28 (July), pp. 591-605.

Ciscel, D.H. (1974), 'Determinants of Executive Compensation', *Southern Economic Journal*, 40 (April), pp. 613-17.

Clark, P.B. and J.Q. Wilson (1961), 'Incentive Systems: A Theory of Organizations', *Administrative Science Quarterly*, 6 (September), pp. 129-66.

Comanor, W.S. and T.A. Wilson (1967), 'Advertising Market Structure and Performance', *Review of Economics and Statistics*, 49 (November), pp. 423-40.

Coombes, R.J. and R.B. Tress (1977), 'The Financial Implications of Corporate Share Reacquisitions', *Abacus*, 13 (June), pp. 40-51.

Coombes, R.J. and R.B. Tress (1979), 'Return of Capital: A Legal or Market Process?', *Australian Journal of Management*, 4 (October), pp. 85-96.

Cosh, A. (1975), 'The Remuneration of Chief Executives in the United Kingdom', *Economic Journal*, 85 (March), pp. 75-94.

Craig, R.M. (1979), 'An Institutional Investor's View of Takeovers', Address to an Australian Institute of Accountants seminar, Sydney, December.

Crichton-Brown, Sir R. (1980), 'The Australian Equity Market — Quo Vadis?', *The Australian Director* (June), pp. 12-16.

Crough, G. (1980), 'Small Is Beautiful But Disappearing: A Study of Share Ownership in Australia', *The Journal of Australian Political Economy*, 8 (July), pp. 3-14.

Daems, H. (1978), *The Holding Company and Corporate Control*, Leiden, Martinus Nijhoff.

Davies, J.R. and D.A. Kuehn (1977), 'An Investigation into the Effectiveness of a Capital Market Sanction on Poor Performance', in A.P. Jacquemine and H.W. de Jong (eds.), *Welfare Aspects of Industrial Markets*, Leiden, Martinus Nijhoff, pp. 329-44.

Davies, P.H. (1982), 'Equity Finance and the Ownership of Shares', in Australian Financial System Inquiry, *Commissioned Studies and Selected Papers Part 3*, AGPS, Canberra, pp. 259-442.

Davies, J.R. and D.A. Kuehn (1977), 'An Investigation into the Effectiveness of a Capital Market Sanction on Poor Performance', in A.P. Jacquemine and H.W. de Jong (eds.), *Welfare Aspects of Industrial Markets*, Leiden, Martinus Nijhoff.

Demsetz, H. (1973), 'Industry Structure, Market Rivalry, and Public Policy', *Journal of Law and Economics*, XVI (April), pp. 1-9.

Dobbins, R. and M.J. Greenwood (1975), 'Institutional Shareholders and Equity Market Stability', *Journal of Business Finance and Accounting*, 2 (No. 2).

Dobbins, R. and T.W. McRae (1975), 'Institutional Shareholders and Corporate Management', *Management Decision*, 13 (No. 6), pp. 373-408.

Donaldson, G. (1961), *Corporate Debt Capacity*, Boston, Harvard University Press.

Drucker, P.F. (1976), *The Unseen Revolution*, Heinemann, London.

Duesenberry, J.S. (1958), *Business Cycles and Economic Growth*, New York, McGraw-Hill.

Dyas, G.P. and H.T. Thanheiser (1976), *The Emerging European Enterprise: Strategy and Structure in French and German Industry*, London, Macmillan.

Elliot, J.W. (1972), 'Control, Size, Growth and Financial Performance in the Firm', *Journal of Financial and Quantitative Analysis*, 7 (January), pp. 1309-20.

Edwards, C.E. and J.G. Hilton (1966), 'A Note on the High-Low Price Average as an Estimator of Annual Average Stock Prices', *Journal of Finance*, XXI (March), pp. 112-15.

Fama, E. (1980), 'Agency Problems and the Theory of the Firm', *Journal of Political Economy*, 88 (April), pp. 288-307.

Fama, E.F. and M.C. Jensen (1983), 'Separation of Ownership and Control', *Journal of Law and Economics*, 26 (June).

Farrar, D. and R. Glauber (1967), 'Multi-collinearity in Regression Analysis: The Problem Revisited', *Review of Economics and Statistics*, 49 (February), pp. 92-107.

Fisher, I.N. and G.R. Hall (1969), 'Risk and Corporate Rates of Return', *Quarterly Journal of Economics*, 82 (February), pp. 79-92.

Fitch, R. and M. Oppenheimer (1970), 'Who Rules the Corporations?', *Socialist Revolution*, Pt. 1, No. 1, pp. 73-107; Pt. 2, No. 5, pp. 61-104; Pt. 3, No. 6, pp. 33-94.

Florence, P.S. (1961), *Ownership, Control and Success of Large Companies*, London, Sweet and Maxwell.

Foote, G.H. (1973), 'Performance Shares Revitalize Executive Stock Plans', *Harvard Business Review*, 51 (November-December), pp. 121-30.

Francis, A. (1980), 'Families, Firms and Finance Capital: The Development of UK Industrial Firms with Particular Reference to their Ownership and Control', *Sociology*, 14 (February), pp. 1-27.

Friedman, M. (1953), *Essays in Positive Economics*, University of Chicago Press, Chicago.

Friend, I., M. Blume and J. Crockett (1970), *Mutual Funds and Other Institutional Investors: A New Perspective*, McGraw-Hill, New York.

Galbraith, J.K. (1967), *The New Industrial State*, Boston, Houghton Mifflin Company.

Goldfeld, S.M. and R.E. Quandt (1965), 'Some Tests for Homoscedasticity', *Journal of the American Statistical Association*, 60 (June), pp. 539-47.

Gordon, R.A. (1940), 'Ownership and Compensation as Incentives to Corporation Executives', *Quarterly Journal of Economics*, LIV (May), pp. 455-73.

Gordon, R.A. (1945), *Business Leadership in the Large Corporation*, Washington, DC, Brookings Institution.

Grabowski, H.G. and D.C. Mueller (1970), 'Industrial Organization: The Role and Contribution of Econometrics', *American Economic Review*, 60 (May), pp. 100-104.

Grabowski, H.G. and D.C. Mueller (1975), 'Life-Cycle Effects on Corporate Returns on Retentions', *Review of Economics and Statistics*, 57 (November), pp. 400-409.

Grether, E.T. (1970), 'Industrial Organization: Past History and Future Problems', *American Economic Review*, 60 (May), pp. 83-9.

Grossfeld, B. and W. Ebke (1978), 'Controlling the Modern Corporation: A Comparative View of Corporate Power in the United States and Europe', *American Journal of Comparative Law*, 26 (Summer), pp. 397-433.

Hall, A.R. (1958), 'Institutional Investment in Listed Company Securities', *Economic Record*, 34 (December), pp. 375-89.

Hall, M. and L. Weiss (1967), 'Firm Size and Profitability', *Review of Economics and Statistics*, 49 (August), pp. 319-31.

Hannah, L. (1974), 'Takeover Bids in Britain Before 1950', *Business History*, 16 (January), pp. 65-77.

Hannah, L. (ed.) (1976), *Management Strategy and Business Development*, London, Macmillan.

Harberger, A.C. (1954), 'Monopoly and Resource Allocation', *American Economic Review*, 44 (May), pp. 77-87.

Hart, P.E. and E. Morgan (1977), *Journal of Industrial Economics*, 25 (March), pp. 177-93.

Hay, D.A. and D.J. Morris (1979), *Industrial Economics: Theory and Evidence*, Oxford University Press.

Hayes, S.L. and R.A. Taussig (1967), 'Tactics of Cash Takeover Bids', *Harvard Business Review*, 45 (March-April), pp. 135-48.

Hiller, J.R. (1978), 'Long-Run Profit Maximization: An Empirical Test', *Kyklos*, 31 (Fasc. 3), pp. 475-90.

Hindley, B. (1969), 'Capitalism and the Corporation', *Economica*, 32 (November), pp. 426-38.

Hindley, B. (1970), 'Separation of Ownership and Control in the Modern Corporation', *Journal of Law and Economics*, 13 (April), pp. 185-211.

Hindley, B. (1972), 'Recent Theory and Evidence on Corporate Merger', in Cowling, K. (ed.), *Market Structure and Corporate Behaviour*, London, Gray Mills, pp. 1-17.

Holl, P. (1975), 'Effect of Control Type on the Performance of the Firm in the UK', *Journal of Industrial Economics*, 23 (June), pp. 257-71.

Holl, P. (1977), 'Control Type and the Market for Corporate Control in Large US Corporations', *Journal of Industrial Economics*, 25 (June), pp. 259-73.

Holl, P. (1980), 'Control Type and the Market for Corporate Control: Reply', *Journal of Industrial Economics*, 28 (June), pp. 443-5.

Holtermann, S.E. (1973), 'Market Structure and Economic Performance in UK Manufacturing Industry', *Journal of Industrial Economics*, 22 (December), pp. 119-39.

Hurdle, G.J. (1974), 'Leverage, Risk, Market Structure and Profitability', *Review of Economics and Statistics*, 56 (November), pp. 478-85.

Hymer, S. and R. Rowthorn (1970), 'Multinational Corporations and International Oligopoly: The Non-American Challenge', in C.P. Kindleberger (ed.), *The International Corporation: A Symposium*, Cambridge, Mass., Massachusetts Institute of Technology Press, pp. 57-91.

Intriligator, M.D., S.I. Ornstein, R.E. Shrieves and J.F. Weston, (1973) 'Conceptual Framework of an Econometric Model of Industrial Organization', in J.F. Weston and S.I. Ornstein (eds.), *The Impact of Large Firms on the US*

Economy, Lexington, Mass., Lexington Books, pp. 23-55.

Jacquemin, A. and E. de Ghellinck (1980), 'Familial Control, Size and Performance in the Largest French Firms', *European Economic Review*, 13 (January), pp. 81-91.

Jacquemin, A.P. and L. Phlips (1976), 'Concentration, Size and Performance of European Firms', in A.P. Jacquemin and H.W. de Jong (eds.), *Markets, Corporate Behaviour and the State*, The Hague, Martinus Nijhoff, pp. 55-77.

Jenny, F. (1974), *Profit Rates and Structural Variables in French Manufacturing Industries*, École Supérieure des Sciences Économiques et Commerciales.

Jensen, M.C. (1983), 'Organization Theory and Methodology', *Accounting Review* (April).

Jensen, M.C. and W.H. Meckling (1976), 'Theory of the Firm: Managerial Behavior, Agency Costs and Ownership Structure', *Journal of Financial Economics*, 3 (October), pp. 305-60.

Johns, B.L. (1967), 'Private Overseas Investment in Australia: Profitability and Motivation', *Economic Record*, 43 (June), pp. 233-61.

Kamerschen, D.R. (1968), 'The Influence of Ownership and Control on Profit Rates', *American Economic Review*, 63 (June), pp. 432-47.

Kamerschen, D.R. (1970), 'A Theory of Conglomerate Mergers: Comment', *Quarterly Journal of Economics*, 84 (November), pp. 668-73.

Kamerschen, D.R. and R.B. Kerchner (1978), 'Market Share Valuation of Control', *Industrial Organization Review*, 6, pp. 75-85.

Kania, J.J. and J.R. McKean (1976), 'Ownership, Control and the Contemporary Corporation: A General Behaviour Analysis', *Kyklos*, 29 (Fasc. 3), pp. 272-91.

Karmel, P.H. and M. Brunt (1966), *The Structure of the Australian Economy*, Melbourne, Cheshire.

Khalilzadeh-Shirazi, J. (1974), 'Market Structure and Price-Cost Margins in United Kingdom Manufacturing Industries', *Review of Economics and Statistics*, 56 (February), pp. 67-76.

Knight, F.H. (1921), *Risk, Uncertainty and Profit*, Boston and New York, Houghton Mifflin Company.

Kotz, D.M. (1976), *Bank Control of Large Corporations in the United States*, University of California Press, Berkeley.

Kuehn, D.A. (1969), 'Stock Market Valuation and Acquisitions: An Empirical Test of One Component of Managerial Utility', *Journal of Industrial Economics*, 17 (April), pp. 132-44.

Kuehn, D.A. (1972), 'Takeover Raiders and the Growth-Maximization Hypothesis', in K. Cowling (ed.), *Market Structure and Corporate Behaviour*, London, Gray-Mills.

Kuehn, D.A. (1975), *Takeovers and the Theory of the Firm*, London, Macmillan.

Larner, R.J. (1966), 'Ownership and Control in the 200 Largest Nonfinancial Corporations, 1929 and 1963', *American Economic Review*, 56 (September), pp. 777-87.

Larner, R.J. (1970), *Management Control and the Large Corporation*, New York, Dunellen Publishing Company.

Lawriwsky, M.L. (1978), *The Ownership and Control of Australian Corporations*, University of Sydney, Transnational Corporations Research Project.

Lawriwsky, M.L. (1980), 'Control Type and the Market for Corporate Control: A Note', *Journal of Industrial Economics*, 28 (June), pp. 439-41.

Leibenstein, H. (1966), 'Allocative Efficiency vs. X-Efficiency', *American Economic Review*, 56 (June), pp. 342-415.

Lewellen, W.G. (1969), 'Management and Ownership in the Large Firm', *Journal of Finance*, XXIV (May), pp. 299-322.

Lewellen, W.G. (1971), *The Ownership Income of Management*, New York, National Bureau of Economic Research.

Lewellen, W.G. (1972), 'Managerial Pay and the Tax Changes of the 1960's', *National Tax Journal*, 25 (June), pp. 111-31.

Lewellen, W.G. and B. Huntsman (1970), 'Managerial Pay and Corporate Performance', *American Economic Review*, 60 (September), pp. 710-20.

Lintner, J. and J.K. Butters (1955), 'Effects of Taxes on Concentration', in *Business Concentration and Price Policy*, National Bureau of Economic Research, Princeton University Press, pp. 239-280.

Lintner, J. (1956), 'Distribution of Incomes of Corporations among Dividends, Retained Earnings and Taxes', *American Economic Review*, XLVI (May), pp. 97-113.

Lintner, J. (1960), 'The Financing of Corporations', in E.S. Mason (ed.), *The Corporation of Modern Society*, Cambridge, Mass., Harvard University Press, pp. 166-201.

Little, I.M.D. (1962), 'Higgledy Piggledy Growth', *Bulletin of the Oxford Institute of Statistics*, 24 (November), pp. 387-412.

Lundberg, F. (1937), *America's Sixty Families*, New York, Citadel, 1960.

Machlup, F. (1967), 'Theories of the Firm: Marginalist, Behavioral, Managerial', *American Economic Review*, LVII (March), pp. 1-33.

Manne, H.G. (1965), 'Mergers and the Market for Corporate Control', *Journal of Political Economy*, 73 (April), pp. 110-20.

Marks, J.N. (1977), 'Practical Implications of Takeovers', paper presented at a seminar on company takeovers and mergers held by the Securities Institute of Australia, November.

Marris, R. (1964), *The Economic Theory of 'Managerial Capitalism'*, London, Macmillan.

Marris, R. (1968), 'Galbraith, Solow, and the Truth about Corporations', *The Public Interest*, 11 (Spring), pp. 37-46.

Mason, E.S. (1939), 'Price and Production Policies of Large-Scale Enterprises', *American Economic Review*, 29 (March), pp. 61-7; reprinted in E.S. Mason, *Economic Concentration and the Monopoly Problem*, Cambridge, Mass., Harvard University Press, pp. 55-72.

Mason, E.S. (1949), 'The Current State of the Monopoly Problem in the United States', *Harvard Law Review*, 62 (June), pp. 1265-85.

Masson, R.T. (1971), 'Executive Motivations, Earnings and Consequent Equity Performance', *Journal of Political Economy*, 79 (November/December), pp. 1278-92.

Meade, J.E. (1968), 'Is the "New Industrial State" Inevitable?', *Economic Journal*, 78 (June), pp. 372-92.

Meeks, G. (1977), *Disappointing Marriage: A Study of the Gains from Merger*, Cambridge University Press.

Meeks, G. and G. Whittington (1975a), 'Directors' Pay, Growth and Profitability', *Journal of Industrial Economics*, 24 (September), pp. 1-14.

Meeks, G. and G. Whittington (1975b), 'Giant Companies in the UK', *Economic*

Journal, 85 (December), pp. 824-43.

Mills, C. Wright (1972), *The Power Elite, USA*, Oxford University Press.

Modigliani, F. and M.H. Miller (1961), 'Dividend Policy, Growth and Valuation of Shares', *Journal of Business*, 34 (October), pp. 411-33.

Monsen, R.J., J.S.Y. Chiu and D.E. Cooley (1968), 'The Effect of Separation of Ownership and Control on the Performance of the Large Firm', *Quarterly Journal of Economics*, 82 (August), pp. 435-51.

Monsen, R.J. and A. Downs (1965), 'A Theory of Large Managerial Firms', *Journal of Political Economy*, 73 (June), pp. 221-36.

Moody, P.E. (1979), 'A More Active Role for Institutional Shareholders', *The Banker* (February), pp. 49-52,

Mueller, D.C. (1969), 'A Theory of Conglomerate Mergers', *Quarterly Journal of Economics*, 83 (November), pp. 643-51.

Mueller, D.C. (1970), 'A Theory of Conglomerate Mergers: Reply', *Quarterly Journal of Economics*, 84 (November), pp. 675-9.

Mueller, D.C. (1972), 'A Life Cycle Theory of the Firm', *Journal of Industrial Economics*, 21 (July), pp. 192-219.

Mueller, D.C. (1977), 'The Persistence of Profits Above the Norm', *Economica*, 44 (November), pp. 369-80.

Mueller, D.C. and J.E. Tilton (1969), 'Research and Development Costs as a Barrier to Entry', *Canadian Journal of Economics*, 2 (November), pp. 570-79.

McEachern, W.A. (1975), *Corporate Control and Performance*, Lexington, Lexington Books.

McEachern, W.A. (1978a), 'Corporate Control and Growth: An Alternative Approach', *Journal of Industrial Economics*, 26 (March), pp. 257-66.

McEachern, W.A. (1978b), 'Ownership, Control and the Contemporary Corporation: A Comment', *Kyklos*, 31 (Fasc. 3), pp. 491-6.

McGuire, J.W. (1964), *Theories of Business Behavior*, Englewood Cliffs, NJ, Prentice-Hall.

McGuire, J.W., J.S.Y. Chiu and A.O. Elbing (1962), 'Executive Incomes, Sales and Profits', *American Economic Review*, 52 (September), pp. 753-61.

Nerlove, M. (1968), 'Factors Affecting Differences Among Rates of Return on Investments in Individual Common Stocks', *Review of Economics and Statistics*, 50 (August), pp. 312-31.

Nichols, T. (1969), *Ownership, Control and Ideology*, Allen and Unwin.

Norman, N. (1976), 'Structure, Performance and Policy: Market Shares Under the Law', in J.P. Nieuwenhuysen (ed.), *Australian Trade Practices: Readings*, 2nd edn, London, Croom Helm, pp. 177-204.

North, P.J. (1976), 'A Contribution to Improved Understanding of the Foreign-Owned Manufacturing Firm in Australia', in *Policies for Development of Manufacturing Industry*, Vol. III, commissioned studies of the Committee to Advise on Policies for Manufacturing Industry, Canberra, pp. 115-236.

Nyman, S. (1974), 'Directors' Shareholding and Company Performance — Empirical Evidence', working paper, Nuffield College, Oxford.

Nyman, S. and A. Silberston (1978), 'The Ownership and Control of Industry', *Oxford Economic Papers*, 30 (March), pp. 74-101.

O'Connor, J. (1968), 'Finance Capital and Corporate Capital', *Monthly Review* (December), pp. 30-35.

O'Hara, M. (1981), 'Property Rights and the Financial Firm', *Journal of Law and*

Economics, 24 (October), pp. 317-32.

Ormandy, J. (1980), 'Share Placements and Defensive Tactics: The Implications of the Code for Takeover Targets', in *The New Deal on Company Takeovers*, Melbourne, Business Law Education Centre, pp. 59-66.

Ornstein, S.I. (1975), 'Empirical Uses of the Price-Cost Margin', *Journal of Industrial Economics*, 24 (December), pp. 105-17.

Pahl, R. and J.T. Winkler (1974), 'The Economic Elite: Theory and Practice', in P. Stanworth and A. Giddens (eds.), *Elites and Power in British Society*, Cambridge University Press.

Palmer, J.P. (1972), 'The Extent of the Separation of Ownership from Control in Large US Industrial Corporations', *Quarterly Review of Economics and Business*, 12 (September), pp. 55-62.

Palmer, J.P. (1973a), 'The Profit-Performance Effects of the Separation of Ownership from Control in Large US Industrial Corporations', *Bell Journal of Economics and Management Science*, 4 (Spring), pp. 293-303.

Palmer, J.P. (1973b), 'The Profit Variability Effects of the Managerial Enterprise', *Western Economic Journal*, 11 (June), pp. 228-31.

Palmer, J.P. (1974), 'Interaction Effects and the Separation of Ownership from Control', *Rivista Internazionale di Scienze Economiche e Commerciali*, No. 2, pp. 146-9.

Parry, T.G. (1978), *The Structure and Performance of Australian Manufacturing Industries*, Canberra, Industries Assistance Commission.

Parry, T.G. and J.F. Watson (1977), 'Economies of Firm Size in Australian Manufacturing Industry', *Australian Economic Papers*, 16 (December), pp. 249-66.

Patman Staff Report (1968), 'Commercial Banks and Their Trust Activities: Emerging Influence on the American Economy', Washington, D.C., Government Printing Office.

Pedersen, L. and W.K. Tabb (1976), 'Ownership and Control of Large Corporations Revisited', *Antitrust Bulletin*, 21 (Spring), pp. 53-66.

Penrose, E.T. (1956a), 'Towards a Theory of Industrial Concentration', *Economic Record*, 32 (May), pp. 64-77.

Penrose, E.T. (1956b), 'Foreign Investment and the Growth of the Firm', *Economic Journal*, 66 (June), pp. 220-35.

Penrose, E.T. (1959), *The Theory of the Growth of the Firm*, Oxford University Press.

Peterson, S. (1965), 'Corporate Control and Capitalism', *Quarterly Journal of Economics*, LXXIX (February), pp. 1-24.

Phillips, A. (1972), 'An Econometric Study of Price-Fixing, Market Structure and Performance in British Industry in the Early 1950's', in K. Cowling (ed.), *Market Structure and Corporate Behaviour*, London, Gray Mills, pp. 177-92.

Phillips, R.W. (1978), *Structural Determinants of Profitability in Australian Manufacturing*, unpublished Ph.D. dissertation, Monash University.

Porter, M.E. (1976), *Interbrand Choice, Strategy, and Bilateral Market Power*, Cambridge, Mass., Harvard University Press.

Porter, M.E. (1979), 'The Structure within Industries and Companies' Performance', *Review of Economics and Statistics*, 61 (May), pp. 214-27.

Praetz, P.D. (1979), 'Time Series and Cross-Section Tests of Higgledy-Piggledy Growth on Australian Company Earnings: 1958-73', *Australian Economic*

Papers, 18 (June), pp. 149-59.

Prais, S.J. (1976), *The Evolution of Giant Firms in Britain*, Cambridge University Press.

Qualls, P.D. (1972), 'Concentration, Barriers to Entry and Long Run Economic Profit Margins', *Journal of Industrial Economics*, 20 (April), pp. 146-58.

Qualls, P.D. (1976), 'Market Structure and Managerial Behavior', in R.T. Masson and P.D. Qualls (eds.), *Essays on Industrial Organization in Honor of Joe S. Bain*, Cambridge, Mass., Ballinger Publishing Company, pp. 89-104.

Qualls, P.D. (1977), 'A Note on the Lerner Measure of Monopoly verus the Rate of Return in Structure-Performance Studies', *Industrial Organization Review*, 5 (No. 1), pp. 67-9.

Radice, H.K. (1971), 'Control Type, Profitability and Growth in Large Firms: An Empirical Study', *Economic Journal*, 81 (September), pp. 547-62.

Rae, P.E. *et al.* (1974), *Australian Securities Markets and Their Regulation*, Pt. 1, report from the Senate Select Committee on Securities and Exchange, Canberra, Australian Government Publishing Service.

Rayner, A. and I. Little (1966), *Higgledy Piggledy Growth Again*, Kelley, New York.

Reder, M. (1947), 'A Reconsideration of the Marginal Productivity Theory', *Journal of Political Economy*, 55 (October), pp. 450-58.

Reeder, J.A. (1975), 'Corporate Ownership and Control: A Synthesis of Recent Findings', *Industrial Organization Review*, Vol. 3, No. 1, pp. 18-27.

Revell, J. and J. Moyle (1966), 'The Owners of Quoted Ordinary Shares', published paper 7 of 'A Programme for Growth', Department of Applied Economics, Cambridge University.

Roberts, D.R. (1959), *Executive Compensation*, Glencoe, Ill., Free Press.

Rolfe, H. (1967), *The Controllers*, Melbourne, Cheshire.

Round, D.K. (1975), 'Industry Structure, Market Rivalry and Public Policy: Some Australian Evidence', *Journal of Law and Economics*, XVIII (April), pp. 273-81.

Round, D.J. (1976a), 'The Effect of the Separation of Ownership and Control on Large Firm Profit Rates in Australia: An Exploratory Investigation', *Rivista Internazionale di Scienze Economiche e Commerciali*, 23 (May), pp. 426-36.

Round, D.K. (1976b), 'Profitability and Concentration in Australian Manufacturing Industries, 1968-69 to 1972-73', *Economic Record*, 52 (June), pp. 228-30.

Round, D.K. (1976c), 'Concentration in Australian Markets', *Management Forum*, 2 (June), pp. 93-105.

Round, D.K. (1976d), 'Price-Cost Margins in Australian Manufacturing Industries, 1971-72', *Australian Journal of Management*, 1 (October), pp. 85-95.

Round, D.K. (1978), 'Economies of Firm Size: A Note on their Calculation and Relationship with Concentration', *Australian Economic Papers*, 17 (December), pp. 356-61.

Round, D.K. (1979), 'Industry Structure and Welfare Losses in Australian Manufacturing Industries', *Southern Economic Journal*, 45 (January), pp. 806-20.

Round, D.K. and J. Ryan (1980), 'Market Structure and the Level and Variability of Profits in Australia', University of Adelaide (mimeo).

Samuels, J.M. and D.J. Smyth (1968), 'Profits, Variability of Profits, and Firm

Size', *Economica*, 35 (May), pp. 127-40.

Santow, G.F.K. (1979), 'Defensive Measures Against Company Take-overs', *Australian Law Journal*, 53 (July), pp. 374-84.

Scherer, F.M. (1970), *Industrial Market Structure and Economic Performance*, Chicago, Rand McNally.

Schumpeter, J.A. (1934), *The Theory of Economic Development*, Cambridge, Mass., Harvard University Press.

Scott, J. and M. Hughes (1976), 'Ownership and Control in a Satellite Economy: A Discussion from Scottish Data', *Sociology*, 10 (January), pp. 21-41.

Securities and Exchange Commission (US) (1940), *The Distribution of Ownership in the 200 Largest Non-Financial Corporations*, Monograph No. 29, prepared for the US Temporary National Economic Committee, Government Printing Office, Washington, DC.

Securities and Exchange Commission (US) (1971), *Institutional Investor Study Report*, March, Government Printing Office, Washington, DC.

Shepherd, W.G. (1972), 'The Elements of Market Structure', *Review of Economics and Statistics*, 54 (February), pp. 25-38.

Shepherd, W.G. (1975), *The Treatment of Market Power: Antitrust, Regulation, and Public Enterprise*, New York, Columbia University Press.

Shepherd, W.G. (1976), 'The Elements and Evolution of Market Structure', in A.P. Jacquemin and H.W. de Jong (eds.), *Markets, Corporate Behaviour and the State*, The Hague, Martinus Nijhoff, pp. 169-212.

Sheridan, K. (1968), 'An Estimate of the Business Concentration of Australian Manufacturing Industries', *Economic Record*, 44 (March), pp. 26-41.

Sheridan, K. (1974), *The Firm in Australia*, Melbourne, Nelson.

Sheridan, K. (1975), 'Business Performance of American and British Affiliated Firms in Australia', *Economic Record*, 51 (December), pp. 549-63.

Simon, H.A. (1957), *Administrative Behavior: A Study of Decision-Making Processes in Administrative Organization*, New York, Macmillan.

Simon, H.A. (1959), 'Theories of Decision-Making in Economics and Behavioral Science', *American Economic Review*, 49 (June), pp. 253-83.

Singh, A. and G. Whittington, in collaboration with H.T. Burley (1968), *Growth, Profitability and Valuation*, Cambridge University Press.

Singh, A. (1971), *Takeovers: Their Relevance to the Stockmarket and the Theory of the Firm*, Cambridge University Press.

Smith, A. (1776), *An Inquiry into the Nature and Causes of the Wealth of Nations*, E. Cannon (ed.), New York, Modern Library Inc., 1937.

Smith, C.W. and R.L. Watts (1982), 'Incentive and Tax Effects of Executive Compensation Plans', *Australian Journal of Management*, 7 (December), pp. 139-57.

Smyth, D.J., W.T. Boyes and D.E. Peseau (1975), *Size, Growth, Profits and Executive Compensation in the Large Corporation*, London, Macmillan.

Smyth, R.C. (1959), 'Bonus Plans for Executives', *Harvard Business Review*, 37 (July-August), pp. 66-74.

Snooks, G.D. (1973), 'The Growth Process of the Firm: A Case Study', *Australian Economic Papers*, 12 (December), pp. 162-75.

Soldofsky, R.M. (1971), 'Institutional Holdings of Common Stock, 1900-2000, History, Projection and Interpretation', *Michigan Business Studies*, 18 (No. 3), pp. 1-223.

Soldofsky, R.M. and W.J. Boe (1975), 'Institutional Holdings of Common Stock, 1969, 1972 and New Developments', *Quarterly Review of Economics and Business*, Summer, pp. 47-60.

Solow, R. (1967), 'The New Industrial State or Son of Affluence', *The Public Interest*, 10 (Fall), pp. 100-108.

Solow, R.M. (1968), 'The Truth Further Refined: A Comment on Marris', *The Public Interest*, 11 (Spring), pp. 47-52.

Sorenson, R.L. (1974), 'The Separation of Ownership and Control and Firm Performance: An Empirical Analysis', *Southern Economic Journal*, 41 (July), pp. 145-8.

Stano, M. (1976), 'The Monopoly Power, Ownership Control and Corporate Performance', *Bell Journal of Economics*, 2 (Autumn), pp. 672-9.

Steer, P. and J. Cable (1978), 'Internal Organization and Profit: An Empirical Analysis of Large UK Companies', *Journal of Industrial Economics*, 27 (September), pp. 13-30.

Stewart, I.C. (1977), 'Australian Company Mergers, 1960-1970', *Economic Record*, 53 (March), pp. 1-28.

Stigler, G.J. (1963), *Capital and Rates of Return in Manufacturing Industries*, National Bureau of Economic Research, Princeton, NJ, Princeton University Press.

Strickland, A.D. and L.W. Weiss (1976), 'Advertising, Concentration and Price-Cost Margins', *Journal of Political Economy*, 84 (October), pp. 1109-21.

Sweezy, P.M. (1953), *The Present as History*, New York, Monthly Review Press.

Sweezy, P.M. (1971), 'The Resurgence of Financial Control: Fact or Fancy?', *Monthly Review*, 22 (September), pp. 157-91.

Taussig, F.W. and W.F. Barker (1925), 'American Corporations and Their Executives', *Quarterly Journal of Economics*, 40 (November), pp. 1-51.

Thonet, P.J. and O.H. Poensgen (1979), 'Managerial Control and Economic Performance in Western Germany', *Journal of Industrial Economics*, 28 (September), pp. 23-37.

Towers, Perrin, Forster and Crosby (1980), *Executive Compensation Study*, Chicago, Towers, Perrin, Forster and Crosby.

Turnbull, C.S.S. (1976), 'The Disadvantages of Australian Firms in Capital Creation', University of Sydney, Transnational Corporations Research Project.

Villarejo, D. (1961), 'Stock Ownership and Control of Corporations', *New University Thought*, Pt I (Autumn), pp. 33-77.

Villarejo, D. (1962), 'Stock Ownership and Control of Corporations', *New University Thought*, Pt II (Winter), pp. 47-65.

Vrisakis, A. (1980), 'Towards Effective Companies Regulation in Australia', in *The New Deal on Company Takeovers*, Melbourne, Business Law Education Centre, pp. 9-19.

Ware, R.F. (1975), 'Performance of Manager- Versus Owner-Controlled Firms in the Food and Beverage Industry', *Quarterly Review of Economics and Business*, 15 (Summer), pp. 81-92.

Weiss, L.W. (1974), 'The Concentration-Profits Relationship and Antitrust', in H.J. Goldschmid, H.J. Mann, and J.F. Weston (eds.), *Industrial Concentration: The New Learning*, Boston, Little Brown, pp. 184-245.

Welles, C. (1974), 'The Individual Investor and the Problem of Institutional Power', *Journal of Contemporary Business*, 3 (Winter).

Wheelwright, E.L. (1957), *Ownership and Control of Australian Companies*, Sydney, Law Book Company.

Wheelwright, E.L. and J. Miskelly (1967), *Anatomy of Australian Manufacturing Industry*, Sydney, Law Book Company.

Whittington, G. (1971), *The Prediction of Profitability and Other Studies of Company Behaviour*, Cambridge University Press.

Whittington, G. (1980), 'The Profitability and Size of United Kingdom Companies, 1960-74', *Journal of Industrial Economics*, 28 (June), pp. 335-52.

Wildsmith, J.R. (1973), *Managerial Theories of the Firm*, Martin Robertson.

Williamson, O.E. (1964), *The Economics of Discretionary Behavior: Managerial Objectives in a Theory of the Firm*, Englewood Cliffs, NJ, Prentice Hall.

Williamson, O.E. (1967), 'Hierarchical Control and Optimum Firm Size', *Journal of Political Economics*, 75 (April), pp. 123-38.

Williamson, O.E. (1969), 'Corporate Control and the Theory of the Firm', in H.G. Manne (ed.), *Economic Policy and the Regulation of Corporate Securities*, Washington, pp. 281-336.

Williamson, O.E. (1970), *Corporate Control and Business Behaviour*, Englewood Cliffs, NJ, Prentice-Hall.

Williamson, O.E. (1971), 'Comment' on a paper by L.W. Weiss in M.D. Intriligator (ed.), *Frontiers of Quantitative Economics*, Amsterdam, North-Holland, pp. 408-11.

Williamson, O.E. (1973), 'Managerial Discretion, Organizational Form, and the Multi-Division Hypothesis', in R. Marris and A. Wood (eds.), *The Corporate Economy*, London, Macmillan, pp. 343-86.

Williamson, O.E. (1975), *Markets and Hierarchies: Analysis and Antitrust Implications*, New York, Free Press.

Winn, D.N. (1977), 'On the Relations Between Rates of Return, Risk and Market Structure', *Quarterly Journal of Economics*, XCI (February), pp. 157-63.

Winter, S. (1964), 'Economic "Natural Selection" and the Theory of the Firm', *Yale Economic Essays*, 4 (Spring), pp. 225-72.

Wood, A. (1975), *A Theory of Profits*, Cambridge University Press.

Yarrow, G. (1972), 'Executive Compensation and the Objectives of the Firm', in K. Cowling (ed.), *Market Structure and Corporate Behaviour*, Gray-Mills.

Zietlin, M. (1974), 'Corporate Ownership and Control: The Large Corporation and the Capitalist Class', *American Journal of Sociology*, 79 (March), pp. 1073-119.

INDEX

absolute control
  see strong owner control
administrative structure 10
advertising 6
  see also product differentiation
allocative efficiency 36, 231
alternative theories
  and control type 213
  and product market 40-1
  and shareholder welfare 24-5
  criticised 2, 219
  evidence 34-8
Australian Institute of Directors 227
Australian Institute of
  Management 82
Australian Mutual Provident Society
  and takeovers 218n, 227
  investment 237n
  major shareholder 109
Australian Shareholders Association
  88, 237n
Australian Standard Industrial
  Classification, 20

barriers to entry 23, 39, 67
board of directors
  and foreign control 123
  and institutions 181n10
  and management control 209
  and ownership control 57
  composition 4
  two-tier 4, 226
Bradmill Industries Ltd 218n4
Britannic Assurance 64

Cable and Wireless Investment
  Trust 64
Canada 5
Canadian Tyre Corporation 136n9
capital asset pricing model 37
capital market restraints
  and management control 210-11
  and Marris's model 26
  and persistent profits 164
  discussed 69-70
  effectiveness 153-65
  extent 151-3

  see also external finance, market
    for corporate control
Carpenter (W.R.) Ltd 136n9
Chandler thesis 10-11
character of control
  and capital market scrutiny
    158-60
  and concentration-profits relation
    147
  and external growth rate 151-2
  and market for corporate control
    165-7
  and new equity issues 152
  and performance 90-1
  and size-performance relation
    143-6
  defined 8
  internal restraints 56-66, 187-91
  performance comparisons 201-5,
    210-17
    large firms 210-217
    small and medium firms 201-5,
      213-17
  see also control
Chow test 94
City of London Takeover Panel 228
Companies (Acquisition of Shares)
  Act 229
company control
  and creeping acquisition 150
  and internal restraints 188-9
  and market for control 169-72
  and size-performance relation
    68-9
  and takeovers 167
  behaviour 59-62
  defined 19, 59
  foreign company control 19, 22,
    61-2, 106, 122-6, 189
    and domestic control 61-2
    and growth 22n8
    defined 19
    leverage 106
    local equity participation 22n4
    managerial discretion 122-4
    performance 124-6, 189
    see also foreign ownership joint